Tongue Ties

For Alban,

A small token of Friendship
and esteem,

[signature]

Casa Hispánica 25 nov/03.

New Directions in Latino American Cultures

A Series Edited by Licia Fiol-Matta & José Quiroga

Published in 2003:

Forthcoming Titles:

Tongue Ties

Logo-Eroticism in Anglo-Hispanic Literature

Gustavo Pérez Firmat

TONGUE TIES
Copyright © Gustavo Pérez Firmat, 2003.

First published in 2003 by PALGRAVE MACMILLAN™
175 Fifth Avenue, New York, N.Y. 10010 and
Houndmills, Basingstoke, Hampshire, England RG21 6XS.
Companies and representatives throughout the world.

PALGRAVE MACMILLAN is the global academic imprint of the Palgrave Macmillan division of St. Martin's Press, LLC and of Palgrave Macmillan Ltd. Macmillan® is a registered trademark in the United States, United Kingdom and other countries. Palgrave is a registered trademark in the European Union and other countries.

1–4039-6288-X hardback
1–4039-6289–8 paperback

Library of Congress Cataloging-in-Publication Data
Available from the Library of Congress

A catalogue record for this book is available from the British Library.

Design by Autobookcomp.

First Palgrave Macmillan edition: August 2003
10 9 8 7 6 5 4 3 2 1

Printed in the United States of America.

For John M. Fein

The moment one learns English,
complications set in.

—*Felipe Alfau,* Chromos

Contents

Acknowledgements

The following friends and colleagues read and commented on parts of this book at various stages in its composition: Isabel Álvarez Borland, Andrew Debicki, Roberto Ignacio Díaz, Lucille Kerr, Raúl Marrero Fente, Christopher Maurer, Raymond Souza, Antonio Prieto, and René Prieto. As they have in the past, Jorge Olivares and John Kronik went through the entire manuscript with their customary care and insight. William Holzberger and John McCormick gave me important tips about Santayana. A lunch with Philip Silver provided the stimulus to write about Pedro Salinas; a dinner with Gonzalo Sobejano led me to some crucial bibliographic sources. José Quiroga and Ella Pearce were enthusiastic about the project from the start. Mary Anne Pérez's willingness to be my eyes and limbs freed me from having to spend my time in libraries. Lastly, the students in "language loyalty" seminars at Columbia and Emory helped to untie my tongue when this book was no more than wishful thinking. To them all I am grateful.

Parts of chapters 4 and 7 appeared in *Colby Quarterly* (December 1996) and *MLN* (March 2002).

Introduction

In a letter written toward the end of his life, the Russian novelist Ivan Turgenev remarked that a writer who did not write only in his mother tongue was a thief and a pig.[1] Although Turgenev did not explain the epithets, it is not difficult to figure out what he meant. Since a language is a form of cultural property, a writer who uses words that do not belong to him is a thief; since his theft of the words of others entails the neglect of his own, he is a pig. As it happens, Turgenev wrote this letter in German. Even though his letters are often every bit as literary as his novels, the use of other languages in correspondence apparently did not count as an infraction against his mother tongue. Indeed, it is revealing that Turgenev, in spite of his mastery of several European languages and his many years of residence outside Russia, never seized the opportunity, or succumbed to the temptation, of writing fiction in a language other than Russian. Once, when a reviewer incorrectly stated that one of Turgenev's novellas had been written originally in French, an offended Turgenev pointed out—in flawless French—that he would never stoop to something so base.

Turgenev's attitude toward the Russian language offers an instance of the phenomenon that Uriel Weinreich termed language loyalty, that powerful, deep-seated attachment that many of us feel toward our mother tongue.[2] Although in Western culture feelings of language loyalty go back to the ancient Greeks, who stigmatized users of other languages as "barbarians" (literally, speakers of gibberish, *barbar*), it is only recently that individual languages have acquired the pull and prestige that they now enjoy. As Leonard Forster pointed out, for several centuries multilingualism was the norm rather than the exception among European writers. A sixteenth-century neo-Latin poet felt few qualms about not using his mother tongue for literary composition; even writers who worked primarily in the vernacular also wrote, without apparent damage to their self-esteem, in other languages: Milton composed Italian sonnets, Garcilaso wrote Latin odes. It was not until the rise of modern nation states that native languages became national languages, and thus a privileged cultural possession.[3] For most of us, as for

Turgenev, the language that we speak is a fundamental component of our nationality, and hence of our sense of who we are. That is why, when we want to question someone's claims about his nationality, we often take aim at his language habits: "Funny, you don't *sound* like an American." As Andrée Tabouret-Keller puts it, language acts are acts of identity.[4] We are what we speak.

As for myself, I have always felt a mixture of regret and remorse that I have not done more of my writing, and my living, in Spanish. Sometimes I have even thought that every single one of my English sentences— including this one—hides the absence of the Spanish sentence that I wasn't willing or able to write. And if I handle English more or less well, it is because I want to write such clear, clean prose that no one will miss the Spanish that it replaces (and that it can never replace). Why I haven't tried to write more in Spanish is something that I've wondered about, something that I am wondering about right now, but that I don't entirely understand. I know the practical reasons for my use of English, but I also suspect that there may be other, more murky motives of which I'm only half-aware: anger, fear of failure, maybe even a little self-hatred. If you say "tomato" and I say *tu madre,* the code-switching expletive may be a symptom of the speaker's unhappiness with his mother tongue, with his other tongue, and most of all, perhaps, with himself. And if you say "latino" and I say *la tuya,* this expletive may reflect his unwillingness to accept his switch in loyalties.

The complexity of these feelings suggests that the notion of language loyalty, useful as it is, does not do justice to an individual's attachment to his or her languages. It is not enough to explain, as Weinreich does, that language loyalty is nationalism applied to language. For one thing, tongue ties do not always correspond to national or regional borders. In *The American Scene,* Henry James affirms that a person's "supreme relation" is to his homeland;[5] but James's own life shows that his bond to the English language was stronger than his connection to the United States. More importantly, tongue ties antedate national allegiances. Psychologists have found that already in the first weeks of life infants can distinguish the sounds of their mother tongue, even when they are not uttered by their mothers.[6] Before we can recognize those pockets of sound that we call words, we are already bound to one language by ties too primal, too irreflective, to be subsumed under the notion of loyalty. At least when it comes to language, and perhaps in other areas as well, loyalty is a secondary or subsidiary affect, a translation of more fundamental drives and investments.

In a recent study of loyalty, George Fletcher theorizes that the "matrix of loyalty" always includes three parties: a subject, an object, and a second or alternative object of loyalty that competes for the subject's fealty. He goes on to say: "The competitor is always lurking in the wings, rejected for the time being, but always tempting, always seductive."[7] Rejection, temptation, seduction: Fletcher's scenario evokes tangles of desire that precede and exceed loyalty; even the term "matrix," from the Latin *mater*, hints at complications too deep for the contractual pact that forms the basis of loyalty (from *legalis*, legal). Languages not only inspire loyalty, they also provoke fear, hatred, resentment, jealousy, love, euphoria—the entire gamut of human emotion. From the undergraduate whose difficulties with *ser* and *estar* make him complain that he "hates Spanish," to the exile who clasps her mother tongue in a tight embrace, tongue ties are every bit as knotty as our other affections. And not only because of the role of language in shaping our conscious identity, but also because languages serve to act out and work through conflicts whose origins lie elsewhere, in groups and individuals who not only speak a given language but for whom that language speaks.

Entrenched as it is in all the European languages, the idea of a "mother" tongue simplifies a much more complicated situation. Mother tongues are forked or folded into father and sister tongues, spouse and lover tongues, friend and enemy tongues. Particularly among bilinguals, language kinship is not restricted to the maternal. George Santayana identified Spanish—his "mother" tongue—with his father, and English—the language in which he wrote all of his work—with his half-sister and her American father, whom he never met but after whom he was named. His polyglot Spanish mother he regarded as tongueless. The Baltimore-born Cuban writer Calvert Casey, whose mother's tongue (Spanish) was different from his father's (English), wrote in both but assigned them to incompatible emotional registers. Many nonlinguistic factors, some nearly impossible to detect, shape a bilingual's engagement with languages, his or her *diálogo de las lenguas*. In the course of their lives, bilinguals shape—and are shaped by—their own language family, which has nothing to do with the language families of the philologists. In the Freudian family romance, the child is caught between the male and female parent; in the linguistic family romance, the bilingual subject oscillates between languages that are not always distinguished so neatly. Although the other tongue may indeed be the father's, there will be times when both tongues will be regarded as motherly (or fatherly). In these instances, the competition will involve aspirants to the maternal (or paternal) slot, as if the child, rather than having to negotiate between parents of opposite sexes, had to choose between a parent and a stepparent, or decide which of his "mothers" is the legitimate one. Because we tend to think about bilingualism in terms of the dichotomy "mother-other," we sometimes overlook that the "other" also has a gender (there are she-tongues as well as he-tongues) and can achieve kinship status. Indeed, the test of genuine bilingualism is whether both languages form part of the same family. The true bilingual is not someone who possesses "native competence" in two languages, but someone who is equally attached to, or torn between, competing tongues.

Tongue ties have little to do with linguistic competence. Affective rather than cognitive in nature, tongue ties do not presuppose mastery of a language. Just as it is possible never to have met one's parents, it is possible to be ignorant of one's mother tongue. The maternal denotes attachment, not skill; affinity, not fluency; familialness, not familiarity. Grounded in biographical and historical circumstances, this sense of kinship can precede acquisition of a language and outlive its loss. U.S. Latino writers habitually pledge allegiance to a mother tongue that, for the most part, they no longer possess. Swearing loyalty to Spanish in English, they do not necessarily bear false witness, for even when the words have become unintelligible, even when the attempts at Spanish are riddled with solecisms, the emotional bond remains unbroken. Lack of skill in a "mother" tongue may well affect how a speaker feels about himself, for few sources of self-reproach are more disabling than the linguistic: "If you want to hurt me," writes Gloria Anzaldúa, "talk badly about my language."[8] But a speaker's linguistic ineptness will not alter the kinship status of the language. As we know, virtuosity can be a function of detachment, while someone secure in his linguistic affections may treat his mother tongue with a familiarity that slips into carelessness. And there is a type of inarticulateness that betrays not too little but too much involvement. When I stammer, I'm more likely to do it in Spanish. A tied tongue speaks of tongue ties.

This book examines the affect of Spanish and English in a group of bilingual writers. Although issues surrounding bilingualism are usually studied from a linguistic, cultural, or political perspective, I am interested in something more elusive, in the emotional bonds or "tongue ties" of selected Hispanic writers. Under the large and porous umbrella of "Hispanic" I bring together writers of varying provenance: Spanish, Spanish American, and U.S. Latino. Included among them are an American philosopher (George Santayana), Spanish poets (Pedro Salinas and Luis Cernuda), Spanish-American fiction writers (Calvert Casey, Guillermo Cabrera Infante, María Luisa Bombal), and U.S. Latino poets and memoirists (Sandra Cisneros, Richard Rodriguez, and Judith Ortiz Cofer). The group is heterogeneous and cuts across established disciplinary boundaries, but its members have one thing in common: Their careers are shaped, in whole or in part, by a linguistic family romance that pits against each other the competing claims and attractions of Spanish and English. Although for every one of these writers Spanish is the "mother" tongue, at some point the intrusion of English reshaped the mother-child dyad into a tense triangle.[9] In some cases, the intrusion led to the abandonment or supercession of the mother tongue (Santayana, Rodriguez, Cisneros, Ortiz Cofer), in others, to its fierce reinforcement (Salinas, Cernuda), and still in others, to an anguished alternation between languages (Casey, Cabrera Infante, Bombal).

It may seem odd to include in a study of literary bilingualism such resolutely hispanophone writers as Pedro Salinas and Luis Cernuda, two of the greatest Spanish poets of the twentieth century. I hope to show, however, that there is a "Latino moment" in the careers of these poets, a segment of their work shaped by the uneasy and muted cohabitation of Spanish and English. Building on W. E. B. DuBois's notion of double consciousness, James Clifford has described diasporic experience as comprising "the co-presence of a 'here' and 'there.'"[10] When I talk about the Latino moment in Salinas or Cernuda, I have in mind the linguistic corollary of Clifford's view, a co-presence whose substance is linguistic rather than spatial (although of course bilingualism can be the product of geographical displacement). This mingling of an anglophone "here" and a hispanophone "there," characteristic of Latino literature, will be a constant in the work of all of the authors discussed in this book, whatever the literary canon or national literature to which they are normally assigned. In this respect, my aim is to establish paths of continuity and borders of affinity that supplement conventional approaches. One can read more deeply into Richard Rodriguez's *Hunger of Memory,* usually studied in the context of North-American "ethnic" or "minority" autobiography, by placing it alongside Luis Cernuda's *Variaciones sobre tema mexicano,* a collection of prose poems written in the early 1950s. María Luisa Bombal's lightly regarded efforts at self-translation form part of a larger pan-Hispanic tradition of anglophone writing. George Santayana's marmoreal prose reveals interesting cracks in the backlight of Calvert Casey's stories.

For the most part, the writers in this book take a guarded stance toward the co-presence of Spanish and English. Since several of them were exiles, the traces of a second language in their writings increased their awareness of displacement and made them fear the loss of their mother tongue. But even those writers who are not exiles in the conventional sense, such as those born and raised in the United States, display considerable anxiety about their divided affections. Contrary to some reports, there is no bilingualism without pain. Although bilingualists are often playful, bilingualism is not a game. More often than not, the interlingual puns of bilingual writers are ill-tempered, nasty, aggressive: have pun, will travel. Etymologically, puns are *pullas,* jabs; when we go for the jocular, we go for the jugular—even if it is our own. The bilingual muse is a melancholy muse; it divides and does not conquer.

I am not talking about casual or classroom bilingualism, about the tourist, the scholar, or the student, but about those who live shaping events in their lives—growing up, falling in love, enduring exile, surviving illness—in more than one language. In these circumstances, the celebration of bilingualism is not the dominant mode.[11] For every merry bilingualist who feasts on word play—all roads lead to roam—there is a somber bilingual who bites his tongues, someone for whom, as Santayana once remarked, language belongs to the dark side of life. We are sometimes too quick in singing the praises of bilingualism. "If identity is shaped by language," writes Steven Kellman in *The Translingual Imagination,* "then monolingualism is a deficiency disorder."[12] Yes and no. Yes, identity is shaped by language; but no, languages are not like vitamins. The blurb on the jacket of Kellman's book sounds a similar note: "Monolingualism is a form of oppression. Join the future, read this book." I don't deny the damage done by coercive monolingualism, which sometimes results in the extirpation of a mother tongue, but bilingualism can engender its own forms of oppression. Calques and barbarisms are only the surface tremors of rifts that reach deeper than syntax or vocabulary. Among bilinguals, nostalgia for monolingualism is at least as common as its repudiation. A Czech proverb teaches: "Learn a new language, get a new soul." Is it always a blessing to be multisouled?

At the other extreme are those who have asserted that bilingualism breeds schizophrenia. "One person, one language," was one French linguist's recipe for psychic wholeness.[13] And this too is overly schematic. There are indeed some multilinguals to whom Babel looks every bit like Paradise. As we will see when we come to Casey and Bombal, emotional balance can depend on alternating between languages, for the use of another tongue sometimes allows a writer to grasp what his or her mother tongue was unable to say. Besides, since bilingualism is not always a choice, preaching against it is often irrelevant, if not cruel. I aim to complicate the usual arguments about bilingualism—for and against—by studying the sometimes joyful, more often painful, and always intricate tying of tongues in half a dozen Hispanic writers. The book is neither a paean to bilingualism nor an exposé of its vexations, but an attempt to understand its psychological and creative entanglements. Bilingual bliss, bilingual blues: Both will find a voice, a *voz*, here.

Linguists sometimes distinguish between a "foreign" and a "second" language according to the context of acquisition. A foreign language, as the term implies, is learned in a setting where the language is not normally spoken, where the "target" language is different from the vernacular. By contrast, a second language is learned where there is no such disparity; the adjective refers to the sequence rather than the context of acquisition. Typically, languages learned exclusively or primarily in the classroom are foreign languages, while languages learned in the countries where they are spoken are second languages. Bilingualism tends to become complicated when the other language is a "second" rather than a "foreign" language, for only a second language can impinge on the dominance of a mother tongue. For all of the writers in this book (the author included), English is a second language. Technically they are "polyglots" rather than "polylinguals."[14] Even if initially a foreign language, exile, immigration, assimilation, or other circumstances eventually raised English to the status of a second language, one woven into the fabric of their lives. Some, like Pedro Salinas, reacted to the ascendance of English by treating it as if it were still a "foreign" language, in this way preserving the old definitions of the foreign and the native. Others, like Luis Cernuda, fled to an environment where English was once again literally foreign. Still others, like Richard Rodriguez, embrace the second language with a passion intended to compensate for the loss of the first; or like Cabrera Infante, write an English so mannered that it parades its foreignness on every page.

I need to clarify what I mean by calling these authors "bilingual writers." As commonly used, the term lends itself to equivocation. Jane Miller writes: "Some of the most powerful twentieth-century writing has come from such well-known bilingual writers as Conrad, Kafka, Borges, Beckett, Julien Green, Nabokov, and Bashevis Singer."[15] This list confounds bilingualisms of different orders. While Nabokov, Beckett, and Green wrote major work in more than one language, Conrad and Kafka did not. Borges also wrote exclusively in Spanish, with a few minor forays into English. Julien Green, whose parents were American, had a family connection to English—it was his "heritage language"—but neither Nabokov nor Beckett had any such ties to their other languages. For Kafka to write in German, a language that he heard and spoke all of his life, is different than for Conrad to write in English, which he did not learn until he was a grown man. Though often used indiscriminately, the phrase "bilingual writer" can mean three different things: 1) that the writer knows more than one language; 2) that he writes sometimes in one language, sometimes in the other; 3) that the writing itself mixes two languages. Bilingualism in the first sense is extraordinarily common; in the second sense, rare; in the third, rarer still. All of the writers in this book are bilingual in the first sense; only a couple are bilingual in the second sense; and except for brief interludes, none is bilingual in the third sense.

I have chosen to concentrate on the first type of writer, "bilingual" but not "biscriptive," because this situation is the most common and the least studied. I hope to show that even in writers who write in only one language, the other language (be it their "second" or their "first") exerts a determining if often tacit pressure. This type of writing incorporates a "latent bilingualism," to use Claudio Guillén's phrase, that manifests itself in deeper, often more disturbing ways than code-switching or interlingual play. In several chapters of the book, my effort will be to read bilingually in seemingly monolingual contexts, to examine how the absent or lost language shapes the writer's transactions with his vehicular tongue.

Bilingualism involves a relation not only between speakers and languages but between the languages themselves. The bilingual is the site where two languages meet, the medium or membrane that engages them in conversation. This conversation doesn't have to be loud, it doesn't have to be long, it doesn't always sparkle with the hybrid wit of a Nabokov or a Cabrera Infante. Sometimes the dialogue of languages is like that of a Calvert Casey story—awkward, brief, but nonetheless eloquent. The two languages may not be equally talkative. At times one language speaks so fast or aggressively that the other is reduced to silence; at times each language politely waits its turn to speak; at times they interrupt each other. Because of the asymmetry of these encounters, none of the writers that concern me is a "balanced bilingual." Even among people who have been raised bilingually, the relation of languages is usually not symmetrical. The notion of balanced bilingualism or *equilingüismo* is as much of a pedagogical fiction as that of bilingualism without pain. Bilingualism tends to be unbalanced, asymmetrical. Again, I am not talking about fluency but about affect. When George Steiner writes that he experiences his first three tongues (English, French, and German) as "perfectly equivalent centres" of himself, I'm impressed but I do not quite believe him.[16] It's not his fluency that I doubt, but the claim of existential equivalence. Steiner was born in Paris and emigrated to the United States with his family when he was eleven years old. He was educated in this country and has lived most of his adult life either in the United States or in Great Britain. Even if during his Parisian childhood the three languages were affectively indistinguishable (but how could this be?), his forced migration from one language world (French) to another (English) as a result of actions by the country of a third (German), is likely to have jarred the equivalence. Then also, the books that we write change our relation to the language in which we write them, and Steiner has done most of his writing in English, not French or German. Even by asserting in English the equivalence of his three languages, Steiner is already tipping the scale in the direction of Shakespeare rather than Voltaire or Goethe. In his case, as in others, the conviction of multilingual balance may well compensate for deeper disequilibriums.

Tongue ties are dynamic; they tighten or slacken over time. A foreign language could well evolve into a conjugal tongue; the sounds that cradled us in infancy could haunt us in adulthood. Jacqueline Amati-Mehler and her colleagues put the matter well: "[T]he 'ideal' bilingual or polylingual speaker, who is equally and consistently fluent in two or more languages, is a conventional abstraction. In fact, the linguistic endowment of an individual is not a solid and stable system but, rather, an ever-changing constellation in which the supremacy of one language over the other, the internal hierarchy, and the absolute and relative degree of mastery, vary continuously over time and space."[17] These variations cannot always be fully explained by the private circumstances of an individual's life. The specific languages involved in the bilingual relation, as well as the cultural and political context in which the relation unfolds, can also play a decisive role. It is not the same to be bilingual in Spanish and English in Chapel Hill, North Carolina, where the two languages barely brush against each other, and in Miami, Florida, where they do. In literary culture, Spanish and English have been in contact at least since the early fifteenth century, when for the first time an English-language phrase—"Mother of God, help!"—sneaks into a Spanish-language poem.[18] In the Americas, the two languages are and have been for centuries not only in contact but in competition. This competition goes on around us every day. As the English-only and English-first movements try to curtail the spread of Spanish in the United States, in Latin America—and particularly in border countries like Mexico and Puerto Rico—equally vigorous (and no less futile) efforts are made to stem the inflow of anglicisms. In a classic essay on the psychology of bilinguals, James Bossard studied what he termed the "enemy tongue problem," the situation that arises when a bilingual's languages represent countries at war.[19] Doing research on bilingualism during the 1940s, Bossard discovered that for his subjects, first or second generation German Americans, the two wars between the United States and

Germany had created a great deal of psycho-linguistic turmoil. For these German Americans, the "balance" of languages was unlike that in other bilinguals. Before World War II, some of Bossard's subjects might well have claimed English and German as equivalent centers of their experience; during and after the war, equivalence was replaced by strife. In a seldom-cited but insightful essay on bilingualism, Paul Christophersen summed up the situation this way, "A war will often afflict a bilingual person particularly severely because it may be to him almost a civil war."[20]

In the New World, English and Spanish represent countries and cultures that, when not engaged in outright war, have been consistently hostile to each other. This makes Spanish-English bilingualism tense, conflictual, adversarial, as can be often glimpsed in the poetry of U.S. Latinos. "Words are a war to me," writes Cherríe Moraga, echoing Christophersen and internalizing cultural and political conflicts.[21] George Santayana, who lived through the Spanish-American War in Boston, wrote one of his most ambitious poems, "Spain in America," inspired and dispirited by Spain's defeat in 1898. In the poem he lists the Spanish language among Spain's gifts to the New World. But Santayana, whose native language was Spanish, wrote his poem in English, to that extent undermining his homeland's cultural legacy. Even if the poem's subject is "Spain in America," its language proclaims the presence of America in Spain. The Chilean María Luisa Bombal, who regarded the English language as "diabolical and mysterious,"[22] spent several decades trying to become an anglophone novelist. Such paradoxes exact an emotional toll. Santayana's renunciation of Spanish diminished him; Bombal's embrace of English, even as it allowed her to transcend traumatic episodes in her life, cut her off from her past. The Cuban Calvert Casey wrote his best story in English in the late 1960s, a time of unprecedented animosity between the governments of Cuba and the United States. Among other things, Casey's switch to English was an act of political spite, a way of reinforcing geographical exile with linguistic expatriation. By contrast, Pedro Salinas's mounting hostility toward the American vernacular during his exile in Baltimore reflected his estrangement from the American muse of his love poetry as well as his nostalgia for Spain's imperial past.

My focus on Spanish-English bilingualism also raises the issue of the "intrinsic" differences between the two languages. For these differences, much anecdotal evidence will vouch. All of us have heard (and sometimes repeated) the clichés: English is factual, Spanish is florid; English is plain, Spanish is ornate; English is the language of business, Spanish the language of love (and of music and food and *abuelitas*). The American

Association of Teachers of Spanish and Portuguese (AATSP) sells T-shirts emblazoned with the logo, "El español es la lengua del alma" [Spanish is the tongue of the soul]. Such sentiments are not limited to promotional hype. As we will see, U.S. Latino writers often endorse the view that Spanish is more soulful than English. According to Judith Ortiz Cofer, who writes only in English, her mother tongue is characterized by "flowery adjectives and passionate verbs."[23] Rosario Ferré, who now writes in both languages, corroborates: "When I write in Spanish, my sentences are often as convoluted as a baroque retablo. When I write in English, Locke is locked into every sentence."[24]

Anyone who knows the two languages cannot but feel that these characterizations, however reductive, contain a grain of truth. Languages do guide and goad their users. They shape what we can and cannot say or think or feel in ways obvious and profound. The existence of kinship terms in Spanish that have no equivalents in English *(compadre, comadre, concuño)* may well reflect differences in how each culture defines the family unit. When Borges gave one of his poems a French title, "Le regret d'Héraclite," he may have been acting on the intuition that there is no good Spanish synonym for the French or English "regret," the emotion expressed in the poem. Some years ago Esmeralda Santiago published an account of her childhood in Puerto Rico under the title *When I Was Puerto Rican*. When the memoir appeared in Spanish, translated by the author herself, the title became *Cuando era puertorriqueña*. Every word in the English title has a match in the translation—every word but one, that is, the first-person pronoun "I," which the Spanish title elides because of the language's tendency to delete subject pronouns (the so-called "pro-drop" feature). But as a result, the Spanish title doesn't make clear that the phrase should be read in the first person; *Cuando era puertorriqueña* could be construed as "When she [*ella*] was Puerto Rican" or "When you [*usted*] were Puerto Rican." And yet, it would seem that whatever else one may omit when translating an autobiography, the one grammatical element that can't get lost in translation is the first-person pronoun. (Interestingly, what the Spanish title does add is gender marking, since it identifies the grammatical subject as female.) It has often been remarked that the literature of Spain and Spanish America is not rich in self-writing. Could one reason be the language's relative inhospitableness to subject pronouns? When the language itself makes the writer's "I" grammatically redundant, autobiography verges on solecism, and self-disclosure risks becoming a slip of the tongue.

Let's assume that, flouting normal usage, Santiago had inserted a "yo" in her Spanish title: "Cuando yo era puertorriqueña." Would the

Spanish and English titles then be cognate? Perhaps not. "I" is an open vowel; graphically, it is singular, erect, indistinguishable from the Roman numeral I. According to Elias Canetti, no word packs a greater wallop than the English "I."[25] By contrast, the hispanophone "yo" rounds your lips to a murmur. At least in the Caribbean, the "y" is pronounced so softly that it tends to disappear into the throat. In English, I read "I" and I hear, "Yes!" In Spanish, I read "yo" and I think, "and/or," because I cannot see a "yo" without slashing the pronoun: "y/o." It may be, as Derrida has suggested, that of all the parts of speech, the most resistant to translation is the first-person pronoun.[26]

The view that a language creates its own worldview has come to be known as the theory of linguistic relativity. Although its origins go back to Wilhelm von Humboldt and the German Romantics, it was popularized in the twentieth century by the American linguists Edward Sapir and Benjamin Whorf. Sapir summarized his still controversial hypothesis this way:

> The fact is that the "real world" is to a large extent unconsciously built up on the language habits of the group. No two languages are ever sufficiently similar to be considered as representing the same social reality. The worlds in which different societies live are distinct worlds, not merely the same world with different labels attached.[27]

For his part, Whorf wrote:

> The categories and types that we isolate from the world of phenomena we do not find there because they stare every observer in the face; on the contrary, the world is presented in a kaleidoscopic flux of impressions which has to be organized by our minds—and this means largely by the linguistic systems in our minds. We cut nature up, organize it into concepts, and ascribe significance as we do, largely because we are parties to an agreement that holds throughout our speech community and is codified in the patterns of our language.[28]

One rather intractable difficulty with linguistic relativity, as has often been pointed out, is that it seems impossible to verify, since the language of the verification will necessarily "skew" the results. If Sapir and Whorf are right, the differences between the "English" and "Spanish" pictures of the world will themselves differ according to whether they are formulated in Spanish or English (or any other language). For instance, Whorf's crucial distinction between the phenomenal world—that "kaleidoscopic flux of impressions"—and his postulated "nature" may not be available in all languages.

For my purposes, however, the ultimate validity of the Sapir-Whorf hypothesis is irrelevant. What is crucial is that many bilinguals relate to their languages in ways that enact some version of this hypothesis. What may not be true for Spanish and English in any objectively demonstrable way may be true for an individual's apprehension of Spanish and English. Although the notion that Spanish is more "passionate" or "baroque" than English may not stand any sort of rigorous test, individual writers or speakers, believing this to be so, may use the two languages in ways that make it true for them. My interpretation of the differences between "I" and "yo" is probably nonsense, but a comparison of my writings in English and Spanish might show that I have incorporated these differences into my authorial persona in each language. In other words, there is a "special" or "restricted" linguistic relativity rooted in the historical tongue ties of individuals or communities. The perception of difference between or among languages is always intensely personal. As Steiner mentions, it ranges all the way from the somatic to the cerebral, from the sound and "feel" of languages to the user's view of them as contrasting structures.[29] Although nearly every writer included here will have something to say about the disparities between Spanish and English, their comments generally reveal more about the writer than about the language. Interestingly, their assertions of difference tend to contradict one another, thereby undermining essentialist claims about the two languages. Ortiz Cofer and Ferré may regard Spanish as passionate and convoluted, but for Calvert Casey it is the medium for impassive, minimalist notation, as if Locke had bolted free and found his way to Old Havana. And while English, not Spanish, gives Casey the means to give vent to desire, to write about passion passionately, for Luis Cernuda physical and emotional intimacy seems to require a hispanophone relation. He could not have composed his beautiful *Poemas para un cuerpo* to anybody (or any body) who didn't speak or comprehend Spanish.

When the Franco-Argentine novelist Héctor Bianciotti states that bilingualism compels us to lie, he is alluding to this sensation of linguistic difference, the bilingual's impression that, whatever the dictionary equivalences, the leap across languages involves a change in emotional register. Bianciotti states: "When naming an object, one is conscious of the changes that the object itself undergoes according to the language that names it. 'Oiseau' is warm, smooth, shining; 'pájaro' flies like an arrow." Santayana gives a different example: "To my sense, 'bread' is as inadequate a translation of the human intensity of the Spanish 'pan' as 'Dios' is of the awful mystery of the English 'God.'"[30] The key phrase in Santayana's statement is "To my sense," which captures the subjective nature of such assessments. This is why no translation is more treacherous than self-translation. Although a biscriptive writer may be able to translate himself, he cannot translate into one language his relation with the other. Each of his languages entails a unique set of associations, burdens, predispositions. His bilingualism is rather diglossia, the linguists' term for the use of separate languages in different contexts and for different purposes.[31] What passes for balanced bilingualism is more often diglossia in disguise.

To understand the intricacy of tongue ties, I have found it useful to distinguish three ways of looking at language. I should make clear that this typology arises not from the formal features of a language, but from the attitudes of its users. Rather than linguistic theory, I offer psychological conjecture. From the perspective of language affect, the grammar or vocabulary of a language matter as little as whether a particular mode of speech is a pidgin, a dialect or a creole. More important is the user's personal "sense" about his words, his degree of intimacy with them, their perhaps not entirely conscious role in his psychic life. For this purpose, languages can be classified into *lenguas, idiomas,* and *lenguajes* (I use the Spanish terms because—to my sense—they make the distinctions clearer).

LANGUAGE AS *LENGUA*

A tongue is language incarnate, as body part, an organ rather than a faculty. By calling our language a tongue, we highlight our bond to it, which is why we use possessives with *lengua* more often than with *lenguaje.* By the same token, the use of a possessive next to the name of a specific language—*"mi español perdido"* [my lost Spanish], as in Juan Ramón Jiménez's famous suite of aphorisms—indicates that the speaker conceives of his language as a tongue. Although not all tongues are motherly, only tongues can achieve kinship status. *Lenguajes* can be native and *idiomas* can be national or regional, but only a *lengua* can be familial. There are no "mother languages" or "father idioms," for all relations of language kinship pass through the tongue. This means, also, that the mesh between desire and language, Eros and Logos, incarnates in tongues rather than languages. The site of logo-eroticism is the tongue. In a poem entitled "Dulzura," Sandra Cisneros asks her lover: "Make love to me in Spanish. / Not with that other tongue." The racy switch in prepositions, from "in" to "with," signals the looseness of tongues, how fluidly they allow us to slide from Logos to Eros. "I am just a cunning lingual," puns the Chicano poet El Huitlacoche in "Searching for La Real Cosa," once again logo-eroticizing, mingling verbal and erotic play in the folds of his tongue. Tongues tie in ways that languages never do, and no language can match the looseness of a tongue.

Not that relations with our tongues are always cordial, however. As I have said, a tongue can also inspire hatred, anger, despair, resentment. The Cuban Edmundo Desnoes, who achieved fleeting fame in the 1960s with his novel, *Memorias del subdesarrollo* (1965), recently gave Spanish a tongue-lashing: "Spanish, the most self-centered Western language, should become aware of the golden cage in which singing changes nothing and divest itself of its baroque ballast. Only what is empty can be filled."[32] Then, remixing already mixed metaphors, he proceeds to say that Spanish is a "black hole" that has swallowed Spain as well as Spanish America. And a black hole it may well be, but only for Desnoes, who has not published another novel in almost four decades. The diatribe against his mother tongue—the essay is entitled, "Born in Spanish"—barely conceals Desnoes's disgust at himself for his legendary case of writer's block. The golden cage is of the writer's own making; the baroque ballast, evident even in his English prose, bears the weight of his own sterility. Because tongues are body parts, Desnoes cannot disparage his without lapsing into self-hatred. Several centuries ago, the Spaniard Cristobal de Villalón wrote: "Harto es enemigo de sí quien estima más la lengua de los otros que la suya propia"[33] [Whoever esteems another tongue more than his own is his own worst enemy]. Some of us make love with our tongues; others slit their throats with it.

Imaged as tongue, language is resolutely phonocentric. Prosodic rather than prosaic, tongues do not have syntax or vocabulary. Those who "speak in tongues" take language back to its origins as glossolalia, inarticulate phonation. Since appeals to language as *lengua* transport us to the realm of sound before words, to the world of infancy (literally *in-fari*, speechlessness), they are always regressive. Recalling his Spanish-only childhood, Richard Rodriguez writes: "Tongues explored the edges of the words, especially the fat vowels. And we happily sounded that military drum roll, the twirling roar of the Spanish *r*. Family language: my family's sounds." Push a tongue back, and you hear babytalk, so-called "motherese." Push it back further, and what you hear is lalling. When Rodriguez adds that he and his siblings "burst syllables into fragments of laughter," he is evoking the preverbal, phonophiliac force of his lingual (rather than linguistic) Spanish. Thus, there are two tongues in any mother tongue: the mother's and the child's. Our first language is the tongue we suck in, in both the active and passive senses of the verb.

Living in exile in Washington D.C., Juan Ramón Jiménez fantasized that the only person who had ever spoken genuine Spanish ("el español que yo creo español" [the Spanish that I believe to be Spanish]) was his mother, whose voice he still heard beneath his own.[34] Although a tongue does not have to be identified exclusively with the female parent (Rodriguez's drum-rolling *r* evokes his father), Juan Ramón's fantasy exemplifies the regressiveness inherent in the notion of a tongue. The exiled Juan Ramón, who believed that for every word of English that he learned he would forget several in Spanish, thought of himself as *deslenguado,* "untongued," because of his physical separation from his mother's (and thus his mother) tongue. The loss of a tongue is felt as an amputation.

A tongue should not be confused with an idiolect, for an idiolect—the sum total of an individual's speech habits—is a subset of one or several languages. The distinction between a tongue and a language is qualitative, not quantitative. A tongue is not a "personal dialect" or the sociolect of a society of one; what distinguishes it is not lexis but cathexis. This is why linguistic ineptness does not undermine a tongue's kinship status. Just as illiteracy is not aphasia, grammatical or lexical deficiencies do not invalidate claims of language kinship. There are no tongue tests, no proficiency exams for membership in a language family.

Language as *Idioma*

If *lengua* bespeaks kinship, *idioma* reveals national or regional allegiances. When the exiled Pedro Salinas states, "el idioma es la mejor memoria de mi país," his use of *idioma* rather than its near synonyms, *lengua* or *lenguaje,* is prompted by the proximity of *mi país.*[35] The idiomatic is the "genius of the local,"[36] words marked by place. In Spanish, *idioma* carries this meaning already in Sebastián de Covarrubias's *Tesoro de la lengua castellana o española* (1611), the first Spanish dictionary, where *idioma* is defined as "la propia lengua de cada nación" [each nation's own tongue]. What a tongue is to an individual, an "idiom" is to a people. When Borges entitled his book on Argentine Spanish *El idioma de los argentinos* (1928), he was drawing on this semantic tradition. When Juan Marinello, in a memorable reflection on New World Spanish, concluded, "Somos a través de un idioma que es nuestro siendo extranjero" [we exist through an *idioma* that is our own while being foreign], the choice of *idioma* over *lengua* or *lenguaje* was once again dictated by the cultural emphasis, his view of Spanish as the bearer of Iberian culture, what he terms "el lenguaje de Castilla."[37] *Idioma* is native language rather than mother tongue. Sealing the bond between person and place, it evokes the country or region where we are born or raised, the *patria (grande* or *chica)* of which we are native or "natural," as one says in Spanish. In Latin, the mother tongue was *patrius sermo,* the speech of the homeland, which Juan Ramón Jiménez correctly translates as "[el] Sacrosanto Idioma de la Patria."[38]

Unlike a tongue, an *idioma* is external to the user. I hold my tongue, I bite my tongue. I cannot hold or bite my *idioma.* When a tongue rises to speech, it discloses the inner self. As Walter Ong points out, voices reveal interiors; and tongues (in the sense in which I am using the term) are organs of sound.[39] That's the reason the AATSP slogan referred to Spanish as "la lengua [rather than *el idioma*] del alma." An *idioma* does not speak for my soul but for my community's. Although an *idioma* too is usually thought of in acoustic terms, its sounds are ambient, not intestine; their locus is the ear, not the mouth. The Spanish phrase "el suelo del idioma" [the ground of language] displaces from the personal to the social, from soul to *suelo.* Like "idioms" in the more restricted sense, the idiomatic alludes to modes of speech that evolve independently of any individual user, that flourish on common ground. In the preface to *Todo más claro* (1949), Pedro Salinas states that he has weathered his years of exile "abrazado a mi idioma como a un incomparable bien"[40] [clutching my idioma as it were an incomparable good]. The metaphor supposes the autonomous, external existence of Spanish, his substitute homeland.

Whereas a speaker possesses his tongue entirely, an *idioma,* no matter how native, is possessed incompletely. Only of my tongue can I confidently say, "it is all mine." I possess my tongue because it exists by virtue of my possession of it. Detached from me, it withers; without me, it is a mouthful of air. In this sense, the expression "mi lengua" is already a redundancy, for in Spanish one does not use the possessive adjective with personal body parts. Being external to the user, an *idioma* reverses the possessor-possessed relation: One belongs to an *idioma* as one belongs to a culture or a community or a country, but my tongue belongs to me. What is more, it belongs *only* to me. While it may seem that others can share my tongue, it is not exactly "my" tongue that they are sharing, for the emotional tenor of my tongue ties, the ways in which I am wont to possess my tongue, are mine alone. Just as it is impossible for two people to love the "same" man or woman, it is impossible for anybody but me to have my tongue. If I were to lose my tongue, it would not be to another speaker, but to another tongue.

Since family ties usually run deeper than national allegiances, there is a perceptible depreciation in the passage from *lengua* to *idioma.* Because of its etymology, *idioma* connotes limitation or peculiarness; like other words that share the same Greek root—idiosyncracy, idiocy—*idioma* gives off the scent of the substandard, the not-quite-right. For this reason, appeals to language loyalty as the defense of a tongue will always be stronger than those expressed in terms of an *idioma*. But such appeals, based as they are on the mistaken assumption that tongues can be shared, are fundamentally bogus. The collective defense or promotion of a *lengua* always subserves a political or a social agenda. The real purpose of the AATSP slogan is to put more students in Spanish classrooms.

LANGUAGE AS *LENGUAJE*

If a *lengua* is corporal and *idioma* is locative, *lenguaje* is language detached from both person and place; that is, language as structure, as an abstract and rational system, somewhat like Saussure's *langue*. If a speaker's relation to a tongue is affective, and that to an *idioma* is cultural, his or her relation to *lenguaje* is cognitive. Silencing the tongue and ungrounding the idiomatic, *lenguaje* sublimates and universalizes. It is unusual to hear someone say, "*mi lenguaje*," for languages are not possessions but acquisitions. Moreover, one does not "belong" to a *lenguaje* as one belongs to an *idioma*. Although a *lenguaje* also exists independently of individual speakers, it is not identified with a particular region or nationality, unless it is the virtual community of all the speakers of the language. Pedro Salinas entitles his defense of the Spanish language "Aprecio y defensa del lenguaje" in order to depersonalize and delocalize his argument, as if his subject were language in general rather than his mother tongue and the *idioma* under siege in Puerto Rico, where he delivered his address. By identifying Castilian Spanish with *el lenguaje*, he is not quite suggesting that Spanish is a universal language, but he does insinuate that his own *lengua* and *idioma* are richer—more articulate, more resourceful, more poetic—than either Puerto Rican Spanish or the American English from which he was fleeing when he left Baltimore for San Juan.

Such appeals to linguistic solidarity typically avoid the rhetoric of the idiomatic, since they aim to subsume regional or national variation under a transnational standard, which Salinas (but not only Salinas) identifies with Castilian usage. He could certainly have availed himself of *lengua*, as in Andrés Iduarte's "De la lengua y su día" (1955), a parallel text, to make similar claims. But had he done so, his title would then have laid the groundwork for a personal appreciation of Spanish, as in Iduarte's speech, rather than for a logical and philological "defense." As we will see, Salinas does mount an impassioned plea for the survival of a certain variety of Spanish, but he does so covertly, in the guise of linguistic and cultural argument, wielding the tools of the professor to shore up the vocation of the poet. But in the end, when he says *el lenguaje,* he really means *mi lengua.*

Although the distinction between *lengua* and *lenguaje* sometimes translates into that between speech and writing, in a literary setting these terms are often used to differentiate between writing that is "alive," words with a voice, and mute letters. In the work of Richard Rodriguez, this distinction is then mapped onto Spanish and English, so that a sonorous tongue (Spanish) competes with, and eventually gives way to, a voiceless language (English). Contrary to what *Hunger of Memory* wants to assert, however, the contest between Spanish and English is resolved in favor of the former, for *lenguajes* cannot rival *lenguas* or *idiomas* in their hold on individual speakers, including Rodriguez. In the sixteenth-century *Diálogo de la lengua,* Juan de Valdés enjoins his countrymen to "ilustrar y enriquecer la lengua que nos es natural y que mamamos en las tetas de nuestras madres"[41] [improve and enrich our natural tongue, the one we sucked at our mother's breasts]. His statement draws on the aura of *idioma* (our "natural," that is, native language) and *lengua* (the tongue we imbibe with our tongue). Having no such aura, a *lenguaje* can appeal to us intellectually or aesthetically, but it cannot bind us like a tongue or house us like an *idioma.*

Some of the writers in this book will deliberately reduce a *lengua* or an *idioma* to a *lenguaje* as a protective reaction against alien encroachments. When a foreign language becomes a second language, it threatens to take over areas of experience occupied by our mother tongue and our native idiom. In such a situation, individuals will sometimes try to silence the intrusive language, either by denying its status as a language or, less radically, by suppressing its lingual and idiomatic force. Relegated to Tomos, anxious that the "hostile sounds" and the "fierce voices" around him will corrupt his Latin, Ovid inveighs against the Tomitans' *barbara lingua,* a nearly oxymoronic phrase, for a barbaric language is hardly a vehicle for human speech (*Tristia,* 5.2.67). For his part, Juan Ramón Jiménez compared the sounds of English to animal noises. (Decades earlier, upon arriving in New York City, the Nicaraguan poet Rubén Darío had remarked on "the barking Yankee slang.")[42] And yet Juan Ramón (like Darío) had no difficulties with literary English, of which he was an avid reader; but the poetic diction of Shelley or Yeats was neither *lengua* nor *idioma,* only *lenguaje.* It did not bellow in his ear like the speech of his American neighbors. Echoing Ovid, Salinas also disparaged the American vernacular as a sublanguage, rudimentary to the point of inexpressiveness; but he too read widely and deeply in English poetry. Only when language incarnates as alien sound, as xenophony, is it necessary to take defensive measures.

In the 1950s, Luis Cernuda abandoned a secure and well-paying job at Mt. Holyoke College in large part to get away from sounds that he perceived as hostile—the "uncultured" and "rancorous" voices of Americans. He framed his return to a hispanophone setting as the recovery of the long-lost harmony between the music of his soul and that of the outside world. This re-audition of the mother tongue, whether desired as a fantasy or enjoyed as a reality, will be a recurring motif. Because many of the writers I discuss spent part of their lives away from their homeland, the experience of exile is woven into the fabric of their tongue ties. As Joseph Brodsky points out, for a writer exile is a linguistic event.[43] Even when the dislocation is not spatial but temporal—aging is also a process of exile—the estranged writer will long for, and mentally rehear, the sounds and voices she heard in childhood. Hearing the mother tongue again, as Cernuda did in Mexico or as Cisneros and Ortiz Cofer do in some of their poems, becomes the distinctive form of return or *desexilio*. Logos, Eros, Xenos—these are the three actors that together play out the *trama* and the trauma of tongue ties.

It should be clear that my emphasis will fall on languages rather than on Language, on the intricacies of Spanish-English bilingualism rather than on language as a universal human faculty or an artistic medium. It should also be clear that I am interested, above all, in the writer in the writing. In *Three Philosophical Poets,* George Santayana remarks that he writes as a pupil of his authors. Although my goals are more modest than Santayana's, I have tried to do the same. After reading and listening to "my" authors, I have tried to articulate the lessons they have taught me about their negotiations in and with their tongues. I have proceeded by what Santayana called "imitative sympathy,"[44] the activity of trying to understand, from within a writer's own circumstances, the literary and affective dynamics of his or her investment in Spanish and English. When it seemed productive to do so, I have not hesitated to delve, at times speculatively and perhaps indiscreetly, into a writer's life. If the term did not have unpleasantly clinical connotations, I would call the chapters that follow "case histories" of these writers' logo-erotic affections (and, at times, afflictions). Although historical events such as the Spanish-American War, the Spanish Civil War, and the Cuban Revolution form part of the background of my discussion, I begin and end with the linguistic situation—the linguistic entanglement—of an individual writer and his or her distinctive quality of voice.

I am well aware, however, of the tenuous borderline between imitation and projection, a threshold I may well have crossed on occasion.

Santayana coined the notion of "animal faith" to designate our unavoidable common-sense commitment to the world as it is. I bring his animal faith with me when I go into the classroom or the library. I teach and read and write from the conviction that when I speak, I speak; and when I listen, someone else—you or he or she—speaks to me, whether from a book or a desk. I cannot do justice to this body of writing, to my conviction of its excellence and relevance, to the ways in which it has helped me unravel my own tongue ties, except by taking it personally. Which to me means not reducing writers and their readers to subject positions or textual constructs. Naiveté also means naturalness. One of the lessons I have learned from Santayana and company is that a writer must find the words—be they *lengua, idioma,* or *lenguaje*—that will allow him or her to keep on writing. I write from the globular rather than the global. Mine is not a cultural study but a survival guide. I map contact zones that exist within the writers themselves, internal rather than regional topographies. It is only when I look away from the big picture and put away the large scale that my tongue feels free. Then I can understand what it was like for one writer to lose her mother tongue, or for another to cling to it, or for a third to refuse to choose.

Chapter 1

Saying Un-English Things
in English

George, digo Jorge Santayana, ese español ajeno y perdido en su patria y otras patrias.
[George, I mean, Jorge Santayana, that alien Spaniard, lost in his and other homelands]

—Juan Ramón Jiménez

In the afternoon of November 8, 1951, the Spanish poet Jorge Guillén paid a visit to George Santayana at the clinic of the Blue Nuns in Rome, where the old philosopher had lived for ten years. At the time, one year before his death, Santayana's reputation in the Hispanic world was broad but shallow. Although some of his principal books had been translated into Spanish, he remained an enigma, a philosopher less known for his philosophy than for his nationality. Even after his death, Santayana's compatriots remained primarily interested in his *españolidad*, whether or to what extent his work reflected a "Spanish" or "Latin" outlook on the world. According to some, even though Santayana wrote in English and resided abroad for most of his life, he had never stopped listening to "the voice of his Spanish blood."[1] As Ramón Sender pointed out, had Santayana stayed in Spain he would have been a member of the Generation of 1898 (he was one year older than Miguel de Unamuno), and even in English his work was similar enough to that of his peers to make him the "evasivo fantasma del 98"[2] [the evasive ghost of 1898]. Others took the position that, his parentage and his place of birth notwithstanding, Santayana was no more Spanish than he was American, or anything else, for his was a philosophy of *desasimiento*, Stoic detachment.

Initially among the skeptics, Guillén came away from the meeting impressed by how Spanish Santayana looked and sounded. Not only did he speak the language "naturally," he even used such colloquialisms as *duro* for dollar and *fonda* for restaurant. From the moment that Guillén had walked into the room, Santayana had begun talking in fluent Spanish, and he had not stopped until an hour and a half later. He was no more and no less than "a Spaniard from Ávila" who even remembered the exact date that he had entered the clinic because it had been St. Theresa's feast day. Reconstructing the conversation for his friend Pedro Salinas a couple of days later, Guillén concluded that Santayana was "a charlatan like us!"[3]

During their meeting, Santayana explained to Guillén that while he had written his prose works in English to reach a broader audience, his poetry would have turned out better in Spanish, an opinion he repeated throughout his life. For the mature Santayana, the verses he wrote as a young man were marred both by his philosophic temper and by the fact that English, not being his mother tongue, did not reach down to his "centre."[4] And yet, on the few occasions when he referred to his adoption of English, he spoke casually about it, as if the change in languages also did not reach his center. Regarding himself as "an unattached man who writes in the English language," Santayana believed that English no more defined him than the *fondas* he patronized or the countries he visited.[5] In a letter to his Harvard friend Henry Ward Abbot, he states: "I sponge systematically and on principle, not feeling my dignity compromised thereby any more than if I were a monk or a soldier."[6] His use of English was another form of sponging. For the writer who entitled the last chapter of his autobiography "My Host the World," English was a host language rather than a kinship tongue, a hotel not a homestead, rooms that he occupied but to which he had no vital attachment or obligation.

Santayana's laxity about his tongue ties was part of a more general indifference. Other than scattered aphorisms, two chapters in *The Life of Reason* (1905–1906) and another in *The Realm of Essence* (1927) are the sum of his sustained reflections on language. Although he composed much of his mature work during the ascendancy of analytic philosophy (Wittgenstein's *Tractatus* was published two years before *Scepticism and Animal Faith* [1923], the volume where Santayana introduced his mature system of philosophy), Santayana's kernel notions—animal faith, essence, matter, spirit—do not hinge on his views on language, which is one reason he is often regarded by professional philosophers as a throwback, "the last bright autumn of the old philosophy."[7] According to Timothy Sprigge, one of his keenest and most sympathetic recent commentators, Santayana is at his weakest philosophizing about language, an odd circumstance for someone who grew up bilingually.[8] But he regarded arguments about the meaning of meaning as no more than "verbal dialectics."[9] Even in his literary criticism he paid scant attention to rhetoric or style; he could write sparkling pages about Lucretius, Dante, or Goethe—his trinity of "philosophical poets"—without saying much of anything about their verbal artistry. Less interested in the arrangement of words than in the vision that underlay them, he valued poetry, as he valued religion, for its "sane and steady idealization" of human life. A poetry that relied on beauties of expression was of a lower kind. The writings of Epicure or St. Thomas Aquinas contained not one word of poetry, even though their doctrines were supremely poetic. And whatever modest merit his own verses possessed had to do not with their diction but with "the poetry of the subject-matter."[10]

As someone who wrote all of his work in a non-native language and spent most of his life in xenophone settings, Santayana was a logical candidate for the heightened linguistic awareness characteristic of polyglots. But he never felt, or was reluctant to admit that he felt, the interest and delight in the sound and fabric of words that arises from a knowledge of several languages. He intensely disliked word play, for puns were to him a "grotesque example" of the abuse of language; and the kind of poetry that showcased the material properties of words was no more than "mere piping."[11] Nothing in Santayana's English prose evinces that "xenity" or foreign feel that one spots even in the most accomplished bilingual writers.[12] The multiplicity of the world's languages distressed him, and contemporary experiments with Spanglish would have horrified him. More like Beckett than like Nabokov, he strove to eliminate all traces of his other languages from his style. His English had no memory of his Spanish, as if his language didn't know his tongue. It may be an overstatement to assert that Santayana "repressed" language—how can a writer repress his medium?—but it is at least fair to say that he neglected the issues raised by his own background and linguistic practice, like a man who looks constantly in a mirror without ever seeing the mirror itself.

How Santayana came to stand before that mirror is a story worth retelling. Born in Madrid in 1863 of Spanish parents, he was his father's first and only child, but his mother's sixth. Before marrying Agustín Santayana, Josefina Borrás had been married to George Sturgis, the scion of a wealthy New England family, whom she had met in the Philippines and with whom she had five children. Some years after Sturgis's death, during a visit to Spain, she ran into Agustín, the retired former secretary to the general governor of the Philippines. Although they had little in common other than their youthful memories of the Pacific, Agustín and Josefina married in 1862 after a brief courtship. According to their only son, the marriage was passionless and irrational, the result of an "irresistible daemonic force, a drift of circumstances and propensities" (*PP*, 50).

"I am glad to say," he reports in a letter written during his college days, "that neither my father nor my mother have ever been in love either with each other or with anybody else."[13] At the time of the marriage his father was over fifty and his mother was almost forty. He was a hypochondriacal and somewhat misanthropic old bachelor who lived on a modest government pension; equally set in her ways, Josefina disliked Spanish society and depended financially on the Sturgises. What's more, she had promised her late husband to raise their three surviving children in the States. When Santayana was five years old, his mother suddenly moved back to Boston with his half-siblings, leaving George in Ávila with his father. Three years later, in 1872, Agustín decided that his son would be better off with his mother. He took George to Boston and returned to Ávila. Although Agustín later said that he intended the separation to be temporary, he and his son did not see each other again for ten years, and only rarely after that.

When eight-year-old George arrived in Boston, he did not know a word of English. His half-sister Susana, who was twelve years older, was his first English teacher. The home lessons were reinforced in school, and before long he was speaking the language without an accent, an accomplishment that he attributed to his good ear and "flexible tongue." (Years later a British acquaintance would remark that Santayana's fastidious diction made him sound like Queen Victoria). Although he continued to speak Spanish at home, by the time he saw his father again, in the summer after his freshman year at Harvard, he no longer felt comfortable in his native language. For many years Agustín had expected that his son, after completing his education in Boston, would settle in Spain to pursue a career in the diplomatic service; but in spite of his father's reassurances, the adolescent Santayana worried that his deficient Spanish would be an impediment to a successful career in his homeland.[14] After much soul-searching (and considerable pressure from his mother, who wanted her son to remain by her side) he began graduate studies in philosophy at Harvard.

By not returning to Spain, Santayana not only sealed the rift with his father, who lamented but did not oppose his son's decision, but also turned himself into a chronic exile. Henceforth he would consider himself a "*déraciné*, a man who has been torn up by the roots" (*PP*, 362), a condition that in his view provided certain intellectual advantages but imposed severe limitations, including childlessness. As he put it, with uncharacteristic bluntness, "I refuse to be annexed, to be grafted, to be abolished, or to be grafted to any plant of a different species" (*PP*, 363). Although in his old age he complained with some bitterness that he had been "involuntarily uprooted" from his homeland, the truth is that when he had the opportunity to reroot himself, he decided against it. Like his father, Santayana tended to take the path of least resistance, which usually meant the one not blocked by his mother. Having to choose between "sticking to her and sticking to his father and his country," it was inevitable that he would choose the former (*PP*, 22). Even if his father was his "natural centre," his mother had much the greater influence on him, not least because she controlled the purse strings. Santayana respected his father, but he submitted to his mother. Explaining his father's tendency to abdicate, he writes: "I am afraid that my father, unlike my mother, was not brave" (*PP*, 17). Perhaps inadvertently, the father's cowardice resurfaces in the son's fear.

Although he stayed in Boston, Santayana embraced the Spanishness that he had chosen not to exercise. As he insisted countless times, Spain, where he spent the first nine years of his life, rather the United States, where he would live for more than forty, was his "real country."[15] Anytime he ran afoul of authority or convention, both as a student and as a professor, he pulled out the excuse that he wasn't American. If he did not hunker down as much as his classmates, it was his "Latin" lassitude; if he did not seem as ambitious as his colleagues in the philosophy department, it was because he hailed from Old Castile, where human aspirations come to dust. When William James, his mentor at Harvard, remarked that Santayana's *Interpretations of Poetry and Religion* (1900) gave voice to a "moribund Latinity," Santayana did not object; he only answered that as a representative of that dying race his mission was to propagate "straight thinking" among the future masters of the world, including James himself.[16]

But Santayana's loyalty to Latinity did not extend to living in Spain or speaking its language. Believing that he could not master two languages at once, he deliberately abandoned Spanish, rarely reading Spanish books and using the language only when he was forced to. The divorce of language and nationality deepened and complicated his exile, for it deprived his Spanishness of a material symbol and support. Exiles seldom abandon their mother tongue, the one portable piece of their homeland. But Santayana was an odd type of exile. When he stated, in English, that he was an exile, the language of the assertion was in large measure its rationale. Recollecting his second visit to Spain in 1886, he writes: "There was no question any longer of a career in Spain; I was too old and too much expatriated by my English language and my American associations" (*PP*, 321). The passive voice dissembles Santayana's agency in the expatriation, as if he had been overcome by linguistic forces over which he had no control. It is truer to say that Santayana grew distanced from Spanish, as from his father, partly by chance and partly by choice.

That the separations were amicable did not make them less traumatic. The simultaneous disappearance of his father and emergence of English would have profound consequences for Santayana's attitude toward his two languages. Agustín Santayana was a talkative, opinionated man who, according to his son, wrote "admirably" and spoke "the purest" Spanish.[17] In his youth he had translated Seneca's tragedies and authored a little book about the Philippines. His many letters, some of them quite eloquent, bear out the son's judgment of his father's literary talents. Intellectually curious and full of strong if crotchety opinions, Agustín had read widely and could turn a phrase. It is not unusual to find him writing to his son about esoteric subjects such as Romantic poetry, Cardinal Newman's defection from Anglicanism, or the merits of a particular Spanish translation of Horace. By contrast, his mother was a hardened, practical woman whose eventful life had left her with an uncertain command of both Spanish and English. The daughter of a restless Catalan free-thinker who had lived in Scotland and Virginia before settling in Barcelona, during her childhood Josefina spoke Catalan as well as Spanish and English. According to Santayana, the great sorrow of her life had been the death in infancy of her first-born son, "Pepín" Sturgis, a tragedy that established in her household a "reign of silent despair" (*PP*, 42). Pepín's death, combined with her linguistic insecurity, made Josefina "prevailingly silent," a woman of "few words and terrible glances" who regarded her other children as inferior (*PP*, 31). A nosy Boston acquaintance once asked her how she spent her time; she replied, "In summer I try to keep cool, and in winter I try to keep warm."

Because his mother wasn't comfortable in any language, Santayana identified Spanish with his father, the author of the never-ending stream of letters from Ávila. Spanish became for him less a "mother" than a "father" tongue, a vital link to the garrulous father rather than to the mute mother. When he states that he was "expatriated" by the English language, the verb aims at the *pater* inside the *patria*. His expatriation amounted to linguistic patricide, a way of formalizing the separation from his father. As the years went by, both father and son realized that English was not the least of the obstacles that stood between them. When Santayana turned sixteen, his father wrote him the customary birthday letter. But on this occasion Agustín decided to write in English and to address him as George, the only time that he did so. In closing he says: "I do promise not to write again in English. This is a Caprice born of the desire of signalizing your birthday."[18] By "signalizing" (a transla-tion of the Spanish *señalar*) the birthday in English, Agustín recognizes that his son's identity is now bound up in a different language. What is caprice in the father is fate in the son. On the cusp of adulthood, "Jorge" has become "George" even for his Castilian father.

Not that this fate was completely unexpected, for in a sense "Jorge" had been "George" all along. His sister Susana, who was also his godmother, had chosen her brother's Christian name in memory of none other than her late father, George Sturgis. Santayana speculates that Agustín did not object because he possessed an "ironical turn of mind" and half-expected his son to grow up into a "simpleton" like his wife's first husband (*PP*, 65). For her part, his mother was too wrapped up in her dumb misery to pay much attention to her children's names. Abdicating to Susana, Santayana's parents gave their son over not to his mother's or father's tongue, but to that of the man known in the household as "Papa George," Santayana's "stepfather by anticipation" (*PP*, 65).

Susana's role in shaping Santayana's tongue ties was crucial. In her brother's eyes "Susie" (as he always called her) was a Sturgis, not a Borrás, her warmth and liveliness a marked contrast to their mother's dour temperament. As the person most involved in George's upbring-ing, she was his "second mother," the "greatest power" and "strongest affection" of his life (*PP*, 77). Indeed, as he once put it, Susana was "psychologically my mother, and one might almost say, my wife."[19] Elias Canetti, who learned German from his mother at the same age that Santayana learned English from his sister, calls German his "belated mother tongue"[20]; for Santayana English was rather a "deuteromaternal" tongue, the language of godmothers and half-sisters, which distanced him from both his parents even as it fulfilled the anglophone promise of his baptismal name. When Santayana states that English did not reach down to his center, he is right insofar as his father was his center. But given enough time exiles grow or acquire other centers, other attach-ments; Susie Sturgis and her Boston family also formed a center, an alternative set of cultural and family allegiances. However casually Santayana may have spoken about it, his acquisition of English implied an existential and cultural relocation. He not only adopted English, he was adopted by it, in the full sense of the verb.

That he may have been more ambivalent than he allowed about the adoption comes across in one of the few examples of his Spanish-language correspondence, a thank-you note he wrote to Miguel de Unamuno upon receiving *El sentimiento trágico de la vida* (1913). After heaping praise on the book (which of course he hadn't read), Santayana adds: "Siendo español y encontrandome en este momento en ciudad tan puramente castellana cómo Ávila, no he querido escribir á V. sinó en la lengua materna, aunque sea con la torpeza propria de quien se sirve habitualmente de otro idioma"[21] [Being a Spaniard and finding myself at the moment in such a purely Castilian city as Avila, I wanted to write to you in my mother tongue, even if with the awkwardness typical of someone who habitually makes use of another *idioma*]. The apologetic tone reveals that even the prince of detachment felt embarrassed about his abandonment of Spanish, an embarrassment justified by the unintended orthographic lapses (such as "proprio" instead of "propio"). Since the two men shared other languages, including English, Santayana might have written the letter in his second-mother tongue, or he might have opted for a neutral linguistic venue, such as French. But not to have addressed the author of *En torno al casticismo* in Spanish would have been an admission of denaturalization, a crime of *lesa españolidad*. That he wrote in Spanish to Unamuno, someone whom he knew to be a leading figure in Spanish intellectual life, suggests that the distinction between language and nationality collapsed under pressure. Note Santayana's choice of words: while Spanish is his "lengua materna," English is his "idioma." Since on the scale of human affect a *lengua* ranks above an *idioma,* he privileges Spanish, to which he has an affective rather than an instrumental relation. English may be his literary medium, the language of which he "makes use" or to which he "helps himself" (the two senses of "se sirve") but Spanish is his tongue. Not surprisingly, he signs the letter with his full Spanish name, "Jorge Ruiz de Santayana."[22] What better guarantor of our nationality than the language of our name?

Some years later Santayana elaborated his instrumental view of English in a passage from "A Brief History of My Opinions" (1930), an autobiographical essay where he discusses his switch in languages. Referring to his father's expectation that he would return to Spain after finishing his undergraduate studies at Harvard, he explains:

We should both of us have liked the Spanish army or diplomatic service, but for the first I was already too old, and our means and our social relations hardly sufficed for the second. Moreover, by that time [1883] I felt like a foreigner in Spain, more acutely so than in America, although for more trivial reasons: my Yankee manners seemed outlandish here, and I could not do justice to myself in the language. Nor was I inclined to overcome this handicap, as perhaps I might have done with little effort: nothing in Spanish life or literature at that time particularly attracted me. English had become my only possible instrument, and I deliberately put away everything that might confuse me in that medium. English, and the whole Anglo-Saxon tradition in literature and philosophy, have always been a medium to me rather than a source. My natural affinities were elsewhere. Moreover, scholarship and learning of any sort seemed to me a means, not an end. I always hated to be a professor. Latin and Greek,

French, Italian, and German, although I can read them, were languages which I never learned well. It seemed an accident to me if the matters which interested me came clothed in the rhetoric of one or another of these nations: I was not without a certain temperamental rhetoric of my own in which to recast what I adopted. Thus in renouncing everything else for the sake of English letters I might be said to have been guilty, quite unintentionally, of a little stratagem, as if I had set out to say plausibly in English as many un-English things as possible.[23]

Although this passage illustrates the equanimity with which Santayana related the most traumatic events in his life, I'm not sure that his account is persuasive. For one thing, not to be able to do justice to yourself in your mother tongue is not a "trivial" matter; as in the letter to Unamuno, it breeds guilt and embarrassment. For another, who is this translinguistic "self" that demands justice? When Santayana says "myself," does he intend to include within the pronoun the child who only spoke Spanish for the first nine years of his life? If so, how could an English-only self do justice to a childhood that transpired in Spanish? Or is it perhaps that Santayana defines his "self" by acts of exclusion rather than inclusion?

His answer to these questions lies in the distinction between medium and source. As medium, language is rhetoric, form rather than substance, the dress of thought. But since Santayana's source is Spain, it precedes and transcends his medium. English takes a back seat to his "natural affinities," to his "temperamental rhetoric," which allow him not only to recast what he receives but even to say "un-English things in English." I'm not sure whether Santayana is arguing, contra Whorf, that languages do not constrain their speakers, or whether he is only claiming that they do not constrain *him*. A firm believer in rules, Santayana believed equally firmly that he was the exception. The language of an idea, he says, "seemed to me an accident," as if he were articulating a personal quirk, another type of accident, rather than a general principle. He may well have thought that, being a *déraciné*, he was no more bound by languages than by the biblical injunction to be fruitful and multiply, which he advocated for others but not for himself. Roots are entanglements, he once wrote; in his mind, uprootedness may have exempted him from linguistic as well as reproductive entanglements.

Elsewhere in his writings, however, he takes a rather different view. In a letter written late in his life, he asserts that French philosophers "are not so good in the heights and the depths, because they can't be written about in good French, and they don't talk inflated nonsense about those super- or infra-human things, because the French language will not permit it."[24] But if French philosophers can't say un-French things in French, how can Santayana say un-English things in English? Half a century earlier, in *The Sense of Beauty* (1896), he had already expressed a similar opinion: "Not only are words untranslatable when the exact object has no name in another language, as 'home' or 'mon ami,' but even when the object is the same, the attitude toward it, incorporated in one word, cannot be rendered by another. Thus, to my sense, 'bread' is as inadequate a translation of the human intensity of the Spanish 'pan' as 'Dios' is of the awful mystery of the English 'God.'"[25] Santayana here evinces the multilingual's typical sensitivity to connotative nuance and phonic value. In *Dominations and Powers*, he puts it this way: "Each language has its special euphony, as every string or wind instrument has; and its peculiar genius casts over the whole world, which men survey and conceive chiefly through verbal description, a distinctive grammatical and poetic colour, a mode of vibrating and rhyming which only those who use that language can discern in things."[26] But if each language has its own genius and music, if "bread" and "God" are not the same as *pan* and *Dios,* the specific verbal incarnation of an idea is not accidental, not merely rhetorical clothing.

The "Whorfian" Santayana undermines the autobiographer. But one does not have to buy into linguistic relativism to question the distinction between a medium that lacks content and a source that transcends expression. Even in Santayana's "little stratagem" of saying "plausibly" in English as many un-English things as possible, the adverb implies an acceptance of limits—linguistic form conditioning content. This adherence to conventions of plausibility follows from his surprisingly categorical renunciation of "everything" that might "confuse" him in the English medium, a renunciation that betrays a desire *not* to say un-English things in English, and in which we can hear an echo of his mother's linguistic insecurities. Paradoxically, even as Santayana declares his independence from English, he abjures Spanish for its sake. His distinction between medium and source does not hold up, for it is inevitable that, to a greater or lesser degree, medium and source will press on each other. In English, Santayana's un-English things will lose at least some of their un-Englishness. Ultimately everything that can be said in English will be an English thing.

In *Reason in Art,* the fourth volume of *The Life of Reason* (1905–1906), Santayana also takes a rather Whorfian view of language. He begins conventionally by analyzing language (or "speech") into material and semantic components, a "body" and a "soul," adding that the corporealness of words creates a "drift proper to the verbal medium" (*RA,* 70). As he explains, "Euphony, verbal analogy, grammatical fancy, poetic confusion, continually drive language afield" from its denotative function (*RA*, 81). To make speech correspond to intention, speakers must conquer a medium that is "difficult to subdue" (*RA*, 81). The catch, however, is that these difficulties occur primarily in poetry, since prose does not drift or stray to the same extent. "Meager and bodiless," prose "clarifies" the medium to the point of transparency. The "purest prose," he says in an analogous passage from *Interpretations of Poetry and Religion*, "is a mere vehicle for thought."[27] But poetry "keeps communication massive and instinctive, immersed in music, and inexhaustible by clear thought" (*RA*, 100). Only poetry "elaborates the fact in expressing it, and endows it with affinities alien to its proper nature" (*RA*, 75).

In Santayana's thinking, prose and poetry invert the relation between medium and message. Defined by "the immersion of the message in the medium" (*RA*, 77), poetry draws the reader's or listener's attention to the words themselves; like a stained-glass window, a poem arrests attention on itself. By contrast, prose interposes no obstacles to transparence; docile and transitive, it prevents the message from capsizing in the medium. A "clarified poetry," one that removes the stain from the window, one endowed with the transparency of prose, would sacrifice beauties of expression—euphony and euphuism—for the sake of intelligibility. But for Santayana "clarified poetry" is another term for philosophical prose, which, by apprehending facts clearly and humanely, has a beauty all its own. The highest poetry, that of subject matter, is a poetry without poems, such as one finds in the ideas of great thinkers like Spinoza.

Although Santayana's description of a poem as a self-reflexive artifact is typical of Modernist poetics, the distinction between prose and poetry cannot pass the test of his own practice. Twenty years after *The Life of Reason*, he returned to this distinction in *The Realm of Essence* (1927). The uniqueness of poetry, he repeats, lies in the material properties and associations of words; but in prose "words are primarily signs for some fact they serve to record or announce. The sounds themselves, and the other essences, emotional or pictorial, which in intuition convey such information, are passed over. They are mere instruments—the claw with which the intent clutches the potent fact."[28] This vivid metaphor illustrates why prose cannot be distinguished from poetry as Santayana would like to do. Prose, and especially his own, has all the qualities that he restricts to poetry—the cadences, the sound effects, the visual and emotional appeals. Although the image of the claw is intended to express prose's instrumentality, it calls attention to itself instead, especially given that a claw, with its associations of violence and awkwardness, is nothing like Santayana's refined writing. Santayana's sentences do not clutch, they fondle; his polished prose does not scuttle across the page, it glides effortlessly over it. In *Reason in Art,* he writes: "To resist this clarification, to love the chance incrustations that encumber human ideas, is a piece of timid folly, and poetry in this respect is nothing but childish confusion" (105). Once again, the medium gets in the way of the message, for his amplification of the subject phrase by apposition is one of those "chance incrustations" that he condemns. Even if Santayana urged the sacrifice of the body for the soul, of the medium for the message, of matter for essence, one cannot read more than one or two of his sentences without pausing to admire a scintillating lexical choice, a surprising metaphor, a witty or elegant turn of phrase. As much as any modern philosopher, Santayana loved "chance incrustations," relished opulent and shapely sentences. If we read Santayana today, it is as much for his incrustations as for his ideas.

When Santayana argues that poetry has a body, he does so in prose as corporeal as any poem. Even his terse formula for poetry—"the immersion of the message in the medium"—relies on metaphor and gummy alliteration. And his attack on puns is complicated by the words that convey it, the denunciation falling prey to the thing denounced: "In the end, those who play with words lose their labour, and pregnant as they feel themselves to be with new and wonderful universes, they cannot humanize the one in which they live" (*RA,* 86). Not only does Santayana exploit the paradox of play that is also work; carried away by the associations of "labour," he drifts to the analogy with pregnancy, thereby turning his point into a *pointe.* Although for Santayana a pun was a pint-sized Babel, the minimal instance of linguistic confusion, he was not above punning. Language, he says in the same chapter, is a "labyrinth of sounds" (80).

Santayana's distinction between poetry and prose, like that between source and medium, needs to be understood much as he understood philosophy: not as the discovery of the truth but as the expression of a temperament. About his own temperament, his life-long ambivalence toward poetry provides important clues. Although the mature Santayana did not think of himself as a poet, his first book, published when he was a thirty-year-old instructor of philosophy at Harvard, was a volume of poems, *Sonnets and Other Verses* (1894). The little book was well-received, especially among the Boston ladies whose company he frequented, and two years later an expanded edition appeared, quickly followed by *Lucifer: A Theological Tragedy* (1899), and a new volume of poems, *A Hermit of Carmel and Other Poems* (1901). It was not until the publication of *The Life of Reason* a few years later, when Santayana was nearly forty, that his standing as a philosopher eclipsed his celebrity as the dandyish author of fashionable neo-Platonic sonnets. After the 1890s, Santayana all but abandoned the writing of poetry and never published another volume of new poems in his lifetime.[29] He gave two reasons for this abrupt end to his poetic career: English was not his mother tongue, and nothing that he wanted to say in poetry couldn't be said better in prose. Since his poetry was a preamble to his philosophical writings, "my philosophy in the making," his true medium was "liquid prose" rather than "the meshes of verse."[30]

Santayana's explanation of his turn toward prose may not tell the whole story. As he construed it, the contrast between poetry and prose included not only the opposition between the bodily and the bodiless, but also that between the "alien" and the "natural." Poetry, he says in *Reason in Art*, overlays the fact "with affinities alien to its proper nature." According to "A Brief History of My Opinions," however, he wished to express his own "natural affinities." Since the natural is also the native, Santayana's abandonment of poetry may also reflect his desire not to risk further alienation from his source. Fearful of enmeshing or immersing his un-English message in an English medium, he chose a venue for his writing that permitted, or so he tried to convince himself, their separation. If he renounced the Spanish language for the sake of his English medium, he renounced English verse so that its medium would not occlude his Spanish source.

As he says in *Reason in Art*, "In the medium the poet is at home" (104). But how could Santayana take up residence in such a home? It would be not only unnatural but denaturalizing; it would imply a rootedness, a kind of repatriation inconsistent with his self-image as an inveterate exile. Had Santayana made a career of poetry, he could no longer have seen himself as "an unattached man who writes in the English language." Like Plato, he was too much of a poet not to recognize poetry's power. In *Reason in Art*, only after remarking on the poet's intimacy with his medium does he launch into a sweeping condemnation of poetry, as such intimacy repelled him. And he wrote *Reason in Art*, which contains one of the most impassioned anti-poetics since Book III of the *Republic*, only after he had stopped writing poems. The sequence of argument duplicates the curriculum vitae. Santayana did not give up poetry, he ran away from it. English verse was not too foreign, but not foreign enough.

By sacrificing poetry for prose, the body for the soul, the alien for the natural, Santayana muted the *voice* of the English language, its embodiment as a tongue. When he states that he gave up Spanish "for the sake of English letters," we need to read "letters" literally. Like Pedro Salinas and Luis Cernuda, Santayana feared English when he listened to it, when it impinged on him as xenophony, alien sound. So long as English remained only *lenguaje,* words bereft of body and sound, he was safe from its clutches. But this involved the sacrifice of poetry, for the poet writes by ear, his music emerging from the labyrinth of sounds inside him. Santayana says that the reason he never mastered English verse is that he "never drank in in childhood the homely cadences and ditties which in pure spontaneous poetry set the essential key."[31] This naive view of the poet's inspiration, expressed in untypically clumsy prose, tells only part of the story. The other part may be that he refused such drink as his second language offered him. In his psycho-linguistic economy, English had to be a bodiless medium so that Spanish could remain a mediumless source.

Because he viewed English as letters, as script, as a language rather than a tongue, Santayana never showed any interest in the speech of Americans, which he derided as the "Yankee vernacular" (*PP,* 134). Although he wrote to Unamuno that English was his *idioma,* he studiously avoided idiomatic and colloquial registers of speech. In *The Last Puritan,* when Oliver Alden begins school and meets other boys his age, the narrator comments that Oliver "soon learned their dialect and slang, but it always remained a foreign language to him, as did common American speech in general" (*LP,* 65). More literally than for his protagonist, for Santayana the American vernacular remained a foreign language, an alien tongue, and just as he avoided hispanicisms, he avoided colloquialisms that might turn his English into a true *idioma,* even to the point of adopting British spelling. Unlike many exiled writers, Santayana never felt his command of his medium imperiled by residence in a country with a different language. Even during the years he lived in Boston, his writing was largely done during periods of residence in France, Spain, or Italy. To write in English Santayana didn't need to *hear* English; he never feared that isolation would make his diction quaint or rarefied. Indeed, he may well have preferred to live in places whose ambient sounds did not stain the transparency of his words. As he bragged to his nephew George Sturgis, he didn't write English, he wrote "Santayanese," his own "special language."[32]

And yet, as we have seen, all one has to do is read a couple of Santayana's sentences to realize that his relation to the English language was far more intimate, far more passionate, far more invested, than he acknowledged. If English was less than a source, it was much more than a medium. He may have detested wordplay, but he liked words and had no qualms about making abundant, sometimes excessive, use of such "poetic" devices as metaphor and alliteration.[33] If the opposite of the natural is the alien, his style is indeed weighed down with alien affinities, but an alienness entirely natural to himself. In another of his autobiographical essays, "The Idler and His Works," he writes: "I like to spend drowsy hours drawing, cleaning or making something, or even mending my clothes. Pleasant is solitude among manageable things. And among manageable things, the most manageable for me are words."[34] His pleasure in making sentences—anglophone sentences—belies his stated indifference to his medium. For Santayana writing was recreation, a form of play, and not merely the vehicle for the propagation of his doctrines. As he freely admitted, his books could easily have been half as long, but he could think of no more enjoyable occupation than putting words together into sentences. This is why reading Santayana for content is often a maddening experience. The liquid prose flows smoothly, evenly, without interruption, but it also meanders, eddies, ripples, seeps into nooks and crannies, occasionally even evaporates.

Santayana's passion for English, for every part of its body, shows through in everything he wrote; but only in rare, somber moments did he recognize that the choice of a language entailed the choice of a self. Because he needed to keep Spain as his source, he struggled against the knowledge that by writing in English he had become some sort of American.[35] Although he wanted to possess English without being possessed by it, a language surrenders only by exacting surrender in return. Words are indeed like claws, and they clutch us. The odd truth is that Santayana, the exquisite stylist whose prose critics like to call "marmoreal" and "pure," had a hard time with language—as hard a time, perhaps, as he had with sex, about which he also spoke with misleading casualness.[36] He wrote easily, but he did not write with ease. He loved easily, but he did not love with ease. The English language distanced him from his father, and this may have been what he wanted, but it brought about its own attachments, including those to his sister and his prenatal "stepfather." If Santayana did not think more about language, it was because such reflection threatened to dismantle the fictions he lived by. For his idea of himself to cohere, for him to "do justice" to the "myself" that he had carefully constructed, he needed the detached, bodiless, language-free identity that he bundled up in the concept of Spirit.

In the opening sentence of "A Brief History of My Opinions," Santayana asks: "How came a child born in Spain of Spanish parents to be educated in Boston and to write in the English language?" His answer is telling for what it omits: "The case of my family was unusual. We were not emigrants; none of us ever changed his country, his class, or his religion." But emigrants also change their language, and in this respect he was indeed an emigrant. When the host language becomes the home language, the exile is no longer only an exile. In *Soliloquies in England* (1922), he makes a similar omission: "Nationality and religion are like our love and loyalty towards women: things too radically intertwined with our moral essence to be changed honorably, and too accidental to the free mind to be worth changing."[37] Since Santayana never loved any woman other than his sister, the epigram rings hollow from the first, but it's suspect also because what it says about nationality and religion could also be extended to language—except that then the epigram's medium would contradict its message. When Santayana states in *Reason in Art* that in prose one "passes over" the words to get to the meaning, he is describing his no-look stance toward language itself. In this light, his emphasis on the priority of subject matter, including his brilliant defense of philosophical poetry, forms part of a concerted effort to discount and disembody language, to turn it into a "manageable thing." Charming as it is, the comparison of writing to dusting or mending belittles language. For a writer, words are more dear than a trusty broom or a pair of old socks.

In *The Last Puritan*, Santayana describes his protagonist's attitude toward language:

> Oliver, in spite of his tendency to believe that whatever was natural in himself was right, was rather disturbed and uncertain on this subject. He couldn't be content, in speech any more than in anything else, with what was wrong or inferior or second best: yet it was most puzzling to decide what the absolutely best was, and so hard, even then, to live up to it. Language, for him, didn't belong to the sunny side of life. It was one of those human troubles in which the curse of original sin, and of Babel, most surely appeared. (126)

Santayana made no secret of the similarities between Oliver and himself, and Oliver's puzzlement surely has its source in Santayana's own feelings as he was learning English. Cioran remarks that someone who uses a foreign language forfeits the right to make mistakes.[38] Puritanical Oliver obviously suffers from a guilty linguistic conscience; but since he was born and raised in Connecticut, his predicament is inexplicable unless one realizes that he speaks for the young Santayana, who arrived in Boston without speaking English. In *Dominations and Powers* (1950), the last book he published during his lifetime, Santayana makes a statement reminiscent of Oliver's: "the existence of foreign tongues seems at first incredible, then ridiculous, and to the end displeasing; and there is nothing in which absurdity looms more obvious and more enormous than in solecisms and verbal slips."[39] Although he always claimed that he had learned English quickly and painlessly, his displeasure with foreign tongues—surprising in someone who knew so many— evokes the linguistic insecurities that bedevil Oliver and silenced Santayana's mother.

Indeed, the myth of Babel casts a long shadow over Santayana's writings. In *Platonism and the Spiritual Life* (1927), he remarks: "Those who know one language, like the Greeks, seem to find language a purer and more transparent vehicle than those of us who notice its idiosyncrasies and become entangled in its meshes."[40] (The same vocabulary that he used to distinguish between prose and poetry now reappears in the discrimination between monolinguals and bilinguals, as if poets and multilinguals shared analogous linguistic entanglements.) In *Person and Places,* he goes further: "Fixity of tradition, of custom, of language is perhaps a prerequisite to complete harmony in life and mind. Variety in these matters is a lesson to the philosopher and drives him into the cold arms of reason; but it confuses the poet and the saint, and embitters society" (103). The multiplication of languages, he said on another occasion, was but another example of man's "long truancies."[41] And the story of his mother's own mutism, which Santayana believed also illustrated the harm of knowing too many languages, was narrated under the Babelian heading of "The confusion of tongues" (*PP*, 31).

Santayana responded to the threat of Babel by eliminating all opportunities for "confusion" (as he put it in "A Brief History") between Spanish and English, an effort that he carried even into his own name, urging publishers to remove his first name from the spine of his books to avoid the "polyglot effect."[42] This dim view of the multiplicity of languages is certainly not unusual; it forms part of a long tradition whose avatars have been studied recently by Umberto Eco.[43] Unlike many thinkers in this tradition, however, Santayana did not react to linguistic fragmentation by fantasizing about a "perfect language," a first-born, prelapsarian *Ur-Sprache* common to all humankind. Rather, he adopted his second language, English, as a nonfoundational *lingua franca,* medium rather than source. Instead of trying to heal the wound of Babel by recovering his first tongue, he accepted what he termed his "handicap" and proceeded to live and write as if it weren't a handicap at all.

In the passage from *The Last Puritan* quoted above, Oliver's reference to the Fall helps to bring into focus other issues underlying Santayana's tongue ties, issues centering on the nexus of language and sexuality. Oliver's view that multilingualism attests to the curse both of Babel and of original sin is puzzling, for in Genesis 2 language is prelapsarian, Adam's innocent gift. Yet Oliver assimilates it to the Fall, as if words themselves were forbidden fruit, as if the knowledge of languages, like that of good and evil, represented an act of disobedience toward the Father. Again acting as Santayana's Alden-ego, Oliver here gives voice to his creator's own guilt at having abandoned Spanish, an event that he had reason to perceive as disobedience of his father. These feelings of guilt were pervasive, if largely unacknowledged. I don't believe, for example, that Santayana didn't read Spanish books because he feared confusion, since he never expressed similar anxieties about reading in other languages. It may be closer to the truth that he avoided Spanish books because they shamed him, as Unamuno's gift of *El sentimiento trágico de la vida* had shamed him. After all, those were the kinds of books that he might have written had he followed his father's wishes and returned to Spain. Rather than returning, he compromised with himself by forsaking the language but embracing the nationality, an unsatisfactory solution, since in the end it deprived him of both language and nationality.

As Santayana's father tongue, Spanish had a body, a male body. By turning away from it, Santayana turned away from his body, like Adam running for cover. And if poetry is "massive and instinctive" while prose is "meager and bodiless," by giving up poetry he was once again running for cover. The two refusals enact different moments of the same repressive gesture, which is why he argues against poetry and multilingualism using similar imagery. Like sex, like languages, poetry too is a human trouble, a bodily act that must be renounced. I have always been struck by the phrasing of Santayana's decision to give up Spanish: "in renouncing everything else for the sake of English letters I might be said to have been guilty, quite unintentionally, of a little stratagem." In this quid pro quo, the "quid" does not match the "quo," since "everything else" encompasses far more than "English letters." Why the disproportion? According to Oliver Alden, the shady side of life includes not only language but all things "accidental and perverse" (117) and "disreputably human" (197), among them history, religion, family secrets, and, most significantly, his own sexuality. For Oliver, as for his creator, sexual urges were also a human trouble, something "to be seen and thought of as little as possible," as Santayana once put it.[44] Although Oliver develops strong attachments to male friends, he never enjoys physical intimacy with a woman—in this, too, like his creator.

While death at an early age put Oliver out of his misery, in his own life Santayana coped with human troubles by making detachment synonymous with The Life of Reason. As he recounts in his autobiography, in the 1890s a series of painful events changed his outlook on life: His father passed away, which severed his deepest link to Spain; his sister married, which ruined his plan to set up house with her; he turned thirty, which made him too old to pal around with his students; and his friend Warrick Potter, a Harvard student of whom he was very fond, died unexpectedly of cholera. Santayana reacted to these misfortunes by undergoing a "metanoia," or conversion, that drove him "from the temporal to the eternal" (PP, 426). Henceforth his attention would be fixed on the "realm of essence," his version of the Platonic world of pure forms. He would live in the world but without partaking of it. Indeed, he would "renounce everything" (PP, 421, 426). Given the absoluteness of the withdrawal, I'm not sure that "conversion" is the right term for his metamorphosis. It may not be a coincidence that Santayana "converted" at about the same age that his protagonist died, for Santayana's conversion implied a severing of vital ties. Forsaking Spanish and desisting from writing poetry formed part of this program of renunciation. "When the thought is absorbing," he once wrote, "the language is not noticed, and seems indifferent" (PP, 371). Lost in thought, absorbed in the steady contemplation of essence, Santayana convinced himself that words did not matter. To secure his conviction, he acted to repress—to "not notice"—its loudest and most threatening manifestations. Let no sound, whether of English or Castilian, pierce the mute chastity of essence. "I need to be quiet in order to be free," he also wrote (PP, 21). In Santayana the word made flesh is the word denied.

Nonetheless, there is always mud in the well, noise in the message. However artful the evasion, however artistic its results, his was a makeshift solution, a way of temporizing. Although Santayana put up a good front, his marmoreal prose—a chiseler's fig leaf—is veined by guilt and melancholy. Even his poetry, for all of its author's disclaimers, occasionally bears eloquent witness to his predicament:

> Ye whose lost voices, echoing in this rhyme,
> My tongue usurps, forgive if I have erred.
> Not as ye uttered, but as I have heard,
> I spell your meanings in an evil time.[45]

This is the opening quatrain of "Invocation," the sonnet that preceded the verse drama Lucifer: A Theological Tragedy (1899), universally regarded as Santayana's least readable work. Addressing the dramatis personae of the poem as well as his precursors (*Lucifer* resonates with Miltonic and Shelleyean echoes), Santayana confesses to being an usurper, someone who has seized what doesn't belong to him, most patently the words with which the poem is written. He has erred not only morally but in the older topographical meaning of the term. Summing up his sin in one source-word—"erred"—the *déraciné* finds the root of his error in errancy. "Wanderings," confirms Oliver Alden's grandfather, "physically, morally and etymologically, are errors" (*LP,* 57). Santayana sins with his wandering tongue, a *lapsus lingua* all the more egregious in that his confession is full of word play and sound effects, those very excesses that he renounced and denounced a few years later in *The Life of Reason.* Like someone who forswears profanity by swearing, the poem asks forgiveness in diction so loud and labored as to be inculpatory.

Usurps, erred, uttered, heard: a labyrinth of sounds that, later in the poem, will issue in "word." Consider the fourth line: "spell" is a multilayered pun (it means "utter" or "decipher," but also "replace," "bewitch," "splinter"), as is "time," which is used in its metrical as well as epochal sense; moreover, the phrase "evil time" is a calque of the Spanish "mal tiempo." And there can be no doubt that this was a very bad time for Santayana, not only because of the personal contretemps of the 1890s, but because the sonnet was written just after Spain's defeat in the Spanish-American War. Accepting the defeat with a mixture of resentment and resignation, Santayana memorialized it in a long poem, "Spain in America" (1901), that contains the only interlingual rhyme in all of his verse: "gone" and "Colón," the name of one of the Spanish battleships sunk in the battle of Santiago. How did Santayana, a Spaniard in America, feel about his surrender to English in light of Spain's defeat? The net of guilt in "Invocation" may stretch farther than first appears. Those "lost voices" may also be Spanish *voces,* and "lost" a punning reference to the catastrophe of 1898.

With Colón (ship and icon) gone, all that is left of Spain in America, according to Santayana's poem, is "Her faith and heart and speech."[46] Of this trio, Santayana retained the first two, but he deliberately abandoned the speech, those "lost voices" that also evoke his own language loss. But since a tongue, unlike a language, does not have to be used to be kept, Santayana's separation from Spanish did not signify its erasure from his emotional life. Even though he became "English-dominant" soon after moving to Boston, Spanish remained dominant in a deeper sense. Like one of those limbs that hurt even after they've been amputated, the phantom of the Spanish language—a fatherly ghost—haunts his English writing.

Put "Invocation" next to the letter to Unamuno and what emerges is the picture of a man uncomfortable in two languages. In its own way his mastery of English distressed him no less than his ineptness in Spanish. Considered in a vacuum, English words were manageable things, but the language itself could only be managed by being ignored. "I wish I might forget that I am I," begins another sonnet, where the obsessive repetition of the first-person pronoun denies the speaker's desire for self-effacement. Just as he wanted to forget himself, he wanted to forget his languages. If letters are fetters, what stronger bind than the capitalized "I," the token of a self and a language that Santayana chafed against but was impotent to shed? That he made music by knocking his chains together is all to his credit, but I can't help wondering what Santayana's life and work would have been like had he given vent to the "polyglot effect" that insinuates itself into the first stanza of "Spain in America." Renouncing Spanish for English was too big a sacrifice; clinging to his *españolidad* was too big a sacrifice. Santayana could have done justice to himself only by risking those entanglements—linguistic, familial, sexual—that he spent a lifetime avoiding. It would be anachronistic to expect him to negotiate his divided loyalties by writing like Nabokov or Cabrera Infante; Santayana is not a post-modern *bricoleur* but a dainty Victorian gentleman. Still, his distaste for immersion, his detachment from both source and medium, his self-imposed deafness to the voices of his dual tongues, ruined him. He never even conquered his hybrid name: "Santayana" didn't approve of "George," and "George" refused to answer to "Santayana." It is as easy to admire his prose as it is difficult not to pity the man who wrote it.

Chapter 2

Love in a Foreign Language

When we made love, two countries made love.

—*Abdelkebir Khatibi*

The legend goes something like this: Santayana was in the middle of one of his impeccable lectures on aesthetics—it is said that he spoke the way he wrote—when someone knocked gently on the door of the classroom. He went over and was handed a slip of paper, which contained the news that his mother had just passed away. After a few moments of silence, he turned to his students. "I have a date with April," he announced. He left the room and never again was he seen in Harvard Yard.

The truth is somewhat less picturesque. When his mother passed away—not in springtime, but in the winter of 1912—Santayana was in England, having left her on her deathbed several weeks before. The telegram with the news of her death was neither unexpected nor unwelcome, not only because Josefina had been ailing for many years but because her son anticipated that his share of her estate would free him from teaching. A few months later, once the amount of his legacy had been determined, he submitted a letter of resignation to Abbott Lawrence Lowell, then Harvard's president. "I hope you will not ask me to reconsider," he wrote. "This is a step I have meditated on all my life, and always meant to take when it became possible."[1] Over the next thirty years, Santayana received many lucrative and flattering invitations from American universities, including Harvard, to teach or lecture, invitations that he invariably declined. Although he didn't stop writing about American culture—*Character and Opinion in the United States* was published in 1920, *The Genteel Tradition at Bay* in 1931—after January 1912 he never again set foot on American soil.

A little more than three decades after Santayana's abrupt departure from his step-fatherland, a group of equally distinguished Spanish writers and intellectuals began arriving in the United States, driven here by the Spanish Civil War (1936–1939). Political rather than temperamental exiles, this wave of emigrés included several of Spain's greatest poets—Juan Ramón Jiménez, Jorge Guillén, Pedro Salinas, Luis Cernuda—all of whom left substantial records of their forced and sometimes traumatic cohabitation with the English language. Unlike Santayana, who believed that he could sever language and nationality, his younger compatriots insisted on their imbrication, and they worried about the impact of exile on their lives and careers. Living in Washington, D.C., Juan Ramón Jiménez thought of himself not only as *desterrado*, expatriated, but as *deslenguado*, untongued; and he described his sense of loss in a handful of anguished aphorisms entitled "Mi español perdido" [My Lost Spanish], in which he relates how he and his wife corrected each other's Spanish "and even consulted the dictionary."[2] Although Juan Ramón's writing during his years in the United States offers no evidence of language loss, he eventually moved to Puerto Rico in search of a more hospitable linguistic environment, a place where, as he put it, he would be enveloped in "atmospheric Spanish."

Years ago José Gaos divided the Spanish Civil War exiles into two groups: *trasterrados*, those who took up residence in Hispanic countries, and *desterrados*, those who ended up in xenophone countries like France, England, or the United States.[3] Unlike *trasterrados*, who lose their territorial homeland but keep their linguistic footing, *desterrados* forsake both, as linguistic estrangement compounds physical exile. Like Juan Ramón, the two writers I will discuss in this and the following chapter, Pedro Salinas (1891–1951) and Luis Cernuda (1902–1963), span both ends of Gaos's distinction by answering *destierro* with *trastierro*. After spending several years in the United States (and Great Britain, in Cernuda's case), they moved to hispanophone havens, safe shelters from alien sounds. Vastly different in texture and tone, their memorials of linguistic exile and return illustrate the intensity of connection to language that Santayana always disclaimed. Although Salinas and Cernuda had far less intimacy with English than Santayana, neither one could keep—or claimed to be able to keep—the American vernacular at bay. For both, atmospheric English impinged on intestinal Spanish; the proximity of someone else's "medium" was enough to infect their "source."

Salinas reflected on these issues in *Aprecio y defensa del lenguaje*, a commencement address delivered at the University of Puerto Rico in May of 1944. Still required reading in many Puerto Rican schools, the speech is a passionate defense of the Spanish language and at the same time a veiled confession of the linguistic anxieties that Juan Ramón openly acknowledged. At the time of the speech, Salinas had been living in Puerto Rico for only a few months. Having left Spain in 1936, he had taught at Wellesley College and Johns Hopkins University before accepting a visiting position at the University of Puerto Rico in 1943. Liberated from the cold Baltimore winters and thrilled to find himself once again in a Spanish-speaking environment, Salinas thrived. Almost as soon as he arrived in San Juan, he began writing poems, something he had not done in several years. In a letter to Jorge Guillén from November 1943, he says that the "first consequence" of his encounter with the sea of San Juan is a three-line fragment of a poem to be called "El Contemplado."[4] A couple of months later he reports that he has written four poems about the sea. By April of 1944 he has completed thirteen poems and is planning to add one more to round out the book and avoid the unlucky number. A month later, *El Contemplado* is finished and he is already at work on other creative and scholarly projects. Indeed, the three years that Salinas spent in San Juan were among the most productive of his extraordinarily productive life. In addition to *Aprecio y defensa del lenguaje del lenguaje* and *El Contemplado,* he wrote monographs on Jorge Manrique and Rubén Darío, the essays gathered in *El defensor* (1948), half a dozen plays, and most of the poems in *Todo más claro* (1949) and the posthumous *Confianza* (1955).

In a brief essay written shortly after his arrival in Puerto Rico, Salinas captures the euphoria of linguistic return. He describes waking up to the cries of "brillo" (shine) from the boot-blacks on the streets of San Juan:

> Persianas. Súbita, por entre dos tablillas, se desliza en el dormitorio, la palabra, vívida, refulgente, entre sonido y saeta.
> ¡Brillo!
> Toda la palabra se deleita en su *r,* se recrea columpiándose en ella, se pasa la mitad de su breve vida, demorándose, allí en su rrr. ¡BrRRRRillo! Tanto chirría como si le hubieran legado los grillos, recién, recién callados, los agrios metales de su noche.[5]

> [Shutters. Suddenly, in between two slats, the word, vivid and resplendent, slips into the bedroom, half sound, half arrow.
> *Brillo!*
> The whole word delights in its "r," swings playfully inside it, spends half of its short life, tarrying, there in its "rrr." *BrRRRRillo!* It screeches as if the crickets, just grown silent, had bequeathed it the harsh trumpets of their night.]

Resonant with alliterations, consonances, and other sound effects, and culminating in an hendecasyllable, Salinas's imitative gloss of this common word offers an example of the incarnation of language as *lengua,* as living sound. Perhaps not since the stories of *Víspera del gozo,* two decades earlier, had he displayed such unmitigated pleasure in tarrying, like the shoe-shine boys, on the music of a single word, or even of a single phoneme, the trilled "r" that he would never have heard on the lips of his neighbors in Wellesley or Baltimore.

The auroral mood of "Brillo" carries over into *Aprecio y defensa del lenguaje,* a commencement address in more ways than one, for Salinas uses the occasion to renew his ties to his mother tongue and asks his audience to do the same. Brimming with intellectual energy, impressively wide-ranging erudition, and a literary zeal that verges on the messianic, the speech bears witness to his resurgence. It is hardly the work of someone who for several years had lamented, in private, the diminishment of his creative powers. The dramatic opening of the speech, where Salinas pictures himself as a man who is able to breathe again after years of asphyxia, dramatizes the salutary effect of an environment where Spanish was, literally, in the air:

> Cuando se siente uno rodeado de su mismo aire lingüístico, de nuestra misma manera de hablar, ocurre en nuestro ánimo un cambio análogo al de la respiración pulmonar, tomamos de la atmósfera algo, impalpable, invisible, que adentramos en nuestro ser, que se nos entra en nuestra persona y cumple en ella una función vivificadora, que nos ayuda a seguir viviendo. Sí, he vuelto a respirar español, en la calles de San Juan, en los pueblos de la isla. (1–2)[6]

> [When one feels surrounded by one's linguistic air, by our own way of talking, our spirit undergoes a change analogous to that of pulmonary respiration; we take something impalpable, invisible, from the atmosphere, something that goes inside us and fulfills a revitalizing function, that helps us to keep on living. Yes, I have breathed Spanish again in the streets of San Juan, in the towns of the island.]

For making it possible for him to breathe in Spanish, Salinas feels a profound gratefulness to the past and the present, to those from whom he inherited his *idioma* and those who continue to speak it "by his side."

In spite of this eloquent testimony, however, the air of Puerto Rico was not quite as healthful as Salinas hoped or expected. Yes, it did vibrate with Spanish sounds, like the cries of *brillo* or the conversation of friends, but it was also laden with contaminants. In the mid-1940s, the signs of Americanization were everywhere on the island, and nowhere more noticeably than in the anglicisms that had crept into newspapers, billboards, and everyday speech. Salinas's daughter recalls that every morning her father would clip from the local newspapers particularly egregious anglicisms, which he would then share with family and friends exclaiming, "¡Qué barbaridad!" For him, San Juan was supposed to be a New

Spain, not a New York. If Puerto Rican Spanish kept drifting toward English, Salinas risked losing his homeland for a second time.

The real subject of his speech, he confided to Jorge Guillén, was the deterioration of Spanish on the island, and the indifference of Puerto Ricans toward the corruption of their mother tongue; but since he didn't want to offend his hosts, he could only broach this topic obliquely.[7] Asserting motives antithetical to the real ones, he thus begins by praising Puerto Rico's hispanophone air, adding that he has elected to speak about language because of the increasing concern for language among ordinary people. "Al hombre le preocupa su idioma" [Man worries about his language], a healthy sign for the future of culture (2). Then he continues to dissemble by framing in general terms what he believes is a specific reality. People who lose their mother tongue, he says, become incapable of articulate thought; they are blind men groping in the dark, or worse, spiritual cripples, "cojos, mancos, tullidos de la expresión" (11). Unlike poets, "the supreme connoisseurs of language," when such people suffer, they cannot say what ails them; when they are happy, they cannot name their joys (12).

These are harsh words to direct at anyone, but at this early point in the speech, his listeners do not realize that Salinas is talking about them. After all, the title does not allude to Spanish, but only to *el lenguaje,* language in the abstract. The human context of his remarks seems to be mankind in general—"el hombre"—rather than any particular group. As the speech progresses, however, Salinas will gradually shift his focus from language to the Spanish language, and from there to the island's *idioma.* To the reader who knows the destination ahead of time, the speech is a marvelous example of reptilian insinuation. Winding his way through thickets of quotations and hedges of allusions, Salinas assumes the magisterial stance of someone who, despite claiming that he is only an amateur, a mere "lover" of language, speaks with the authority of the whole of Western culture behind him.

Puerto Rican Spanish finally comes up, almost as an afterthought, in a discussion of neologisms. After praising the benefit to Spanish of lexical borrowings from other tongues, including English, he returns to teratological metaphors in describing the harmful consequences of this phenomenon: "Naturalmente, alguna desventaja ha venido envuelta: una de ellas los calcos idiomáticos innecesarios, que no responden a una tendencia del español, que desfiguran su fisonomía y la apartan de la lengua española general de América y España" [Naturally, there have been some disadvantages, among them unnecessary linguistic calques that do not agree with the nature of Spanish, that disfigure its physiognomy and distance it from the general Spanish tongue of America and

Spain] (42). Then he zeroes in on what had been his theme from the outset: Puerto Rican Spanish risks "irreparable harm" unless its speakers act quickly to stem the inflow of English. The greatest threat to the survival of Spanish on the island is the lack of awareness *(inconciencia)* of some of its speakers, who passively absorb the stream of imports from the North. At the beginning of the speech, Salinas had stated that "educated peoples" *(pueblos cultos)* were characterized by devotion to their mother tongue (2). If one joins exordium and peroration, the conclusion is inescapable: Puerto Ricans are well on the way to becoming barbarians, in both the linguistic and cultural senses. Taken as a whole, the speech expresses not only the author's *aprecio* for language but his *desprecio* for those who neglect it.

Salinas's defense of Spanish is, more narrowly, a defense of the Iberocentric norm. It is remarkable that an essay that often reads like an anthology of familiar and unfamiliar quotations does not mention or cite a single Spanish American author. In particular, Puerto Rican literature and culture do not appear on Salinas's cultural map of Hispania, a glaring omission. By having only Spaniards speak for Spanish, Salinas belatedly joins ranks with the advocates of the so-called "panhispanic" movement of the beginning of the twentieth century, who compensated for the loss of Spain's American colonies by highlighting, in books with such titles as *La reconquista de América* and *España en América,* the mother country's continued cultural hegemony.[8] Several decades later, Salinas follows the same script by encouraging Puerto Ricans to maintain their "loyalty" to inherited linguistic norms and their "familiarity" with the Spanish literary tradition, which contains "the classics of our language" (58–59).

His Iberocentricism comes across vividly, if perhaps unintendedly, in an ostensibly hypothetical illustration. To explain how a common language brings people together, he composes a little fable whose protagonists are a Spaniard and a Spanish American:

Si en una ciudad extranjera, un español acaudalado oye, en la calle, en un lugar público, a otra persona, de traza modesta, hablar su lengua, aun cuando sea con acento distinto, chileno o cubano, lo más probable es que sienta el deseo de acercarse a él y trabar conversación. Son dos personas de clase social muy dispar, de dos naciones distintas; pero los une algo superior al sentir de clase y nación, y es su conciencia de pertenecer a un mismo grupo lingüístico, la fraternidad misteriosa que crea el hecho de llamar desde niños las mismas cosas con los mismos nombres. (15–16)

[If in a foreign city, a rich Spaniard hears, on the street or in a public place, a person of humble appearance speak his tongue, even if it's with a different accent—Cuban or Chilean—it's likely that he will want to approach that person and start a conversation. They are two people from very different social classes, from two different nations; but they are joined by something that transcends class and national allegiances, their awareness of belonging to the same linguistic group, the mysterious fraternity created by the fact of calling since they were children the same things by the same names.]

My question: Why a "rich" Spaniard and a "humble" Chilean or Cuban? In San Juan, where Salinas befriended some of the most prominent people on the island, he was surrounded by wealthy Latin Americans. Although he does not say so, the speech makes clear that the wealth of his "español acaudalado" is not only financial but cultural. The word *caudal* appears several times, always to designate cultural or linguistic capital, as in the phrases, "el caudal común de lo humano" [the common wealth of humanity] (20), "ese caudal de palabras con que Homero describe las luchas de los héroes" [that wealth of words with which Homer describes the heroes' battles] (54); or as in the sentence, "el lenguaje funciona como una fatalidad, que nos arrastra en su caudal, como el arroyo a la brizna de yerba" [language functions fatefully, dragging us in its current (*caudal*), like a blade of grass in a stream] (32). What sets the Spaniard apart is not affluence but fluency, a thesaurus rather than a treasure, as in the title of Covarrubias's famous dictionary, *Tesoro de la lengua castellana o española*. Implicitly, this disparity in wealth also distinguishes Salinas from his listeners. The anecdote mirrors the speech. Affluent because fluent, opulent because eloquent, Salinas is himself that *español acaudalado* who, filling the auditorium with his precise and copious Castilian, shares and showcases his cultural treasures. That the teacher is also a poet bolsters his status, for as Salinas stresses, once again resorting to class distinctions, poets are the "lords" of language (22).

Though tendered hypothetically, the anecdote is based on an incident in Salinas's life. In a 1941 letter from Berkeley, he tells his wife Margarita that he has just met the Ecuadorian poet Jorge Carrera Andrade, as well as the consuls from Venezuela and the Dominican Republic. Carrera Andrade he likes, but the others are a different story:

Carrera es buen chico y se puede hablar con él. Tiene un culto de la poesía ingenuo, pueril, de la poesía en forma de versos. Para él la poesía es lo escrito, lo literario. Pero los otros dos, son dos perfectos zoquetes, tipo del sudamericano blanducho, soso y degenerado. Y yo me preguntaba al verme hablando con dos individuos de esa especie: "¿Pero por qué hablo yo con esta gente? ¿Qué tengo que ver con ellos?" La respuesta es muy sencilla; porque hemos nacido con el mismo idioma. ¿Qué tendrá un idioma de tan profundamente humano, tan hondo, que crea una forma de lazo entre gentes que por lo demás no tienen nada en común? Esos dos hombres en nada se parecen a mí. Espiritualmente me son extraños, ajenos. Y no obstante, al hablar con ellos me siento en un ambiente familiar, el ambiente de palabras comunes. Llaman a las cosas como yo. Al cielo, cielo; a una mesa, una mesa.[9]

[Carrera is a good kid and one can talk with him. His idea of poetry is ingenuous, puerile, of poetry as verse. For him poetry is what is written down, literature. But the other two, they are perfect blockheads, typical exemplars of the flabby, dull and degenerate South American. And I asked myself seeing me talk with two such individuals, "But why I am talking to these people? What do I have to do with them?" The answer is very simple; because we were born in the same language. What is it about a language's profound humanity that it creates a kind of bond among people who do not have anything else in common? Those two men are nothing like me. Spiritually they are strange, alien to me. And yet when I speak with them I feel I'm in a familiar environment, that of the words we have in common. They call things the way I do. The sky, the sky; a table, a table.]

A few years later, reworking this incident for the speech, Salinas changes the nationality of his interlocutors and strips them of their profession, but he retains the central idea and some of the phrasing, while transforming his sense of cultural superiority into the distinction between rich and poor. Although the use of the same language establishes that "familiar environment" that he also found in Puerto Rico, he has no more in common with the Spanish American consuls than with the boys who shine shoes on the streets of San Juan—or those men and women who listened to his commencement address.

Salinas's Iberocentrism would be only insulting did it not also reflect a profound vocational crisis. The defense is also a self-defense, an impassioned if dissimulated plea for his survival as a writer. It is not just *el hombre* but *un hombre,* Pedro Salinas, who worries about his tongue. *Aprecio y defensa del lenguaje* may be a "great profession of faith," as Claudio Guillén has said,[10] but it is also a complicated admission of anxiety. By the summer of 1944, after nearly a decade in exile, Salinas himself had become something of a contact zone, a "man on the edge," as he put it in one of the poems of *Todo más claro* (1949). His son-in-law, Juan Marichal, has written that Salinas viewed Puerto Rico as frontier between "ser *en* español" and "ser *en* inglés"[11]; but all those years of living in Wellesley and Baltimore had erected a similar border inside him. His American connections had hybridized him, made him "Puerto

Rican" in spite of himself, for the anglophone assaults on Spanish that he witnessed in Puerto Rico he had experienced in his own life.

Salinas's colleagues at Johns Hopkins have talked about his habit of stacking the bookshelves in his office with Spanish grammars and dictionaries. His daughter relates that during their years in Baltimore her father used to read aloud plays by Carlos Arniches, a minor Spanish playwright, in order to suffuse his American household with the Spanish tongue, and, more specifically, with the *madrileño* dialect of Arniches's characters. But Spanish dictionaries and *viva voce* readings of local-color plays were not enough to muffle the sounds beyond his door, which perhaps explains why some of the most strident comments in *Aprecio y defensa del lenguaje* are reserved for the American vernacular, the "inglés de América" that Salinas invariably associated with slogans such as "Time is money," "Keep smiling," and "The bigger the better."[12] He was especially aroused by Basic English, C. K. Ogden's program for an 850-word English-based lingua franca, which in his view epitomized the degradation of language in the modern world. Predictably, he derides Ogden's proposal with teratological and classist invective: Basic English is an "unfortunate monster" *(desdichado engendro)*, and its users are "indigent" (42).

Literary English held no terrors for Salinas. An admirer of English poets ever since his youth, he quoted them often, sometimes in the original. But the English of Shakespeare or Shelley was disembodied speech, antiquarian rather than idiomatic, literary rather than colloquial, *lenguaje* rather *lengua* or *idioma*. It was one thing to quote from Shakespeare's sonnets, as he does in the speech, and quite another to be constantly assaulted by the "vociferous letters" *(letras voceadoras)* of headlines and billboards (49). Reading, as Quevedo put it in a poem that Salinas quotes, is listening with our eyes. Intimate but mute, the written word does not besiege us phonically. Shutting our eyes is a natural reflex, stopping our ears is not. To look away is not to see, but someone who "turns a deaf ear" makes a deliberate effort to ignore what he cannot help hearing.

Because of its ubiquity, the argot of American advertising in particular was a constant source of distress. In a 1941 letter to his wife Margarita, he remarks that Broadway is a wonderful sight, but only if one can't read, for otherwise the words of the neon signs "will kill the spirit."[13] One specific slogan, Western Union's "Wire, don't write," raised him to withering heights of Biblical indignation. In "Defensa de la carta misiva," an apology for letter writing also written in Puerto Rico, he brands the Western Union slogan "factious, rebellious, Satanic,"; "the most subversive, the most dangerous for the continuation of civilized life" because of its "brutal laconism and barbaric energy."[14] In *Elogio y defensa del lenguaje,* the slogan serves as an extreme instance of the "contraction of language" exemplified by Basic English (50). Devilishly clever, the motto promotes telegraphy with telegraphic conciseness, conveying the contraction of language in the language of contraction: Just as "do not" contracts to "don't," "write" contracts to "wire." The letter that separates the two verbs is "t," which stands for Time, the constraint that telegraphy seems to vanquish. But for Salinas, who (like Santayana) loved nothing better than writing, the injunction not to write was anathema. Like greeting cards, which he also detested, telegrams sacrificed leisure, elegance, and originality of expression for speed. As the offspring of the modern god Praktikos, the usurper to the throne of the ancient Graces, the clipped sentences of telegrams, like the aphorisms of advertisements, are little better than grunts or animal sounds (44).

Slogans such as "Wire, don't write" stood at the opposite pole from poetry, since they embodied a utilitarian rather than an aesthetic use of language. As Salinas liked to say, poets had to be lazy, slackers in love with language; *ocio* was their *negocio.* In contrast, the anonymous bards of the advertising agencies were busy men, business men, people who turned phrases to turn a profit.[15] His "Nocturno de los avisos," a poem where the speaker portrays himself hounded by billboards and neon signs, is not only a nightmarish vision of the modern metropolis, a theme with ample precedents in Eliot, García Lorca and Neruda; it is also a poetic manifesto.[16] The punning title juxtaposes the two types of language, the utilitarian and the aesthetic, for the poem itself is an *aviso* about *avisos,* an *advertencia* about advertisements. As an anti-*aviso,* a warning about the impoverishment of language in a profit-driven culture, "Nocturno de los avisos" is both diagnostic and curative. The convoluted syntax of the last few lines, which in a different context would be pointlessly mannered, stands in therapeutic contrast to the directness of billboards and neon signs. Gazing at the heavens, "God's publicity," the speaker lists stars and constellations:

> Orión, Cefeo, Arturo, Casiopea,
> anunciadoras de supremas tiendas,
> con ángeles sirviendo
> al alma, que los pague sin moneda,
> la última, sí, la para siempre moda,
> de la final, sin tiempo, primavera.[17]

> [Orion, Cepheus, Arcturus, Cassiopeia,
> advertisers of supreme stores,
> with angels serving

the soul, to be paid without money,
the latest, yes, the forever fashion
of the final, timeless, Spring.]

Earlier in the poem, the only proper names were product brands: Lucky
Strike, White Horse, Coca-Cola. Now the poet escapes the city not only
by fleeing to the pre-urban, precapitalistic world of classical mythology,
but by rendering this world in a language so labored, so labyrinthine, that
it could never be confused with a promotional slogan.

Because Salinas identified the advertisement industry with the United
States, his irritation toward slogans and popular sayings dovetails with his
mixed feelings about the American vernacular. When he disparages the
"barbarity" of the Western Union motto, he is responding both to its
function and to its language. In "Defensa de la carta misiva," he jokingly
proposes to start a "brotherhood" of "martyrs of epistolography" that
will roam American cities chanting anti-telegram slogans. The brotherhood's counter-slogan is: "¡Viva la carta, muera el telegrama!" [Long
live the letter, death to the telegram!].[18] It is hardly an accident that this
lemma is an emphatic hendecasyllable, the paradigmatic verse line in
Spanish. As in "Nocturno de los avisos," Salinas exorcises English-
language prose with Spanish-language verses. Touched by a poet, Basic
English translates into literary Spanish. The contrasts in language and
genre echo and ratify each other.

In a 1939 letter to Margarita, he describes the electric signs that he
sees from his apartment window in Los Angeles, where he had accepted a
summer teaching position. He explains that he likes to play translation
games with the signs, changing the words from English to Spanish, so
that in his mind "Market" becomes "Arte."[19] Illustrating the old Salinas
dictum that the highest form of interpretation is the *malentendu,* the
hispanicizing pun distills his perception of the differences between the
idioma that surrounded him and the *lengua* of his poems. English is
market language; Spanish is language art.

Exiled to the *orbis ultima* of Tomis, Ovid obssessed that his separation
from Rome diminished his poetic gift. Salinas is less forthcoming, since
in *Elogio y defensa del lenguaje* he deflects his unease onto his audience,
but he too was gripped by the twin fears of language loss and creative
sterility. The American vernacular was his *barbara lingua,* a tongue
whose proximity menaced his tongue. Too close for comfort, it provoked a defensive reaction that betrayed too much rather than too little

familiarity. Of all the languages he knew, only English intruded into his daily life. Only English bellowed in his ear. Only English had evolved from a "foreign" into a "second" language.

Of all the languages he knew, also, only English was Katherine Whitmore's tongue. Salinas, the author of *Reality and the Poet in Spanish Literature*, who believed that the first thing one should study in a poet is "the relation between his poetic world and the real world,"[20] was no exception to the rule that an individual's relations with languages are shaped by nonlinguistic circumstances. If Salinas's aversion to colloquial English during the early 1940s testified to his increasing apprehension about living in a xenophone environment, it also reflected his complicated personal life, in which Whitmore played an important part. No less than Santayana's, Salinas's tongue ties were bound up with private affections.

In August of 1936, when he sailed from Spain to the United States, Salinas was known not only as one of his country's most versatile and enterprising men of letters, but as the author of *La voz a ti debida* (1933), a widely read volume of poetry that instantly made him the heir to Garcilaso de la Vega and Gustavo Adolfo Bécquer, Spain's two greatest love poets. As soon as this little book was published, rumors began to circulate about the identity of the poet's beloved. Salinas, in his early forties when *La voz a ti debida* was published, had been married to Margarita Bonmatí for over fifteen years and had two children. Although in his youth he had occasionally written love poems to Margarita, his earlier collections of poetry were notable for ingeniosity rather than for depth of feeling. While not losing any of his cleverness, in *La voz a ti debida* Salinas reached emotional registers that he had not visited before. Even the title—"the voice owed to you" (borrowed from Garcilaso)— insinuated that this book represented a fresh start affectively as well as literarily.

For decades, the identity of the anonymous "you" to whom Salinas addressed his poems has been grist for Hispanism's rumor mill. In large part because of his children's wish to protect their father's reputation, only recently has it been confirmed that Salinas's muse was an American woman, Katherine Reding Whitmore, whom he met in Madrid in the summer of 1932.[21] Almost ten years younger than Salinas, Whitmore was a professor of Spanish at Smith College and a doctoral student at the University of Madrid, where she eventually completed a doctoral dissertation on the Generation of 1898.[22] Within a few weeks of first seeing her in one of his classes, Salinas began showering Whitmore with long, impassioned letters written with green ink in an almost indecipherable script. Overwhelmed by such attentions from a famous writer, she responded with love letters of her own. Although Salinas and Whitmore saw each other only when she visited Spain and he was able to get away from his family, their love deepened. In February of 1935, Salinas's wife (who had believed, somewhat improbably, that she was her husband's inspiration) learned of the affair and tried to drown herself. Shaken but undeterred, Salinas continued seeing an increasingly reluctant Whitmore and writing the poems that went into *Razón de amor* (1936), a second volume of love poetry, which contained "Salvación por el cuerpo," the most sexually explicit of all his poems.

Early in 1936, perhaps as a result of Whitmore's efforts, Salinas was offered an appointment at Wellesley College. As a young man in Spain, he had been enamored of fast cars, tall buildings, big cities, and even telephones (of which he had two in his Madrid home, as he once bragged to Jorge Guillén). Sailing to the United States in August of 1936, he could barely contain his excitement at getting to know first-hand the country responsible for many of these inventions, a country for which he had always felt "the highest spiritual curiousity."[23] Rather than a forlorn exile who had left his family behind in Spain, he was "eager-hearted Pedro," as Katherine Whitmore dubbed him, the avid traveller who looked forward to experiencing first-hand the marvels of American civilization. Typical of his enthusiasm is a letter written in English to Whitmore on Thanksgiving day 1936, a couple of months after his arrival, in which he jokes that he is starting a "Brotherhood for the restauration [*sic*] of the sense of wonder" whose mission is to "see through the practical utilization of cars, phones, radios, etc" to appreciate "the wonder that is at their bottom."[24] Nearly antithetical to the anti-telegram league that he thought up years later, this brotherhood includes only two members, "a silly boy and a silly girl"—Pedro and Katherine. Even his letters to his family and friends back in Spain are surprisingly cheerful, as he raves about everything from the George Washington Bridge—"¡Cántico!"—to the mail chutes in New York hotels.

In November of 1938, he writes to Whitmore that he does not regard himself as an exile: "No soy un *desterrado*. América no es para mí un destierro, donde viva por obligación o disgusto, no. América es para mí un país bueno, generoso, donde me rodea una atmósfera agradable y serena" [I am not an *exile*. America for me is not a place of exile, where I live by force and unhappily, no. America for me is a good, generous country, where I am surrounded by a pleasant and serene atmosphere].[25] Even though he says he misses Spain, he adds that the two years he has spent in the States have only increased his "desire" to "cohabit" (*convivir*) with his new country as much as was "possible and discreet."[26] The choice of words suggests that, for Salinas as for many other exiles and immigrants, acculturation to a foreign country was facilitated by personal liaisons. He articulates his relation to the United States in terms that refer to his affair with Whitmore.

However discreet and desirable, the project of *convivencia* did not go smoothly. In 1937, when Salinas decided that his wife and children should join him in the States, Whitmore called off the affair. The break-up prompted the poems of *Largo lamento,* a book whose existence was at first denied by Salinas's family and that was only published in its entirety many years after the poet's death. Evenly divided between laments over the break-up of the relationship and entreaties for its resumption, the poems—many of which Salinas sent to Whitmore—seemed to have worked, for Whitmore agreed to continue the relationship, at least platonically. (No less than ads, poetry can be a powerful rhetorical tool.) But in March of 1939, finally convinced that Salinas would never leave his wife, Katherine married Brewer Whitmore, a colleague at Smith who had courted her for several years. Believing that she should have been content to be his mistress and muse for life, Salinas did not understand her decision. After her marriage, he continued to write to her (addressing the envelopes with her maiden name!), apparently with Mr. Whitmore's knowledge and compliance.

In the summer of 1943, when Salinas moved to Puerto Rico, his letters to Whitmore abruptly stopped, and she did not hear from him again for most of the three years that he spent on the island. On the back of an envelope, Whitmore records her reaction to his silence: "After the death of my husband [Brewer Whitmore died in 1943 in an automobile accident] Pedro's letters stopped and in that time when I was so alone, so sad, this silence which I did not understand (since through the years of my brief marriage I had continued to hear from Pedro) made me bitter and dumb. These letters explain. He was in Puerto Rico and feared *la censura.*"[27] Salinas's explanation of his three-year silence strains credibility, given the risks that he had always been willing to take to pursue the relationship. If his wife's near-suicide had not deterred him, it's hard to believe that the unlikely possibility of exposure by *la censura* would have. Moreover, he had remained incomunicado even after the war had ended and the mail was no longer inspected.

Censorship there was, though it wasn't only external. Hard-pressed to explain why he had not resumed writing after the war, he cited a mysterious force: "Me he estado, Katherine, meses y meses, como atado, trabado, ligado, por una fuerza invisible y sin embargo superior a mí" [For months and months, I have been, Katherine, bound, trammelled, tied by an invisible and yet superior force].[28] Salinas is equivocating, but he is not lying. The truth is that he went to Puerto Rico to get away from the United States—from its movies, its billboards, its skyscrapers, its eating habits, its language and, not least, his "honey girl" (as he called her), who was no longer his honey. He wanted not simply to recover Spanish as a companiable presence, as a living tongue, but to escape from what he termed the "mundo KP,"[29] whose collapse had paralyzed him. As he grew distanced from Katherine, the wonder of America was replaced by something like terror. Almost every aspect of what he called "the American system of living" upset him: the speed, the size, the impersonality, the pursuit of material gain.

He was not joking when, soon after Whitmore's marriage, he told her that now that his muse had turned into a bourgeois wife, he could no longer write poetry.[30] During the late 1930s and early 1940s, his correspondence is peppered with references to the waning of his poetic gift. In a 1940 letter to Whitmore, he says bluntly: "No, no escribo" [No, I'm not writing].[31] To Jorge Guillén he complains that he is "distanced" from his poetry just as he is distanced from Spain. Like his homeland, poetry is "real and possible but inaccessible."[32] During his first couple of years in the United States, Salinas had composed the poems of *Largo lamento*; but after that initial burst of creativity he seems to have run dry, and at times this book reads like a farewell not only to Whitmore, the woman who inspired it, but to poetry itself.

A few months after Whitmore's marriage, in an address to the PEN Club of New York City, he returns to the atmospheric imagery that he used in his correspondence and would use again in *Aprecio y defensa del lenguaje*: "I cannot conceive of the existence of a poet outside his own native linguistic atmosphere. The poet not only hears language; he breathes it. So if the poet is withdrawn from his atmosphere of language, his poetry may be seriously affected."[33] Although Salinas speaks hypothetically, again he is talking personally. No longer enveloped by the "pleasant and serene" atmosphere that Whitmore had created, he falls victim to asphyxia. One of the poems of *Largo lamento* employs the same metaphor but applies it to the end of their love affair: "El aire es apenas respirable / porque no me contestas: / tú sabes bien que lo que yo respiro / son tus contestaciones. Y me ahogo" [The air is barely breathable / because you don't reply to me: / You know that what I breathe / are your replies. And I am choking.] (530). Here the poet's asphyxia is caused not by separation from Spain or the Spanish language, but from his beloved. Only after Katherine became Mrs. Whitmore, once his deepest link to the United States had been sundered, did Salinas begin to feel the full impact of exile.

Although he states at the end of *Aprecio y defensa del lenguaje* that he has set forth a political project ("un proyecto de política del lenguaje," 58), the context of his arguments—and concretely his attack on American speech habits—is not only political but personal. All of Salinas's writings demonstrate his remarkable receptivity to language. He loved words, whatever their provenance, and English was no exception. In an early poem, "Underwood girls" (from *Fábula y signo,* 1931), the English language is synonymous with typewriters, one of those modern gadgets he admired. A few years later English would become identified with one "girl" in particular, Katherine, who gave his anglophone tongue ties an intimate twist. In his early letters to her, he parades his increasing fondness for the language, sometimes doing it in English: "Do you know that english is becoming my favorite language? Why? Perhaps you'll be clever enough to guess."[34] In the same letter he jokes that his friends are alarmed that he is "getting crazy with english," that he is becoming an "anglicano."[35] He doesn't share their worries, though, for his knowledge of English only foments what he calls, mixing languages, their "*togetherness* de alma."[36]

Early in 1936, preparing himself to come to the United States, Salinas hired an English tutor and began to listen to language-instruction records *(Brush up your English, Everyday Sentences, English Songs).* Every few weeks, Katherine would send him the *Reader's Digest,* which he liked because of the variety of topics. As he told her in a March 1936 letter, "hago *my utmost* de rodearme de inglés" [I'm doing my utmost to surround myself with English]. Once at Wellesley, he no longer needed phonograph records or English tutors to surround himself with English, and his letters from the late 1930s are peppered with English words and American slang. Delighting in interlingual play, he called survey courses "sorbetes," alley cats "alicates," and Edgar Allan Poe's tomb, not far from his home in Baltimore, "la mismísima tumba Poe-tica."

In *Love in Two Languages,* Abdelkebir Khatibi writes that to love someone is to love that person's body and language; but perhaps it's not necessary to distinguish between body and language, because to love someone's body is already to love her tongue, her language conceived as a body part. Because the tongues that people speak also speak for them, they become acoustic images, voice prints, of their users. Reading books in English, Salinas wrote to Whitmore, was like looking at her picture: "If I like english, if I read english it is only by its similarity with you. I read english as I'd look to picture of you."[37] In the letter to his wife about his meeting with the Spanish American consuls, he remarks that to talk *in* Spanish is to talk *to* Spanish, to converse not only with individual speakers but with the language itself.[38] The opposite is no less true: By engaging with or detaching from a language, we engage with or detach from people with whom the language has become identified. If Santayana abandoned Spanish as a reaction to his father's abandonment of him, Salinas embraced English in order to embrace Katherine. Although he had learned the language as a young man, only after falling in love with Katherine did it become *her* language, the tongue she used in her letters, the tongue he loved and made love to.

Salinas's tongue ties cannot be understood apart from his relations with his American lover and his Spanish wife. Spanish was not only his maternal but his conjugal tongue; English was not simply another language but his "other" tongue, in the charged sense in which Katherine was the "other" woman. The force that manacled him, preventing him from writing to her, was invisible but not mysterious; the same force kept him bound to his wife, to his country, and to his language. In her letters to Salinas, Whitmore complained of his tendency to retreat from promises of marriage and "turn back to M."[39] Regress as well as *regreso*, the Puerto Rican years represented a dramatic turning back "to M," understanding "M" not only as Margarita, but more generally as the maternal, the homegrown, the native (and Madrid, the city where he was born and that he regarded as the capital of Hispanic culture). Even if Salinas's fear of exposure was genuine, the most aggressive acts of censorship originated within himself.

In *Aprecio y defensa del lenguaje*, he states that he has spent thirty years in "daily and close cohabitation" (*diaria y estrecha convivencia*) with his tongue (5). The time span is a little odd, given that he was in his fifties at the time he delivered his speech, and that his first poems had been published well over thirty years earlier. He seems to be dating his tongue ties from 1915, when he began teaching Spanish literature at the University of Paris. But 1915 was also the year that he and Margarita married. Living with one implied living with the other. Later in the speech, his attacks on the "adulteration" of Spanish (43) and his appeals to "faithfulness" to its norms (57) also waver equivocally between the linguistic and the matrimonial. When he argues against the "convivencia" of Spanish and English (40), he is arguing against his own divided affections. When he concludes his address, which Margarita attended, by exhorting his listeners to give to the Spanish tongue "the love that she deserves" (65), one hears in his words the subdued echo of a private pledge. To say that Salinas was wedded to Spanish is more than a metaphor. The panegyric is also epithalamium, for Margarita hovers over the entire speech, as Katherine had hovered over the poetry he wrote between 1932 and 1938.

Margarita also hovers over *El Contemplado,* the book of poems that he composed during his first months in Puerto Rico, when he was no longer wiring or writing Whitmore. As the poetic correlate of the speech, *El Contemplado* also yokes private and public agendas. Not enough attention has been paid to the ways in which these poems erase or exorcise the trilogy of love poetry initiated by *La voz a ti debida.* In his edition of *El Contemplado,* Díez de Revenga remarks that everything in the book "breathes order, concert, inner and outer peace."[40] He gets the verb right, but glosses over the emotional turmoil that not only antecedes but underlies the book. In one of his letters to Whitmore, Salinas divides his poetry into two periods, "B.K." and "A.K.," "Before Katherine" and "After Katherine."[41] The poems of *El Contemplado* leap back over the After Katherine era to situate themselves in the Before Katherine era. Permeated by literal and figurative "oceanic feeling," they also "turn back to M," in every sense of the initial (which now includes "mar," the sea). In 1938, during a trip to Mexico, Salinas reports that he is "living backwards"[42]; the *vivir hacia atrás* that he glimpsed in Mexico he fulfills in San Juan. These poems turn back even metrically, for in contrast to *Largo lamento,* they avoid free verse and resurrect traditional metrical forms.

But the poet who turns back is not the same one who had turned away. For a volume that breathes order and peace, *El Contemplado* is surprisingly full of references to stress and suffering. Although the book has often been described as celebratory, a "hymn of joy,"[43] the poet's joy has a somber underside. Beginning with the epigraph from Jorge Guillén's *Cántico* about a light that "never suffers," the poems repeatedly allude to the poet's recovery from trauma. "You cured my madness," he says to the sea (619). In Variation XII, the only one that refers explicitly to his life in the United States, he portrays himself as someone who has "escaped miraculously from so much agony" (645). From the first to the last variation, the mood is recuperative, convalescent. As the other epigraph from *Cántico* avers, the book is an "attempt at harmony" *(tentativa de armonía),* a record of the poet's efforts to heal himself. If *Largo lamento* was an outpouring of grief, *El Contemplado* gives voice to the precarious peacefulness that follows upon such catharsis.

Robert Havard has suggested that Salinas's "more complacent" attitude toward language in *El Contemplado* indicates that by then the poet had "won his battle" with words.[44] But it may be more accurate to say that he had stopped fighting, because the battle wasn't with words to begin with. The poet's new-found equanimity may arise less from his triumph over language than from a switch in subject matter. One of the odd things about *La voz a ti debida* and *Razón de amor* is that the dominant emotion is not love or lust or longing, but a kind of restlessness, of discomfort, whose origin is not erotic but cognitive. The poet's insistent question to his beloved is not "How do I love thee?" but rather "What do I make of you?" The English-language epigraph of the book—"Thou Wonder, and thou Beauty, and thou Terror"—a tip-off to the beloved's identity, also suggests her intractability.[45] Although Leo Spitzer was factually wrong in asserting that Salinas's beloved was not a flesh-and-blood woman, he was right in perceiving that the poet had transformed her into "a pure concept."[46] The famous resort to pronouns instead of proper names, beyond the obvious motive of concealment, amounts to an admission that the poet is not up to the task that he has set for himself.

Taking the cue from one of the poems in *La voz a ti debida* ("Amor, amor, catástrofe"), I would suggest that the trilogy exemplifies what may be called a "catastrophic" view of language. Literally a catastrophe is an overturning, a sudden upheaval or collapse: in this sense each of the seventy stanzas of *La voz a ti debida* is a cata-strophe, the poetic residue of epistemological failure. The line, "Amor, amor, catástrofe," traces a sequence of events, like the acts of a play ("catastrophe" originally designated the dénouement of a tragedy); but what Salinas chronicles is not the course of a love affair but his vanquishment—not as suitor, not as lover, but as knower. The last word in "Amor, amor, catástrofe"—*caos*—encapsulates in one echoing sound the collapse of his enterprise, even as it timidly insinuates Katherine's name.

Because Salinas believed that naming and knowing were cognate acts, the poet's supreme gift was his ability "to name realities fully, to draw them out of that enormous mass of the anonymous."[47] Yet, *La voz a ti debida* does not name, it points; deictic gestures replace cognitive appropriations. When Salinas, in the most famous lines in all of his poetry, emotes about the "joy" of living in pronouns, I'm not sure that I believe him. This passion for pronouns does not appear in the rest of his work, where he delights in neologizing. It also does not appear in his correspondence with Whitmore, striking for Salinas's obsessive repetition of her first name, Katherine, which he labels "la palabra por excelencia" [the word par excellence].[48] Less a resource than a ruse, his "tú" is a stab in the dark, an insufficient substitute for the real thing, the proper name. Wrenchingly ambiguous, the title of *La voz a ti debida* expresses the poet's debt to his beloved even as it reveals that he has no word, no *voz* in the other sense, with which to name her.

By contrast, *El Contemplado* relieves him of cognitive stress. The title, Salinas's cognomen for the sea of San Juan, already announces that the poet has recovered his nominal gift. Since the initial "theme" and each of the fourteen "variations" consecrate the onomastic bond between the poet and the objects of his gaze, here language functions sacramentally, not catastrophically. Glossing a letter by Gershon Scholem, Derrida remarks that, for Scholem, the power to name makes language sacred.[49] Salinas would have agreed and added that the reason poets are the supreme connoisseurs of language, as he asserts in the speech, is that they are name-givers. The sacralizing dimension of the poet's gift becomes explicit in Variation III, "Dulcenombre," in which the poetic act of naming is itself named: "Obra, sutil, el encanto / divino del cristianar" [Subtle work, the divine / enchantment of christening] (616). Evoking the evangelical zeal of the Spanish conquest, the term "cristianar" reprises the imperial agenda of the speech; but it also reaffirms the poet's loyalty to his maternal and conjugal tongue, since *cristiano* is a colloquial synonym for the Spanish language. For the poet of *El Contemplado,* to name is to name in Spanish, *en cristiano,* as if his tongue were coextensive with language itself. No longer is his Spanish shadowed by Katherine's English. In the sea of San Juan, baptisms are monolingual immersions.

Near the beginning of *Aprecio y defensa del lenguaje,* Salinas tells the story of a young girl who, upon first seeing the Mediterranean, exclaims, "¡Mar, el mar!" He explains:

> La voz es pura defensa. La criatura ve, ante sí, algo que por sus proporciones, su grandeza, su extrañeza, la asusta, casi la amenaza. Y entonces, pronuncia como un conjuro, estos tres sonidos: "mar." Y con ellos, sujeta a la inmensa criatura indómita del agua, encierra la vastedad del agua, de sus olas, del horizonte, en un vocablo. En suma, se explica el mar, nombrándolo y al nombrarlo pierde el miedo, se devuelve a su serenidad. (8)

> [The word is purely defensive. The child sees in front of her something that because of its dimensions, its greatness, its strangeness, scares her, almost threatens her. And then she pronounces, as if it were a spell, these three sounds: "sea." And with them she subjects the immense untamed creature of water, she encloses the vastness of water, its waves, its horizon, in one word. In sum, she explains the sea, naming it, and by naming it she loses her fear, regains her calm.]

This passage provides a gloss of *El Contemplado,* which arises from the admirative and defensive naming described in the anecdote, as well as a diagnosis of what goes wrong in the trilogy, where taming by naming fails. In the poems to Katherine, Salinas is an eager but defenseless *criatura,* defenseless because he lacks words with which to christen her. Unexpectedly, he finds himself in a world of irreducible alterity— wondrous, beautiful, but also indomitable. Not so in *El Contemplado,* whose beloved, the anthropomorphic sea, bends to the poet's onomastic will. Even when the sea incarnates in a female figure, as it does in several variations, she is defined by her passivity: *amada* rather than *amante*, beloved rather than lover (Variation IX).[50]

Although the ostensible subject of *El Contemplado* is the sea that Salinas looked at every morning from the terrace of a beach club in San Juan, the book is no more about the sea than the commencement speech is about "el lenguaje." The poems spring from a commonplace and a conceit: The commonplace is that of "the sea of language," *el mar del idioma,* or what he calls in the speech "las aguas hondas de la lengua materna" [the deep waters of the mother tongue] (6); the conceit, anchored in the Atlantic Ocean's role in the colonization of the New World, construes the sea as a metaphor for Spanish culture. The book's onomatopoetics is not only Adamic, as has often been said, but Columbian. In "Verbo," another poem from the Puerto Rican period, Salinas asserts that he is the "beach" that receives the waves of the "Castilian sea."[51] Land-locked Castile has no sea, which only makes his meaning more transparent. The lapping of the sea of language onto the poet engenders the words of Salinas's poems, including "Verbo" itself. In *El Contemplado,* the equivalence of sea and poem will be previewed in the book's subtitle, "mar, poema" (which plays on *poemario*), and developed by scriptural metaphors (in Variation VI, for example, the seaspray contains "white signs" that imprint a "magical text" upon the "golden sheets" of the sand [623]). Like *Aprecio y defensa del lenguaje,* only more explicitly and elaborately, *El Contemplado* celebrates and renews the poet's ties to his mother tongue. Initially an object of contemplation, the sea becomes a mirror of the poet's mind in the act of creation as well as the vehicle through which he verbalizes what he sees. A stark counterexample to Santayana's severance of source and medium, the unvarying theme of Salinas's variations is the identity of message, medium, and source. *Poema, poeta, poesis*—all three converge in the metapoetic sea; the *mar castellana* is contemplated *en castellano* by Salinas, *poeta castellano.*

For the reinvigorated poet, every word is new, every onomastic act is inaugural, an *estreno* (611). Only this subjective impression of initial achievement makes plausible his elation with his rather commonplace nickname for the sea. As a verbal find, *el contemplado* is no more remarkable than the cries of *brillo* from the shoe-shine boys, especially for someone as clever with words as Salinas. But in his excited state, any Spanish word, any hispanophone sound, would have induced euphoria. In the latter part of the book, as the variations succeed one another, his excitement tempers before the sobering realization that, once embedded in their cultural matrix, his debuts are actually encores. Adam the neologizer is also Funes *el memorioso*. Names have a history, even a personal history, as in Variation XIII, "Presagio," which turns back to Salinas's first book, *Presagios* (1924), or as in Variation III, "Dulcenombre," an epithet applied to the Virgin Mary's name that Salinas had also used apropos of his wife, whose actual name surfaces in Variation VII: "Venus verdes, tendiéndose en la umbría; / menea un airecillo sus cabellos, / herbazal, juncos, altas margaritas" [Green Venuses, lying in the shade; / a soft breeze stirs their hair, / grasses, reeds, tall daisies *(margaritas)*] (624).[52]

In the concluding poem of *Razón de amor*, "La felicidad inminente," written when Salinas had already decided to join Whitmore in the United States, the speaker shudders with "a great tremor of anticipation and dawn" at the realization that his love will require severing ties with the past (445). Undoing the undoing of the trilogy, *El Contemplado* reattaches the poet to his personal and national history.[53] In the last variation, as he remembers his parents, his "brothers" (Salinas was an only child), his literary precursors, all those who have used the language before him, Salinas redefines his mission as the perpetuation of their "inexhaustible legacy." In the previous variation, he had described his new-found sense of purpose in terms nearly identical to his explanation for not writing to Whitmore from San Juan. As in the letter, he says he has been overcome by an irresistible force: "Poseído voluntario / de esta fuerza que me invade" [Involuntarily possessed / by this force that invades me] (647). The difference between letter and poem is that his surrender to this force, to the ligatures of language and family and community, is now voluntary. As voluntary, in fact, as the decision to stop writing to her.

Having lost his battle with foreignness, with Katherine's xenophone "Thou," Salinas retreats to safer ground, to holy ground, to the sanctuary of San Juan, a haven of homogeneity where (as he said about language communities) he could name "the same things" with "the same names": not Salinas in Beauty- and Terror- and Wonder-land, but *Pedro por su casa*. "¡Gloria a las diferencias!" he exclaims in *Razón de amor*, but these differences required a work of translation—translation *to* as well as translation *from*—that he was not capable of. For Spitzer, the speaker of *La voz a ti debida* is a Narcissus who looks for his reflection in his beloved. Yes, but he is a frustrated Narcissus, one who cannot see what he seeks. In a note to one of his letters, Whitmore explains why: "Beautiful letter in which he assures me that he loves me *as I am*—which, poor dear, he could never do except when my actions coincided with his ideas."[54] Comfortable only when contemplation turned into self-regard,

Salinas has no such difficulties with the sea of San Juan, which never failed to reflect his bright ideas.

Mar/Margarita, Katherine/*Catástrofe*: As a symbol of his "B.K." self, of attachments and obligations that antedated his love for Katherine, the sea of San Juan offered Salinas a steady, restorative affection, very unlike the shattering, logoclastic passion of the trilogy. The first adjective that he applies to the sea is *constante*, and constant it remains amidst all of the poet's variations. The tongue that he saved, saved him in return.

Or did it? Salinas's relationship with Whitmore did not end with his departure for Puerto Rico. In February of 1946, a few months before returning to his position at Hopkins, he unexpectedly received a letter from Katherine, who wrote to ask for a copy of . . . *Aprecio y defensa del lenguaje*. Interpreting her request as an icebreaker, he immediately forgot the vows contained in the speech and began writing letters again, though he was careful to ask her not to reply. As deft with excuses as he was with poems, he pleaded with her to forgive him: During those years of silence she was constantly in his thoughts, often in his dreams; he may have stopped writing her, but he had never stopped loving her; on her birthdays (October 25), his torment became unbearable. Katherine of course forgave him—she always did—and their friendship, though not their love affair, resumed. But the Salinas who returned from Puerto Rico was not the same man she had known. Already ill with cancer (though he didn't realize it), he had lost the "eager-heartedness" that had characterized him. Even though he continued to write, he never again matched the literary excellence of the trilogy or the exuberant productivity of the Puerto Rican years. In "La amada de Pedro Salinas," a brief memoir included in Whitmore's bequest to the Harvard Library, she describes their last meeting:

> The few times I saw Pedro after his return from Puerto Rico he seemed strange to me, alien. The last time was in the spring of 1951, the year he died. He had come to Northampton to give a college lecture and we found a few minutes to talk. I had always hoped that he would come to understand why I had to break with him. And so I asked him again, "Don't you see now why it had to be?" He looked at me sadly and replied, "No, I really don't. Another woman in your place would have considered herself most fortunate." That, dearest Pedro, is doubtless true but "yo no soy más que lo que soy" [I am not more than what I am].[55] He took his leave—I did not know that he was ill and I would never see him again.

Chapter 3

Spanish-Only Body Talk

Canta tus aires fielmente.
[Sing your airs faithfully.]

—Luis Cernuda, *"Amor en música"*

Unlike Pedro Salinas, who had been his mentor and eventually became his nemesis, Luis Cernuda spent his years in the United States hiding, deliberately closed off from Americans and their culture. Salinas's diatribes against the utilitarian lapidariness of the American vernacular could not disguise his fascination with it; indeed they were its symptom. But Cernuda, who also spent time in Scotland and England, felt no such fascination. He turned a deaf ear to ambient sounds as much as Salinas made a point of recording and recoiling from them. Although Cernuda learned English well enough to write knowledgeably about English poetry, he had no interest in the English spoken in Great Britain or the United States. The two great poems of his American exile, "Nocturno yanki" and "Retrato de poeta," portray him incommunicado, in soundproof isolation. In "Nocturno yanki," the speaker walls himself up in his apartment, windows closed and the shades drawn, listening out for the voices of absent friends; all he hears is the beating of his blood and the hissing of the radiator. In "Retrato de poeta," he takes refuge in the Boston Museum of Fine Arts, where he begins a one-sided conversation with El Greco's portrait of the seventeenth-century Spanish poet and preacher, Paravicino. In the comparable poems by Salinas, "Nocturno de los avisos" and "Hombre en la orilla," the speaker is equally alone, equally alienated, but he is out and about, walking the streets of New York City and taking in the sights. Famous for verse colloquies with himself—"soliloquios contigo," as he puts it in "Nocturno yanki"—Cernuda goes outside only to look for the self that he carried within.

When Cernuda left Madrid in February of 1938 to deliver a series of lectures in London, he had the reputation of being something of a *poète maudit,* the result of his sullen temperament and his defiant acknowledgement of his homosexuality. Born and raised in Seville, he (along with Jorge Guillén and Pedro Salinas) was identified with the group of poets that clustered around José Ortega y Gasset's influential journal, *Revista de Occidente,* where Cernuda published his first poems. Even though his first book, *Perfil del aire* (1927), received mixed reviews, some years later his collected poetry, *La realidad y el deseo* (1936)— which included several sections inspired by homosexual relationships— was praised warmly by many of the leading literary lights of the day, including Juan Ramón Jiménez and Pedro Salinas, who had been his teacher at the University of Seville and to whom Cernuda had dedicated *Perfil del aire.* Never the type to have many close friends or promoters—a contemporary once described him as "cold, distant, cut off from life"[1]— by the mid-1930s Cernuda was nonetheless widely regarded as one of his generation's most talented and original poets.

After finishing his lecture engagement in London, he travelled to Paris, from where he planned to return to Spain, but the impending loss of the Republican side in the civil war persuaded him that return was not feasible. For the next five years he taught Spanish in Glasgow, a city he loathed, and eventually moved on to similar employment in Cam-bridge and London. During these years he published an expanded edition of *La realidad y el deseo* (1940) and wrote the prose poems of *Ocnos* (1942). In 1947 he accepted a position at Mt. Holyoke College. Initially sanguine about his prospects in America, he soon became disenchanted with life in a New England college town. Unlike Salinas, who greeted his first New England winter with a panegyric to snow, Cernuda hated the climate from the start.[2] The snow was stain upon the earth, and the bare trees and freezing temperatures were nothing like warm and green Andalusia. He endured Mt. Holyoke until 1952, when he decided to forego the security of a tenured teaching position to live in Mexico City. Lacking steady employment, he roomed with friends and eked out a precarious living writing and lecturing for the remaining decade of his life.

The turning point in Cernuda's move from *destierro* to *trastierro,* from an anglophone to a hispanophone environment, occurred barely two years after his arrival in the States. In the summer of 1949, eager for a change from Mt. Holyoke, he spent a month in Mexico. Like Salinas in Puerto Rico, Cernuda immediately felt at home. In Mexico he too could "live backwards," as Salinas had put it, for the country seemed to him a new Spain. Over the next few years, he returned to Mexico as often as his job allowed. These visits acquired a special urgency after the summer of 1950, when he fell in love with a young Mexican named Salvador, who was half his age.[3] Henceforth Mexico would be identified not only with the recovery of his homeland, but with the revival of his body. In

Massachusetts his body was "cuerpo en pena," a variation on "alma en pena," a soul in purgatory ("Nocturno yanki"). In Mexico, it came back to life, like the Lazarus of the Gospels (154).[4] By falling in love, the middle-aged Cernuda retrieved what he called his "summer self" *(ser estival),* the youthful, vigorous man that had lain dormant under the New England snow.

Variaciones sobre tema mexicano (1952), a collection of prose poems, contains the record of Cernuda's creative and corporal rebirth. Written after his first and second trips to Mexico, and published a few months after he moved there permanently, *Variaciones* occupies in Cernuda's career a place analogous to that of *Aprecio y defensa del lenguaje* and *El contemplado* in Salinas's. Like Salinas's texts, *Variaciones* is joyful, celebrative, conjunctive, a testimony to the merging of self and other. In this respect, this book differs from most of Cernuda's earlier and later poetry, which (as he was one of the first to point out) centered on the conflict between reality and desire. The paradox in the title of his collected poetry, *La realidad y el deseo,* is that the conjunction must be read disjunctively, for poem after poem bears witness to the difficulty of merging the two terms. If anything, the title expresses the reality *of* desire, the poet's stubborn search for what he called "the complete image of the world."[5]

As soon as Cernuda set foot in Mexico, after more than a decade of uninterrupted residence among English speakers, the new country registered as homophony, familiar sound. Like Salinas, his first impression was linguistic, or, more precisely, lingual. In "Retrato de poeta," the seat of the poet's nostalgia had been his ears, "empty shells" that resonated with the distant murmurs of home. Once in Mexico, his ears are filled with hispanophone voices:

—Tras cruzada la frontera, al oír tu lengua, que tantos años no oías hablada en torno, ¿qué sentiste?
    —Sentí como sin interrupción continuaba mi vida en ella por el mundo exterior, ya que por el interior no había dejado de sonar en mí todos aquellos años. (625)

["After crossing the border, upon hearing your tongue, which for so many years you had not heard spoken around you, what did you feel?"
    "I felt as if through it my life continued without interruption into the exterior world, since in my interior it had never stopped sounding during all those years."]

As inner speech becomes public discourse, *lengua* expands into *idioma.* In the introduction to the book, Cernuda notes that Mexico "resonates" with "our echoes" (622). Now, in the first vignette, as he begins playing variations on this theme, the echoes are not only those of his nation but those of his own voice. Abolishing the barrier between outside and inside, between *mundo exterior* and *mundo interior*, Mexico triggers an experience of *acorde*, as Cernuda would call such epiphanic moments, an accord whose substance is musical, harmonic. This is homecoming as consonance, as musical chord, as the merging of "la música afuera y el ritmo de la sangre dentro" [outer music and the blood's inner rhythm] ("El acorde," 614).[6] That the epiphany should take the form of a dialogue underscores the intersubjective or communal nature of the experience. No longer does Cernuda address mute interlocutors, as in "Retrato de poeta." The *frontera* that he mentions not only separates countries and languages, but also the poet and his *entorno*. Crossing the border, he lets his inner life flow into the world around him. In a memorable line from *Los placeres prohibidos* (1931), he writes that desire is a question without an answer (178). The coupling of question and answer—"what did you feel?" "I felt"—confirms that this variation records one of those rare moments of *acorde*, of realized desire, that Cernuda spent his life in search of. In a subsequent variation, he asserts that Mexico is a question to which he provides the "consonant answer" (*consonante respuesta*; 653).

True to the book's title, Cernuda strikes the musical chord repeatedly. Although it would be inaccurate to downplay the visual impact of Mexico, his primary organ of perception is the ear, not the eye. In addition to using such headings as "Músicos rústicos," "Dúo," and "La concha vacía," he will fill the vignettes with song lyrics, snippets of conversation, and the cries of street vendors. These persistent acoustic references give continuity and coherence to his otherwise fragmentary reflections. As Jaime Gil de Biedma points out, *Variaciones* traces an asymmetrical narrative of arrival, departure, and return.[7] Of the twenty-nine variations, the first twenty-six relate Cernuda's initial impressions of Mexico. Narrated in the present tense, they span the brief, intense interlude between the "yesterday" when he arrived and the "tomorrow" when he will leave (638). The twenty-seventh variation, "Centro del hombre," describes the tearful flight back to the United States. The twenty-eighth, "La concha vacía," finds him in Mt. Holyoke again, nostalgically evoking his Mexican stay. The last, "El regreso," rejoices in a return that feels like a new homecoming. All three stages are woven together by aural motifs. If Cernuda's first impressions of Mexico are phonic, upon his return to the States he obsessively replays in his memory a "tune" he learned in Mexico (155). A year later, back in Mexico, the echoes revert to voices:

Otra vez estás en una tierra cuyo ritmo y acento se acuerdan con aquellos de la tuya ausente, con los tuyos entrañables. ¿No los escuchas? Confundidos unos y otros, ¿no parecen sonar en tus oídos tras el eco de aquella joven voz varonil, que acompañándose en la guitarra, al cruzar la frontera, oíste cantando en un barracón de la aduana? (654)

[Once again you are in a land whose rhythm and accent accord with those of your absent homeland, with those inside you. Can't you hear them? Mixed together, don't they seem to resonate in your ears with the echo of the young manly voice that, accompanying itself on the guitar, you heard singing in the customs house?]

Reprising the first variations in the last, the allusion to the "rustic musicians" of the third variation (121) stresses the iterative nature of the experience. The iteration operates on two levels, for going back to Mexico involves returning to the place of return, to the country where a year earlier he had already experienced the sensation of retrieving his homeland. Because the "rhythms and accents" of Mexico accord not only with his own, but with those of his "absent homeland," the harmony of outer and inner voices is enriched by the consonance of past and present. This consonance is both historical and personal: Just as Mexico is a New Spain, the young Cernuda revives in the mature poet. As he says in an earlier variation, in Mexico the man that he is embraces the child that he was (648); that "young manly voice" that he heard when he first arrived echoes his own youthful voice. *Regreso* is also regression, a way of cancelling what he elsewhere calls "the double distance," age and exile.[8] By travelling to Mexico, Cernuda brings together not only the *mundo exterior* and his *mundo interior* (here called "entrañable"), but also his *mundo anterior,* that "Andalusian corner" (149) where he spent his happiest years.

In the passage quoted above, the unusual construction "se acuerdan con," which blends the harmonic *(acordar con)* with the mnemonic *(acordarse de),* conveys the intricacies of his multileveled *regreso.* The expression exploits the resemblance between etymologically distinct but phonically similar families of words: on the one hand, *cuerda* and *acorde* (from *chorda,* string); on the other, *acuerdo, recuerdo,* and their paronyms (from *cors,* heart).[9] Derived from the harmonious sounding of musical tones, *acordar con* implies simultaneity; *acordarse de,* which refers to the recollection of past events, implies succession. By combining the two phrases, Cernuda fuses simultaneity and succession, space and time, into a unitary experience: "there and then" are reborn as "here and now." Elsewhere in his work, he plays on the resemblance between *acordar* and *acordarse*: in "Desengaño indolente" (1925), "el sonido acordado"

(768) names a concordant as well as remembered sound; in "El intruso" (1945), the speaker's "conciencia desacordada" suffers from a lack of memory and harmony (391); in "El retraído" (1946), "recuerdos" are likened to "las cuerdas" of a guitar (400); in "Música cautiva" (1956), the "desacuerdo" between reality and desire designates absence of *acorde* as well as of *acuerdo* (hence the musical title).

In *Variaciones,* however, *acorde* triumphs over *desacuerdo.* The insistent sounding of the spatiotemporal chord separates this book from the rest of Cernuda's work, including *Ocnos,* the other collection of prose poems to which *Variaciones* is usually compared. Composed in 1940 while he was living in Glasgow, *Ocnos* is also reconciliatory, conjunctive, but the poet's quest for harmony is satisfied only in memory, only as an *acordarse de,* since the world that surrounds him--"hateful Scotland" (608)—does not enter into the accord. If the poet mentally retreats to his Andalusian youth, it is to escape the "prison" of Glasgow (76), memorialized in such somber vignettes as "Ciudad Caledonia" and "Elegía anticipada." But in *Variaciones,* there is no discord between the outward and the backward glance—to look out is to look back—as there is no discord between the outward and the inward glance—to look out is to look in. *Ocnos* makes up for exile with recollection, while *Variaciones* offers the additional compensation of relocation, a form of return enabled by Spain's reincarnation in Mexico, "los ecos nuestros que aquí resuenan, intactos a pesar del tiempo" [our echoes that resonate here, intact in spite of time] (622).

Because voices ride on the breath, Cernuda's lingualism, his stress on Spanish as sound, provides the occasion for respiratory imagery similar to those in *Aprecio y defensa del lenguaje.* As in the speech, respiration becomes a metaphor for the continuity of self and world. Once again, *lo exterior, lo interior,* and *lo anterior* converge, except that now the dominant idiom is respiratory rather than musical:

> Viendo este rincón, respirando este aire, hallas que lo que afuera ves y respiras también está dentro de tí; que allá en el fondo de tu alma, en su círculo oscuro, como luna reflejada en agua profunda, está la imagen misma de lo que entorno tienes: y que desde tu infancia se alza, intacta y límpida, esa imagen fundamental, sosteniendo, ella tan leve, el peso de tu vida y de su afán secreto. (648)

> [Looking at this corner, breathing this air, you find that what you are seeing and breathing outside you is also within you; that there in the bottom of your soul, in its dark circle, like the reflection of the moon in deep water, is the very image of what you have around you: and that from your infancy there arises, intact and limpid, that fundamental image,

holding up, in spite of its slightness, the weight of your life and your secret longing.]

Another example:

> Sí, ahí lo tienes, frente a tus ojos, al objeto de tu amor: míralo, que pocas veces halagó tu mirada la vista de lo que has amado. Esta llanura, este cielo, este aire te envuelven y absorben, anonadándote en ellos. El amor ya no está sólo dentro, ahogándote con su vastedad, sino fuera de ti, visible y tangible; y tú eres al fin parte de él, respirándolo libremente. (654)

> [Yes, there it is, before your eyes, the object of your love: look at it well, because few times has your glance enjoyed the sight of what you have loved. This plain, this sky, this air envelop and absorb you, losing you in them. Love is no longer only inside you, choking you with its vastness, but outside you, visible and tangible; and you finally have become a part of it, breathing it freely.]

As we have seen, exiles sometimes experience xenophony as asphyxia. In "Nocturno yanki," Cernuda's apartment resembles an airless tomb rather than a cozy corner, which is why he adapted the poem's metrical scheme from the best-known elegy in Spanish literature, Jorge Manrique's *Coplas por la muerte de su padre*.[10] In "Retrato de poeta," the speaker goes to the portrait of Paravicino in search of air, "queriendo resurgir, buscando el aire / Otra vez" [wanting to revive, seeking air / Again] (450). That's what he finds in Mexico, pulmonary freedom, breathing space, the type of environment in which Paravicino thrived, where the "beloved word" achieved its "power and magic" (451).

One suggestively ambiguous word summarizes the source of Cernuda's well-being—*aire*. Air is the language one breathes in, Juan Ramón's atmospheric Spanish, but in "La concha vacía," it is also the Mexican song that he hums to himself back in the States—"este aire, esta tonada" (652). Behind the elemental and the musical lies a third sense, for *aire* is also a toponym, the name of the street in Seville where Cernuda spent his adolescence, *calle Aire*, evoked in the title of his first book, *Perfil del aire*. When Cernuda states that by breathing Mexican air he feels rejuvenated, when he realizes that the breeze that sways the branches in a Mexican garden is the same "aire" that swayed other branches in other gardens (645), a ghostly Andalusian topography lurks in Mexico's landscape. Although the role of the four elements in Cernuda's poetry has been discussed extensively, *aire* differs from the others because of its personal significance. Stung by criticisms of his first book, Cernuda omitted *Perfil del aire* from his collected poems, but he compensated for the omission by infusing his poetry with air.[11] Regardless of the date of composition, every section of *La realidad y el deseo* bathes in the aura of *calle Aire,* which Cernuda associated with the lost paradise of youth. A late poem, "Lo más frágil es lo que dura" (1955), encapsulates the scope of Cernuda's theme-word: "Un olor de azahar, / Aire. ¿Hubo algo más?" [A scent of orange blossoms, / Air. Was there anything else?] (468). Even literary immortality consists in being remembered as "un nombre, un son, un aire" [a name, a tune, an air] (368). Like these, many other examples could be cited.[12]

When Cernuda entitles the poem marking his arrival in the States "Otros aires" (1948), he is using the noun in three senses—the elemental, the musical, and the toponymic. The title alludes to the landscape of grey skies and barren fields; but it also announces the expectation of creative renewal, of hearing the "hidden music" of the bare new England landscape (417), as well as the desire of making a home—another *calle Aire*—in America. "Aire" even turns into a proper name in "El indolente" (1929), a story whose protagonist, a young man named Aire, personifies the mythical Andalusian town of Sansueña. The word that Cernuda suppressed as a title he abundantly cultivated as allusion and metaphor, and nowhere more explicitly than in *Variaciones,* a book that records not only the recovery of his native linguistic air but the triumphant return of *Perfil del aire.* Indeed, each of the variations is an "air" in both musical and atmospheric senses. The expansive versicles of the prose poems, which stand in stark contrast to the unrhymed *coplas*—songs without music—of "Nocturno yanki" or the dreary stanzas—*octavas irreales*—of "Retrato de poeta," mime the relaxed, roomy rhythms of the experiences they record. Technically flawless, Cernuda's verse poetry during his years in South Hadley has a constricted, claustral feel quite unlike the plein-air spaciousness of the prose poems, whose pattern of "tema y variaciones" afforded him, as it did Salinas in *El contemplado,* the opportunity for unhurried digression. The versicles of *Variaciones* contain Cernuda's truly "free" verse, as the poet's languid enjoyment of Mexico is matched by the leisurely pace of his evocations.

The different function of this element in Cernuda and in Jorge Guillén, the other great Spanish poet of air, illustrates why these two poets had such different reactions to anglophone exile. Unlike Cernuda, Guillén uses *aire* as a symbol of what is not individual or local; and by entitling his collected poetry *Aire nuestro,* he intended to designate shared human experience. For Guillén, "aire" is not a toponym or a proper name or even a metaphor for his mother tongue, but the commonest of nouns. In a fine study of exilic literature, his son, Claudio Guillén, has distinguished between two fundamental responses to exile, the Ovidian and the Plutarchan. While Ovid responds to banishment with longing for Rome, his spiritual and literary center, Plutarch reminds himself that the same sun shines on exile and non-exile alike.¹³ Like Plutarch's sun, Jorge Guillén's air is a metaphor for what transcends locality, nationality, history. Nothing could be further from the sensibility of Cernuda, who had difficulty using the possessive *nuestro* even when referring to the tongue that he shared with his countrymen.¹⁴ A rancorous Ovid, Cernuda never sought or achieved the detachment that Guillén (or Santayana) made such a central part of their writerly stance. Even when he was railing at his country and his countrymen, as he sometimes did, his rancor was his bond. *Español sin ganas* he may have been, but a Spaniard nonetheless. And since *Aire* was, in effect, another name for his *tierra*, he did not use it with Guillén's universalizing intent.

For Cernuda, Guillén's Plutarchan indifference to the local, his dilution of local airs, was not capacious but narrow, confined in its abstractness. All of the poems of *Cántico*, he said, were written from the same vantage point, that of the notorious *beato sillón* of one of Guillén's *décimas*, a comfortable reading chair that could grace the parlor of any bourgeois household in the world.¹⁵ In the scathing chapter about Guillén and Salinas in his *Estudios sobre poesía española contemporánea* (1957), Cernuda singles out for criticism "El aire," the next to the last poem in *Cántico*; he remarks that the poem illustrates the author's tendency to write without having anything to say ("hablar por hablar, o para decirlo de otra manera: rizar el rizo").¹⁶ Unlike the vibrant, melodious airs of *Variaciones*, the air in Guillén's poem is soundless, and life transpires quietly within it: "Y la vida, sin cesar / Humildemente valiendo, / Callada va por el aire" [And life, without stopping / modestly worth living / Quietly goes through the air]). To Guillén's vaporous assertion, "Soy del aire" [I belong to the air], Cernuda could have replied with biotopographic justness: "*I* am the one who hails from, or belongs to, *el aire*." For Cernuda, *aire* is not a "secret being" or a platonic "Idea," as in Guillén's poem, but the name of the street where he lived.

In his study of Guillén's poetry, Cernuda makes the shrewd observation that the former's diction is based on the written rather than the spoken word, a suggestion born out by the title of one of the sections of *Aire Nuestro*, "Tiempo de leer, tiempo de escribir" [Time to read, time to write]. The exiled Juan Ramón boiled down poetic inspiration to four words: "¡A oír, a hablar!" [Listen, and talk!]¹⁷ But for Guillén poetry is not talk; and it follows upon reading, not listening. Like Juan Ramón, Cernuda conceived of poetry as speech rather than script, as *lengua* and *idioma* rather than *lenguaje*. When Cernuda reflects on poetry, he invariably resorts to the lexicon of orality: Poetry "speaks," its medium is a "tongue," the poet's words are "echoes."[18] Discriminating between the "musical mode" of his poetry and the "sculptural mode" of Guillén's, Cernuda simplifies, but he does not misjudge.[19] A poet who conceives of poetry as speech uses music as his model, as Cernuda did, taking inspiration from "jazz airs" and cultivating what he called the *poema-canción* [song-poem]. A different type of poet, like Guillén, thinks of poetry as writing, of writing as sculpting, and likens his life's work to a finely chiseled block of marble, as in the dedication to *Aire nuestro*: "Contigo edificado para ti / Quede este bloque ya tranquilo así" [Edified with you and for you / let this block rest peacefully like this]. Cernuda generally put the poems in his books in the order in which he wrote them, a "temporal" arrangement; Guillén worked tirelessly on the architecture of *Aire nuestro,* making sure that each piece occupied the right niche in the total edifice—"cathedral work," as Salinas put it.[20] One kind of poet sings; the other crafts. One arranges airs; the other, building blocks.

These contrasts help to explain why Guillén adapted more easily to life in exile. At Wellesley College, where he succeeded Salinas and taught for many years, Guillén found a "pleasant retreat"; a few miles away, in South Hadley, Cernuda felt himself to be living in limbo.[21] Since Guillén did not need to be cradled by the sounds of the language in which he wrote, he did not suffer the linguistic estrangement, the asphyxia, of some of his Spanish contemporaries. Cernuda, who thought of himself as a *vocero,* as someone who inherits and perpetuates the voices of his forebears, could not endure the silence of his mother tongue. As he acknowledged, had he not moved to Mexico he might have stopped writing poetry altogether. But linguistic repatriation, which left such a profound imprint on Cernuda, as it did on Salinas and Juan Ramón, barely made a ripple in Guillén. Describing his return to Spain after an absence of more than ten years, he mentions that the "novelty" of hearing his mother tongue wore off within twenty-four hours.[22] Many months after his arrival in San Juan, Salinas was still enraptured (and sometimes enraged) by the Spanish he heard around him. Every time he returned to Mexico, Cernuda was seized by phonic bliss. Not so Guillén, who in order to keep on writing only had to keep on reading. Paris, Montreal, Wellesley, or Madrid—no matter where he lived, he was breathing the same air.

Predictably, Cernuda's sensitivity to ambient sounds led him to demonize colloquial English. Almost pathologically shy, he did not engage in public diatribes, à la Salinas, though he also developed what we might term a "malarial" view of the American vernacular. Like his former teacher, Cernuda regarded the speech of Americans as *mal aire,* air infected by the utilitarianism of its users, the "protestant industrialists" whom he refers to *Variaciones* (631–632). One of the most beautiful variations, "Los ojos y la voz," contrasts anglophone and hispanophone voices:

> Muchos años viviste entre gentes de ojos apagados y de voz inexpresiva. Y no es que algunas dejaran de estar bien; pero sus ojos, cuando más, eran aguas estancadas, y cuando menos, tragaluces. ¿Había algo dentro? Si lo había, que no pocas veces dudaste, estaba muerto.
>
> Y sus voces, o rencorosas o desdeñosas; entre ambos extremos, ruido, ruido, ruido. Temblor ninguno. Voces incultas eran aquellas (cultura: patrimonio de voces desinteresadas), sin modulación, sin caricia; voces para el negocio o la necesidad, nada más. (640–41)

> [For many years you lived among people with dull eyes and unexpressive voices. And it's not that some of these people were not alright; but their eyes, at best, were stagnant waters, and at worst, fanlights.[23] Was there anything inside? If there was, which you often doubted, it was dead.
>
> And their voices, either rancorous or disdainful; between the two extremes, noise, noise, noise. Not a quiver. They were uncultured voices (culture: a patrimony of disinterested voices), without modulation, without caress; voices to do business or meet wants, nothing more.]

By contrast, the speech of even the humblest Mexican is refined and cultured:

> Pocas o ningunas voces son aquí incultas; por humilde que sea quien habla, es en lenguaje delicado. Un habla precisa, una lengua clásica, sin modismos vulgares ni entonaciones plebeyas. Y cómo suenan estas voces, claras, sedosas, con el rumor frío y airoso de la seda. (641)

> [Few or any voices here are uncultured; no matter how humble the speaker, he speaks a delicate language. A precise speech, a classical tongue, without vulgar idioms or plebeian intonations. And how these voices resound, clear, silky, with the cold and airy murmur of silk.]

Like Ovid, for whom the language of the Getes was a rumble of hostile sounds, for Cernuda the speech of his American neighbors consists of *voces incultas,* barbarous voices/words. As neither *habla* nor *lengua,* spoken English is no more than noise. (In *Ocnos* he also disparages anglophony as "offensive noise" [610].) Mexican *voces* not only embody a melodious tongue, their sound is "airy," an adjective charged with all the beneficent, life-affirming connotations of *aire.*

Only in one place does Cernuda allow the English language to creep into his text. "Dúo" is an intriguing variation, not only because of the intrusion of English but also because Cernuda suppressed it from the only edition of the book published in his lifetime. Found among his papers after his death (along with a notation indicating where it should be inserted), "Dúo" relates a sexual encounter with a Mexican boy—"a dark little body on the threshold of adolescence" (643)—with whom Cernuda spent a passionate afternoon. As he lounges in bed after the lovemaking, the late afternoon shower reminds him of an anonymous sixteenth-century English lyric, "O Western Wind," which he then reproduces in the original language:

A tu mente acuden entonces unos versos viejos de siglos (O Western wind, when wilt thou blow / That the small rain down can rain? / Christ, that my love were in my arms, / And I in my bed again!), y ante el recuerdo literario inoportuno no puedes reprimir tu disgusto. ¿Literatura? ¿Aquí? Avergonzado de tu memoria, impertinente en este trance de animalidad pura, quieres desechar, olvidar los versos. (643)

[Your mind then recalls some verses aged by centuries (O Western wind, when wilt thou blow / That the small rain down can rain? / Christ, that my love were in my arms, / And I in my bed again!), and confronted by the inopportune literary reminiscence, you cannot repress your disgust. Literature? Here? Ashamed by the memory, impertinent in this moment of pure animality, you want to discard, to forget the verses.]

As always happens with poetic condemnations of poetry, Cernuda's disgust is self-refuting, for by narrating the incident Cernuda is also making literature, transposing animal moments into literary occasions. More importantly, the true "here" in his account is the present of writing, not the recollected *après-midi*. Although the variations as a whole foster the illusion of presentness, of the simultaneity of event and transcription, not a single one was written in Mexico; all were composed in South Hadley in the winter and fall of 1950, after his first and second visits. While the persona of the variations may be the poet's summer self, it is the invernal Cernuda, the shut-in of "Nocturno yanki" and "Retrato de poeta," who composed them. Although the book appears to be corroborative, it is actually compensatory. This rift between scriptive record and mental *recuerdo* comes to the surface in "Dignidad y reposo," where after noting that "here" in Mexico bodies take more naturally to restful poses than in "Anglo-Saxon lands," Cernuda adds: "Pronto, pronto. Antes que olvides, recuerda, entre otras, algunas" [Hurry, hurry. Before you forget, remember some of them] (627). What's the hurry? If he is living in Mexico, amidst those very bodies, why the urgency to recall, an urgency opposed to the leisurely life that he is praising?

No less than *Ocnos*, and unlike *Aprecio y defensa del lenguaje* and *El contemplado, Variaciones* is the work of an exile rather than a *revenu*. Like the fear of forgetting, the irruption of English into "Dúo" bespeaks the anglophone atmosphere in which the book was written. The erotic duet disguises existential duality: between the poet's summer and winter selves; between his inner voices and those of the world around him. It is Cernuda who is *impertinente*, who doesn't belong where he is. In fact the English lyric comes closer to reflecting his real *trance* or situation than the protracted lovemaking. When Cernuda translated this English lyric into Spanish (a translation also written in South Hadley), he called it, "El amante en invierno hace proyectos para la primavera" [The lover in winter makes plans for spring] (850). Not part of the original poem, this title reveals the amount of wishful thinking hidden in Cernuda's variations. If he reacts with disgust to the English lyric, it's because he cannot prevent the encroachment of xenophony, of offensive noise, on his exile life. Writing "Dúo," he is closer to the English poet than to the Mexican boy. Rather than sexual, the real duet in the variation is literary—a counterpoint of English and Spanish, of verse and prose poetry.

In "Los ojos y la voz," when Cernuda complains that anglophone voices do not "quiver" or "caress," he is calling attention to the corporealness, the fleshiness of his mother tongue. This too sets *Variaciones* apart from the corresponding works by Salinas, which differ in their presentation of the link between mother tongue and sexuality. Both in the speech and in his own collection of poetic variations, Salinas invokes his nuptial bond with Spanish. In *El contemplado*, this bond finds expression in the many references to the love between the poet and the sea. At first this love seems entirely narcissistic, with the sea giving back the poet's own image; but as the variations unfold, the poet discovers that the sea also contains other presences, other voices, and his narcissism recedes: "soy mucho más cuando me quiero menos" [I am much more when I love myself less].[24] This change brings about a regendering of the sea, which initially had been portrayed as exclusively male—"el contemplado." Starting with Variation VII, that is, exactly halfway through the book, female figures enter the poem: first the "Green Venuses" *(Venus verdes)* of island vegetation, among them the "tall *margaritas*"; then, in the following variation, the "true Venus" *(la Venus verdadera)*, which rises from the sea of San Juan (Salinas is playing on the resemblance between *verde* and *verdadera*). Her rebirth is supplemented in the Variations VIII and IX by a chorus line of mythological female spirits—undines, sylphs, nymphs, nereids. All these "women" have one thing in common: None has a material body. As "sketches of Aphrodites," they are as fleshless and insubstantial as the foam from which they emerge and into which they vanish. Aphroditic rather than aphrodisiac, these born-again Venuses inspire the poet's admiration, affection, and loyalty, but not his desire.

In Salinas's variations there is sexuality, but no eroticism. For the poet of *El contemplado*, the "turn back to M" involved, perhaps required, a turning away from the body, his own not less than Katherine's. In a 1946 letter to Whitmore, he warns her that during the years in Puerto Rico he has put on a lot of weight because of "indifference" toward his appearance and "demoralization" about his physique.[25] It's not accidental that Salinas's indifference toward his body coincided with his separation from hers. When it came to sex, his tendency had always been to value the idea of possession more than the physical act. Even at the height of their affair, effusing about their love gave him far more pleasure than the lovemaking, about which he had almost nothing to say. Sometimes it seems as if the more Salinas didn't see Whitmore, the better he liked it. When she refused to have sex with him, after he was joined in the States by his wife and his children, he quickly—too quickly—transmuted his disappointment into a new achievement. If having sex with her was good, not having it was even better! Clearly, eager-hearted Pedro was not the kind of writer who does his best work in bed. Katherine inspired him because she excited him, but it was the inspiration that he prized above all. Once in San Juan, out of touch with Whitmore, he was able to give his penchant for sublimation free rein, redirecting it toward the kind of beloved who did not excite or expect physical passion.

Cernuda's temperament was far different. Visiting Mexico, he also made a "turn back to M," but his recovery of a maternal space, linguistically and psychologically, did not divert or blunt sexual desire.[26] There are no spirits in his variations, no ocean gods or goddesses, only "el fluir agolpado de los cuerpos" [the crowded stream of bodies] (630), "la turbamulta de los cuerpos" [the chaotic multitude of bodies] (630), "los cuerpos que rondan en torno" [the bodies milling around] (635), "criaturas de cuerpos negros y cabellos rubios" [children with black bodies and blonde hair] (636). Cernuda's irrepressible desire for young male bodies is evident on almost every page, whether or not he is overtly talking about sex. Looking at a boy selling flowers, or at a young man playing a guitar, or at a *chamaco* sitting on the steps of a church, his glance is always erotic. Not one to dissemble about such things, he acknowledges that when his body speaks, his spirit always gives way (635). Unwilling or unable to separate Logos and Eros, Cernuda knots the lingual and the sexual in the *bonaire* of his Mexican *acorde*: if bodies talk, tongues caress. In "Dúo," lovemaking is likened to a musical duet; in "Los ojos y la voz," sexual attraction arises from the combination of looks and sounds; in "El acorde," written in Mexico in 1956 and added to the 1963 edition of *Ocnos,* the "mystical chord" begins as sexual urge (*prefiguración sexual*; 614).

For Cernuda, Spanish was mother and lover tongue, his body's native language. At the end of the introduction to *Variaciones,* he reveals that in Mexico, unexpectedly, he fell in love again, a "belated love" that he is reluctant to discuss (622). Almost certainly, it was this "strange prudishness" (strange because uncharacteristic) that induced him to suppress "Dúo," the most sexually explicit of the variations, from the first edition of the book. Several years later, once the affair with the inaptly named Salvador had ended, Cernuda no longer felt such compunction, and he chronicled the relationship in *Poemas para un cuerpo* (1957), which includes some of the most touching verses he ever wrote. Even though these fourteen poems sing of loss rather than possession, even though they are elegies rather than epithalamiums, they resemble *Variaciones* in much the same way as *El contemplado* resembles *Aprecio y defensa del lenguaje.* If *Poemas para un cuerpo* plays variations on Cernuda's desire for Salvador, *Variaciones* intones poems to a body, and not just the "dark bodies" of the young men that Cernuda mooned over but that of his native tongue, the *lengua* that possessed him and that he repossessed as soon as he crossed the border.

There is one crucial difference, however, between possessing a body and a tongue. Discussing the two poetics in Cernuda's work—a poetics of reconciliation, or accord, and a poetics of failure, or discord—Philip Silver has argued that the Cernudian notion of *acorde* is not a feature of the poetic work, but a metapoetic fantasy that reveals the poet's debt to Romanticism. Noting only exceptionally the merging of subject and object, *La realidad y el deseo* testifies much more powerfully to the failure of reconciliation, which makes Cernuda "a demystified poet of non-conciliation."[27] As we have seen, even *Ocnos* and *Variaciones,* his most affirmative works, are evocative rather than constative, partial recollections rather than contemporaneous testimonies, memoirs rather than diaries. In one area, however, the experience of *acorde* coincides exactly with its transcription. In the late poem "Díptico español" (1961), Cernuda ruefully admits that he is bound to Spain by his tongue:

> No he cambiado de tierra,
> Porque no es posible a quien su lengua une
> Hasta la muerte, el menester de la poesía.

[. . .] Poeta alguno
Su tradición escoge, ni su tierra,
Ni tampoco su lengua; él las sirve,
Fielmente si es posible. (503)

[I have not changed homelands,
Because it's not possible for someone joined to his tongue
Until his death, by the task of poetry.
(. . .) No poet
Chooses his tradition, or his homeland,
Or his tongue; he serves them,
Faithfully if possible.]

These lines enact what they enounce. There is no fissure here between the saying and the said, as there is when Cernuda recalls Mexican voices, his afternoon tryst with the Mexican boy, or the love affair with Salvador. If taken in the language to which one is swearing allegiance, language loyalty oaths are always performative. Declaring his intention to serve his tongue faithfully, Cernuda is already performing such service. When he affirms his tongue ties in hispanophone verses, the *acorde* is not metaphor but synecdoche. In *Poemas para un cuerpo,* he writes: "Estas líneas escribo / Únicamente por estar contigo" [I write these lines / only to be with you] (472). If the *tú* that he addresses is Salvador, the lines are compensatory; but if the *tú* is his mother tongue, the lines furnish incontrovertible evidence of the companionship that they seek; *por estar* should then be translated "because I am" rather than "to be."

While it's true that Cernuda's insistence on the ineffability of epiphanic experiences supposes a type of expressive failure, the language in which he expresses the failure never abandons him. His later poetry has sometimes been criticized for its "culturalist" bent, the Guillén-like reliance on earlier works ("Nocturno yanki" recycles Manrique's *Coplas;* "Retrato de poeta" uses not only El Greco's portrait but Paravicino's sonnet about the portrait).[28] But one could imagine a much bleaker future than culturalism—muteness: not the blockage of access to nature or other men, but the loss of the tongue in which the denial of access could be expressed. Silver's classic book *Et in Arcadia ego* (1965) takes its title from the last line of "Luna llena en semana santa" (1961), one of last poems Cernuda wrote, where he once again rejoices in memories of his Andalusian youth, "el tiempo sin tiempo del niño" [the time without time of the child] (538). Consisting of seven quatrains (one for each day of the week), the poem ends with an inter-strophic rhyme; the last word, *ego,* rhymes with the last word of the previous stanza, *eco.* This phono/graphic echo suggests that the Arcadian ego is Arcadian echo, that its substance is musical, a suggestion already present in the "soft air" that opens the poem:

> Denso, suave, el aire
> Orea tantas callejas,
> Plazuelas, cuya alma
> Es la flor del naranjo. (537)

> [Dense, soft, the air
> freshens so many alleys,
> Squares, whose soul
> Is the orange blossom.]

Itself an echo of Rubén Darío's "Era un aire suave," the first line plays on the two senses of air, atmospheric and musical. Elaborating the pun, the second stanza describes the "resonance" of several wind instruments—clarions, flutes, oboes—and reinforces it with the only other rhyme in the poem.

Although Cernuda may be a failed Narcissus, as has often been said, he has the air of a successful Echo. If the sexual *acorde*—the union with a young body that mirrored his adolescent self—was achieved only ephemerally, the lingual *acorde* sounds consistently in all of his exile poetry. When viewed as verbal performance, even the melancholy but masterful "Retrato de poeta" limns the self-portrait of a poet very much at home in his medium. "Retrato" concludes with a couplet:

> ¿Yo? El instrumento dulce y animado.
> Un eco aquí de las tristezas nuestras. (453)

> [Me? The sweet and lively instrument.
> An echo here of our melancholies.]

Omit the first-person pronoun and the penultimate verse scans as a hendecasyllable. Leave it in and the couplet uncouples metrically. The anacrustic *yo* suggests the poet's lack of fit, his dislocation, his "imperti-nence"—which is the point of the poem. To make the verse scan without elisions, the reader needs to run the "yo" into the next syllable, forcibly joining the poet with the instrument. But this too is the point—the poet *is* his instrument, these words that he uses so deftly, the *lengua* that, however distant he may be from his homeland, never leaves him. In Cernuda's Spanish, every syllable is an echo, a respondent *aire*—melody as well as breeze—that ratifies his uneasy membership in the culture and country of his birth. Whatever the uncertainties of his life, he never doubted that, as he affirms in *Variaciones,* just as the first word that he uttered had been in Spanish, so would his last (625). Santayana says, "We triumph, if we know we failed." For a writer like Cernuda, the triumph lay in knowing and owning the words that expressed his knowledge of failure.

The best-known sentence in *Variaciones* asserts that poetry is written with the body (635). Salinas would not agree, for Salinas wrote poetry always with his head, occasionally with his heart, and only rarely with his body. But Santayana, who spent a lifetime running away from his body, would have assented to Cernuda's dictum, which is one reason he stopped writing poems. The identification of poetry with the body, of the body with the mother tongue, and of the mother tongue with same-sex desire, makes Cernuda's *Variaciones* illustrative of the recursive inweaving of a certain kind of tongue tie. The dissonance of Salinas's correspondence with Whitmore, in which he wrote to her in Spanish and she replied in English, would have been intolerable to Cernuda, for whom tongues came attached to bodies like his own, and bodies like his own talked only in Spanish. Anything else was noise—"ruido, ruido, ruido."

Chapter 4

Mother's Idiom, Father's Tongue

You cannot write about the people you love in a language that they understand.

—*Anton Shammas*

Along with Guillermo Cabrera Infante, Heberto Padilla, and Edmundo Desnoes, Calvert Casey (1924–1969) formed part of the generation of Cuban writers and intellectuals who came into prominence with the triumph of the Cuban Revolution in 1959. During those heady days of the early sixties, Casey was everywhere: hobnobbing with visiting writers, making the rounds of book exhibits and cocktail parties, contributing stories and essays to *Lunes de Revolución* and *Casa de las Américas*, and writing a couple of well-received books: *El regreso* (1962; expanded edition, 1963), a collection of stories; and *Memorias de una isla* (1964), a volume of essays. It was also during this period that Casey acquired the nickname of La Calvita [Baldie], a punning reference to his hairline and his homosexuality. But in 1965, during a trip to Poland, Casey decided not to return to Cuba, at least in part because of the Revolution's hostility toward homosexuals. Eventually settling in Rome, a city that he thought of as a two-thousand-year-old Havana, he worked as a translator and continued to write stories. In 1967 Seix Barral published a third edition of *El regreso* and two years later a new volume of stories, *Notas de un simulador*, which turned out to be his last. In May of 1969, despondent over an unhappy love affair and anxious about the possibility that his visa might not be renewed, La Calvita committed suicide by taking an overdose of sleeping pills.

For years after his death, Casey was nearly forgotten. In the eyes of the cultural commissars on the island, there had never been a Cuban writer with the unlikely name of Calvert Casey. Like Cabrera Infante and others, he was not included in the two-volume *Diccionario de la literatura cubana* published in Havana in 1980 and 1984. Even critics of Spanish American literature writing outside of Cuba tended to ignore him. He is not mentioned in Kessel Schwartz's *A New History of Spanish American Fiction* (1971), Jean Franco's *Spanish American Literature Since Independence* (1973), David William Foster's *Cuban Literature: A*

Research Guide (1985), or Gerald Martin's *Journeys Through the Labyrinth: Latin American Fiction in the Twentieth Century* (1989). It was not until 1993, nearly a quarter century after his death, that the Cuban journal *Unión* began Casey's rehabilitation by reprinting several of his stories along with a dossier of critical essays and personal reminiscences.[1] In 1997 a selection of his work appeared in Spain, followed in 1998 by a volume in English of Casey's stories.[2]

Several reasons may account for Casey's lapse into obscurity. One is that he was an exiled Cuban writer at a time, the middle sixties, when it was already unfashionable to be an exiled Cuban writer. His letters to Cabrera Infante amply document how his defection not only strained his friendships with sympathizers of the Revolution like Julio Cortázar and Italo Calvino, but hampered the dissemination of his writings. In 1966, fearful that his status as an exile would spoil his chances of being published by Seix Barral, he told his editor that he was only temporarily away from the island. When the Spanish edition of *El regreso* appeared, the back cover stated that the author resided in Cuba, a lie that would haunt Casey for the rest of his life. Two years later, when *Notas de un simulador* was published, Casey was no longer willing to hide his disaffection with the Revolution, but he worried that his anti-Castro stance would exclude him from "la onda política-snobista-literaria" [the snobbish-political-literary wave].[3] After his death, a news release from the Agencia de Informaciones Periodísticas indicated that Casey had committed suicide "shortly after having announced his desertion from Castro's Communist regime."

A second reason for the neglect of Casey's work has to do with literary rather than political bad timing. In a decade when Latin American novelists were publishing big, booming novels, Casey was writing what he called "notes," seven- and eight-page miniatures without family trees, banana plantations, or showers of butterflies. The Spanish edition of *El regreso* appeared in the same year as Gabriel García Márquez's *Cien años de soledad* (1967); the publication of *Notas de un simulador* coincided with that of Mario Vargas Llosa's *Conversación en una catedral* and Reinaldo Arenas's *El mundo alucinante* (1969). And Casey, because of mixed feelings about his writing, did not help himself much by lapsing into periods of inactivity. As he once said, "Más silencio, menos corrupción" [More silence, less corruption].[4] But there is a more important reason, perhaps, for Casey's obscurity: He is one of those writers whom Turgenev would have considered a thief and a pig, since he wrote fiction in more than one language. Although the bulk of Casey's fiction is in Spanish, two anglophone stories bracket his Spanish-language output. Both his first story, "The Walk" (1954), and his last, "Piazza Margana" (1969), were written in English. What is more, it is now generally agreed that Casey's single most powerful performance is "Piazza Margana," a brilliant short monologue that he composed in the months before his suicide. The Cuban critic Víctor Fowler has gone so far as to assert that this story is "nuestro supremo texto del goce" [our supreme text of bliss].[5] That Cuban literature's supreme text of bliss should be written in English is remarkable, but no less so than Fowler's unselfconscious use of the possessive "nuestro," as if Casey's language and exile were irrelevant to his work's cultural location.

But Casey's case is complicated, because if he was a thief and a pig, it's not clear which language he betrayed and which he stole from. Since he was born in Baltimore of a Cuban mother and an American father, his mother's tongue was Spanish, but his native language was English. Although very little is known about Casey's early years, he spent at least part of his childhood in the States—enough to speak accentless English and write the language fluently. At some point in his childhood or adolescence, he moved to Cuba with his mother and sister. By the time he was fifteen years old, Casey was delivering phone books for the Cuban Telephone Company.[6] Then, in 1946, he left Cuba, travelling in Europe and living for a while in Canada, until he settled in New York City. Apparently it was after returning to the States that Casey began to write fiction; his first story, "The Walk," was published in the *New Mexico Quarterly* in 1954. The biographical note that accompanies the story reads: "Calvert Casey until 1946 lived and was schooled in his native Cuba. He has worked in Canada and Switzerland and, for the past six years, in this country (New York City), as a translator. This is his first published story."[7] Although Casey was not "native" to Cuba, this statement typifies his tendency to dissemble about his American birth in order to remove any doubts about his Cubanness. He once asked a friend, "¿No es verdad que soy muy cubano a pesar de mi nombre?" [Isn't it true that I'm very Cuban in spite of my name?].[8]

After "The Walk," Casey seems to have stopped writing in English. In 1956, still in New York City, he began sending notes and essays in Spanish to the Cuban magazine *Ciclón,* and in 1958 or 1959 he moved back to Havana. He worked odd jobs until he was introduced to Cabrera Infante, at the time the influential editor of the magazine *Lunes de Revolución,* who made him a regular contributor and opened doors to other publishing outlets. As Casey explains in the author's note to the second edition of *El regreso* (1963), he realized that he had to return to Cuba during a visit to Rome:

Aquella ciudad no era Roma, era una ciudad muy remota, era La Habana. Las semejanzas resultaban casi dolorosas. [. . .] Por las arcadas que yo había atravesado momentos antes bajaba la muchedumbre que durante años había visto bajar por los soportales de la Calzada de la Reina; los balcones eran los mismos balcones de cemento de la vieja calzada donde yo había contemplado por primera vez el gran espectáculo del mundo. A la emoción que me produjo el espejismo siguió un pánico infinito (recordé el pánico que sienten los elefantes cuando próximos a la muerte se sienten muy lejos de donde han nacido). Estaba terriblemente lejos de La Habana. Quizás había perdido para siempre el paraíso (y también el infierno) de la primera visión. Aquella mañana terminó mi exilio voluntario. Debía volver al escenario de los descubrimientos, donde todo viene dado y no es necesario explicar nada.[9]

[That city wasn't Rome, it was a very remote city, it was Havana. The similarities were almost painful. (. . .) The crowds that I had seen go under the colonnades of the Calzada de la Reina now walked through the arcades that I had just crossed moments earlier; the balconies were the same cement balconies of the old roadway where I had contemplated for the first time the world's great spectacle. The emotion produced by the mirage was followed by an infinite panic (I remembered the panic that elephants feel when, on the verge of dying, they find themselves very far away from their birthplace). I was terribly far from Havana. Perhaps I had lost forever the paradise (and the hell) of the first vision. That morning my voluntary exile ended. I had to return to the scene of discoveries, where everything is given and no explanations are necessary.]

The literary flavor of Casey's epiphany, reminiscent in content and diction of the opening sections of Alejo's Carpentier's *Los pasos perdidos* (1951), make one wonder to what extent this epiphany is another autobiographical fabulation prompted by his need to showcase his Cubanness. Certainly, the implication that he was born in Havana is false, as is the assertion that in Cuba he would not have to explain himself. Moreover, this visit to Rome occurred in the late 1940s, a decade before he finally moved back to Cuba.

Whatever the reasons for his return, once in Cuba Casey continued to write in Spanish, as he did after going into exile. But toward the end of 1967, a year and a half before his death, he launched into a novel—his first—in English, a language that he had not used in formal writing since the early 1950s. That Casey switched back to English toward the end of his life is all the more puzzling given his insistence that he was a Cuban writer rather than, as some people thought, an American who had emigrated to Cuba. Depending on his mood, he would rail at reviewers for mistaking him for an American, or lacerate himself because of his

equivocal name—"mi eufónico y despreciable nombrecito" [my eupho-
nious and worthless little name].[10] Unlike Santayana, who was dismayed
by the hybridity of his name, Casey resented the anglophone purism of
his. Even though he had been born in the United States, Casey regarded
Cuba as his homeland and Spanish as his mother (and not simply his
mother's) tongue. And yet, not only did he choose English for his last
project, he also said to the Spanish critic Rafael Martínez Nadal that this
novel was his most personal work: "allí estaba, al desnudo, mi íntima
verdad" [there it was, naked, my intimate truth].[11]

It turns out that the same man who dissembled about his birthplace
and resented his anglophone name—"mi nombrecito repugnante" [my
repugnant little name], "nuestro infecto nombrecito" [our infected
name][12]—resorted to English when the time came to write nakedly
about himself. But can a Cuban writer lose his clothes in English?
Doesn't an intimate truth become less intimate when rendered in
someone else's language? And for whom was Casey disrobing? Not for
his natural audience, which was Spanish-speaking. Multilingual writers
sometimes choose their language according to the public they wish to
reach; but Casey seems to have switched to English for the opposite
reason: not to reach an audience but to deprive himself of one. Even as
the appearance in Spain of his two story collections, *El regreso* and *Notas
de un simulador*, was making his work available to a broader readership,
La Calvita was holed up in a shabby Rome apartment making sure those
very readers would not have direct access to his "intimate truth."

The surviving fragment of Casey's English-language novel will help us
understand this equivocal striptease. What we know about the genesis of
the work is this: In the summer of 1967, while living in Rome, Casey fell
in love with a young Italian named Gianni. At the time Casey was in his
mid-forties; Gianni was no more than twenty. The relationship was
passionate but stormy, with rifts and reconciliations that Casey characterized as a cycle of "riñas, besitos, riñas, besitos" [spats, kisses, spats,
kisses].[13] Not long after meeting Gianni, Casey got the idea for a novel
based on their love affair. After a visit to London in September of 1967,
he wrote Cabrera Infante that he had returned to Rome with "a clear
head and the plan for a novel in English." Entitling it "Gianni, Gianni,"
he described it as "una maravillosa novela de amor, terrible, antropofágica,
pues así es como suele ser el amor" [a marvelous love story, terrible,
anthropophagous, for that's how love tends to be].[14] Later that fall he
reported that his novel was progressing slowly and expressed doubts
about its publishability, given its "violent" language.

Almost as soon as Cabrera Infante found out about his friend's new
project, he began to express reservations about it. First he questioned

whether Casey, who had written only short fiction up to that point, was capable of writing a novel. Casey replied that since Cabrera Infante had liked "Notas de un simulador," a novella, he had no reason to think that the novel would be a failure. After reading excerpts, Cabrera Infante told Casey that the novel was a "mistake" and tried to dissuade him from proceeding with it. According to Cabrera Infante, the chapter that Casey sent him, set in India, began by stating that the Taj Mahal was so dirty that it needed to be washed with detergent, a notion that struck Cabrera Infante as foolish.[15] Convinced that the novel's poor taste was the result of Gianni's baneful influence, he objected both to the "Italian realism" of the work and to Casey's new love, whom he and his wife regarded as a "Mediterranean gigolo."[16] Wounded by his best friend's criticisms, Casey responded with a spirited defense:

Me acusas de un realismo italiano sensacionalista de la peor especie. Olvidas que detrás de las páginas que te mandé está Lawrence (D. H.) con su mística del sexo y Miller (Henry). Si te parece sensacionalista porque es homosexual yo no tengo culpa de tus provincianismos mentales; las páginas de la novela no tienen nada que ver con el realismo italiano, contra el cual tengo los mismos prejuicios que tú. Ningún realista italiano se convertía en falo ni se metía dentro del cuerpo del amante, la mente italiana no da para eso, eso está dentro del departamento de mi padre D.H. y de mi tío Henry.[17]

[You accuse me of a sensationalist Italian realism of the worst kind. You are forgetting that behind the pages I sent you is Lawrence (D. H.) with his sexual mysticism and Miller (Henry). If it seems sensationalist because it's homosexual I'm not to blame for your mental provincialisms; the pages of the novel have nothing to do with Italian realism, which I don't like any better than you do. No Italian realist turned into a phallus or went inside his lover's body, the Italian mind doesn't reach that far, that's the territory of my father D.H. and my uncle Henry.]

Going on to say that Gianni, far from hurting his writing, had shown him his "true vocation," he concluded with a jibe at Cabrera Infante's own work. Unlike the author of *Tres tristes tigres,* he refused to be condemned to writing "textos exclusivamente sobre melancolías habaneras" [texts exclusively about Havana melancholies].

Nonetheless, whether because of Cabrera Infante's cavils or his own doubts about the project, by the time that Casey met with Martínez Nadal, on April 23, 1969, he had destroyed most of the novel. Only the last chapter, "Piazza Margana," had been spared. Although Casey instructed Martínez Nadal not to show the manuscript to anybody, he asked him to publish it at an "opportune moment" in a "good British magazine." Handing it over, he explained why it was written in English: "Debí escribirlo en italiano porque en italiano está pensado y sentido, el italiano es su 'habitat,' pero como no domino el idioma, y como en este caso el español no me servía, recurrí al inglés, mi segunda lengua" [I should have written it in Italian because it was thought and felt in Italian, Italian is its "habitat," but since I haven't mastered the language, and since in this particular case Spanish was of no use, I resorted to English, my second tongue].[18]

By suggesting that Spanish was not a suitable vehicle for the story, Casey is evoking the phenomenon that linguists term diglossia, that is, the use of different languages for different purposes. If a bilingual is someone who handles two languages equally well, the diglossic individual is someone whose verbal bilingualism is complicated by a bilingualism of thought and feeling, by the conviction that objects, events, emotions, ideas "speak" a particular language. When Santayana states that the English "bread" cannot translate the human intensity of the Spanish "pan," he is exhibiting the diglossic's intuition of connotative difference, whether or not this difference reflects a real disparity in the languages.[19] When Salinas and Cernuda focus on the utilitarianism of American English, they are doing the same thing. Although Casey did not explain to Martínez Nadal what he meant by saying that Spanish would not do "in this particular case," a writer's choice of a language was a matter to which he had given some thought. One of his first Spanish stories, "El regreso," opens with the narrator's reflection on the difficulties of translating from English to Spanish: "¿Cómo se llamaban esas cosas? ¿Actos fallidos? ¿Alienación del yo? Traducía mal los conceptos psicológicos a la moda, que había leído en inglés sin entenderlos mucho, más bien para impresionar a los demás" [What were those things called? Failed acts? Alienation of the self? He translated poorly the fashionable psychological concepts, which he had read in English without really understanding them, only to impress others] (*Notas,* 80). This linguistic self-consciousness runs through all of Casey's work. Having been raised bilingually, he realized that to speak a language was to occupy a place, to settle into a cultural habitat with its history and contours. Like Cernuda, he believed that a writer speaks for all those who have preceded him in the language. As he put it in *Memorias de una isla,* to say *alpaca* is to let an anonymous Quechua Indian speak with our lips, to say *arar* is to become one with the voice of a Spanish peasant. The issue then becomes, "¿Cómo perpetúo yo los movimientos de millares y millares de labios?" [How do I perpetuate the movements of thousands and thousands of lips?][20]

But if this is what Casey believed, it's all the more puzzling that he chose to sever his ties with the community of Spanish speakers. Whose lips was Casey moving when he elected English as the "habitat" of "Piazza Margana"? Whose voice was he grafting onto his own? These questions are all the more relevant because the theme of "Piazza Margana" is bodily possession. Having written about *espiritismo* in "Los visitantes" and other stories, Casey here takes the idea of inhabiting someone's body to a literal extreme. This is how the story begins:

> I have now entered your bloodstream. I have gone beyond urine, beyond excrement and its sweet, acrid taste, and have at last lost myself in the warm recesses of your body. I am here to stay. I will never leave it. From my vantage point, where I have finally attained bliss, I see the world through your eyes, hear the most frightening and the most enchanting sounds through your ears, taste all tastes with your tongue, feel all shapes with your hands. What else could a man desire? Forever and ever "emparadised in thee." "Envejeceremos juntos, dijiste" [We will grow old together, you said], and we will.[21]

In the paragraphs that follow, Casey explains this dramatic opening: One day, "between spells of mutual hatred," Gianni had cut himself while shaving. Dressing the wound, Casey felt tempted to drink his lover's blood. As the days went by, however, his urge turned into a cannibalistic fantasy; not only did he want to drink his lover's blood, he wanted to eat his flesh. "But then," he says, "I thought I knew better" (181). Instead of devouring Gianni, he decides to lodge himself inside his lover's body. The act of possession completed, the rest of the story recounts Casey's marvel-filled exploration of Gianni's insides. Each organ is described in loving, sometimes delirious, detail: the brain, the ears, the nose, the mouth, the heart, the lungs, the large and small intestines, the testicles, the penis. This fantastic "safari," as he calls it, ends up in his lover's rectum, where the narrator had to dodge large, slow-moving monoliths that threaten to crush him, or rather, *aplastarlo*. Finally finding a safe haven within the "forest of giants," Casey ends his journey, and the story, with the words:

> This is Paradise. I have found it. Unlike Columbus I will not be shipped home in a hold with bound feet. No Canossa for me either. I have entered the Kingdom of Heaven and taken proud possession of it. This is my private claim, my heritage, my fief. I am NOT leaving. (193)

Perhaps we can begin to see why Casey told Martínez Nadal that this work was his most "honest and original."[22] The extremity of the situation, the intensity of the writing, the bluntness—these are all without precedent in his fiction. Since most of Casey's stories were written in Cuba during the 1960s, censorship or self-censorship may well account for his reticence in discussing homosexuality.[23] As he once wrote to Cabrera Infante, he even "heterosexualized" the plot of some of these stories by switching the gender of one of the protagonists (in "Adiós, y gracias por todo," where the narrator says "Marta," we should read "Mario" instead).[24] Casey's struggles with his homosexuality were no secret to his friends. His marriage in the early 1960s to Olga Andreu was regarded by those who knew them as a farcical effort to preserve appearances. Although Casey said that he loved her in spite of what he called his "limitations," he and Andreu were never close, and after leaving Cuba he had little or no contact with her.[25]

But Casey's difficulties with Cuban homophobia, however internalized, don't completely explain why, once he had left the island for a second time, he felt that he could not write his "intimate truth" in Spanish. The issue here would not be censorship or even self-censorship but a peculiar combination of reserve and exhibitionism that made it possible for him to flaunt in one language truths about himself that he could barely utter in another. If the hispanophone Casey is not quite straight, neither does he verbalize his pleasure with the relish displayed in "Piazza Margana."

Not only does the subject matter of "Piazza Margana" set it apart from Casey's previous writing, but its style and diction also separate it from anything he had written before. In "Notas de un simulador" and elsewhere, Casey's Spanish is plain, spare, economical. Influenced not by his "uncle Henry" but by Hemingway and the French *nouveau roman*, he relies on dialogue and objectivist descriptions of Havana cityscapes. "Piazza Margana" has no dialogue; despite the title, the only locale is the pink bioscape of Gianni's organs; and the prose is densely allusive. At the end of the first paragraph, Casey asserts that he has become "emparadised" in Gianni: "Forever and ever 'emparadised in thee.'" Though now archaic, the verb "emparadise" occurs with some frequency in sixteenth- and seventeenth-century English. In Book IV of *Paradise Lost*, Milton describes Adam and Eve as "Imparadised in each other's arms"—a context of use consistent with Casey's. But the word also occurs in religious liturgy, and the phrase in "Piazza Margana" is lifted from a hymn by John Wesley, the founder of Methodism. Entitled "Come, Father, Son and Spirit," the hymn says in part:

> O wouldst Thou stamp it now on mine
> The name and character Divine,

> The Holy One in Three!
> Come, Father, Son, and Spirit, give
> Thy love,—Thyself: and lo! I live
> Emparadised in Thee.[26]

What is the Methodist hymnal doing in Rome, of all places, and on the lips of a gay Cuban writer? As perhaps the only reference in Casey's writings to his American childhood, the quotation points to the part of his life he suppressed to become "Cuban," that part inhabited by his American father. Emparadised inside his beloved, Casey resurrects the man who had always dwelled in his name, whose "stamp" he bore and whose language he was using, but whose existence he never acknowledged publicly. If "El regreso" charts Casey's return to his mother's country, "Piazza Margana" stages an even more radical regress, for the story takes him to a place that, in one sense, he had abandoned long ago, but that, in another, he had never left. As soon as he says "I," Casey leaves his mother's country for his father's land. English is not only his other language, it is also his father's tongue. Rome is not only another Havana, it is also Baltimore. Rather than indulging his Cuban nostalgia, like Cabrera Infante, Casey imagines a wholly ghostly paradisal realm where, as the hymn asserts, he can live enfolded in the Father. Indeed, "Piazza Margana" allows Casey to unite father and son in himself. Becoming one with Gianni, he finds the father he never had, he becomes the son he never was.

The quotation from Wesley also injects into the story a motif to which Casey will return repeatedly, that of the mystical union of the lover and the beloved, of the *Amada en el Amado transformada*. According to several of Casey's friends, one of the last books he read was Miguel de Molinos's *Guía espiritual* (1675), a controversial theological treatise banned by the Inquisition for its advocacy of a passive, nonliturgical surrender to God's grace.[27] Deep inside Gianni, the narrator exclaims: "What infinite quietude, what peace" (192). Molinos's heretical doctrine was called *quietismo*. Imparting a scandalously corporal meaning to the *camino interior* of mystical doctrine, which in this instance runs through Gianni's intestines down to his anus, Casey brings together his "father D.H." and his "uncle Henry" with John Wesley and Miguel de Molinos to institute what he rightly termed "sexual mysticism."

This recovery of the paternal tongue excites a linguistic euphoria that pushes articulateness to the border of bombast. The initial description of his travels inside Gianni consists of a long, rambling, nearly incoherent sentence propelled by sound and sense effects—alliteration, assonance, paronomasia, synonymy, antonymy, hyperbole. The introductory phrase,

"As I write," sets the stage for the verbal performance that immediately follows:

> As I write, travelling at ease in unspeakable merriment through your bloodstream after a protracted summer in the mastoids, always ready to forsake the lymphatic for the parotids, where the frantic humming of your brain reaches and reassures me, I know that I will be with you, travel with you, sleep with you, dream with you, urinate and generally defecate with you, make love *with and through* you, hate with you, think, cry, grow senile, warm, cold and warm again, feel, look, jerk off, kiss, kill, pet, fart, fade, flush, turn into ashes, lie, humiliate myself and others, strip, stab, wilt, wait, wail, laugh, steal, quiver, waver, ejaculate, linger, backscuttle, pray, fall, doublecross, triplecross, ogle, browse, goose, suck, brag, bleed, blow with and through you. (188)

Although the contexts could not be more dissimilar, Casey's exuberance resembles Salinas's in *El contemplado*. Like the Spaniard's poem, "Piazza Margana" celebrates tongue ties, the writer's psychic investment in words that speak for areas of himself from which he had become estranged. Gianni's body is Salinas's sea, the trysting place for old loves and languages.

The intimations of "Piazza Margana" in Casey's hispanophone fiction underscore the uniqueness of this story. In "El regreso," first published in 1961, the protagonist alludes to several male lovers. One of these "idols," as he calls them, is a man named Alejandro, about whom he exclaims, anticipating "Piazza Margana," "¡Ah, poder ser como Alejandro, poder *ser* Alejandro!" [Oh, to be able to be like Alejandro, to be able to *be* Alejandro!] (*Notas*, 82). Once the protagonist of "El regreso" moves from New York to Havana, however, no further mention is made of his homosexuality. In the "Cuban" section of the story, the bond between lover and beloved is replaced by that between victim and scourge. Walking the beach during his first day back, the protagonist is picked up by a car full of men who turn out to be government thugs. Without explanation, they take him to a police station where he is beaten and tortured. When the protagonist tells his torturers his name, they warn him not to "invent foreign names" (*Notas*, 94). Insisting on being told his true identity, one of the men approaches him:

> Un hombre hercúleo lo tomó sin violencia, casi delicadamente, de un brazo y le pidió que le mirara los ojos. Cuando lo tuvo frente a sí y tan cerca que podía sentirle el aliento, se le quedó mirando un momento.

[A Herculean man took him by the arm without violence, almost deli-
cately, and asked him to look into his eyes. When he had him in front of
him, so close that he could feel his breath, he paused to look at him for a
moment.]

Up to here, these sentences could be the prelude to a kiss. But this is
what ensues:

Luego, alzando con un movimiento rapidísimo la rodilla formidable, se la
hundió en las ingles. Cayó al suelo gimiendo y retorciéndose de dolor. "Es
un tiro, Fillo. Eso nunca falla," oyó decir a uno de los hombres. (*Notas*, 95)

[Then, raising his formidable knee very fast, he dug it into his groin. He fell
to the floor moaning and writing in pain. "That's a sure shot, Fillo. It
never fails," he heard one of the men say.]

This incident knots language and sexuality. From the moment he
arrives in Havana, Casey's protagonist sticks out because of his paleness,
his "vague foreign accent," and his "unpronounceable name" (*Notas*,
89)—so unpronounceable, in fact, that the story omits it. Although he
wants to blend in, the people he meets take him for an American,
addressing him in English and remarking on the anglicisms in his speech.
But once he is arrested his torturers refuse to believe that he is indeed a
foreigner. Their punishment, to assault him in the "ingles," is anatomi-
cally and linguistically correct. Move the stress, and "ingles," groin,
becomes "inglés," English. Kicked in the *ingles/inglés*, Casey's fictional
double is simultaneously unmanned and untongued. Later in the torture
session, the untonguing becomes literal when, after several electric
shocks, he realizes that he has bitten off his tongue.

As soon as "El regreso" appeared in *Casa de las Américas*, it became
Casey's most popular story, in no small measure because of its indictment
of the brutality of the Batista regime. As one reads the story today,
though, the murky personal subtext is more intriguing that the transparent political message. As far as I can tell, the first part of the story is
autobiographical, for Casey lived in New York City in circumstances
similar to those of his character. Even Casey's stutter, paleness, and
premature baldness reappear in his unnamed and unnamable protagonist. What is not literally true is that Casey was tortured by Batista's
henchmen. This part is fiction, which may mean that it touches on truths
too intimate, too troublesome, to be acknowledged openly. An apparently trivial detail: When Casey's fictional double is picked up by the
police, he is wearing a long-sleeved *guayabera* sewn from "Irish linen"

(*Notas*, 92, 93). Mentioned twice within a couple of pages, the foreign fabric of this Cuban shirt weaves Casey's Irish-American father, from whom he inherited the unpronounceable name and the pale complexion, into the torture scene. When the protagonist is punished for pronouncing his real name, the father's tongue and the son's genitals are tied together and brutally mangled. That Casey would do this to himself, however figurative the doing, provides a clue to the self-hatred generated by the conflict between his two countries, a conflict especially acute, perhaps, during a period of intense acrimony between the governments of the United States and Cuba. In spite of Casey's desire to be "very Cuban" and of his protagonist's "pathetic efforts to sound like a native" (*Notas*, 89), homecoming leads to mutilation.

The cost of becoming Cuban also comes across in "Notas de un simulador," the off-beat tale of a loner who befriends the terminally ill. Armed with a mirror and matchbox (to detect the last breath of his subjects), the narrator frequents hospitals, the homes of sick friends and relatives, and the plaza where the Havana homeless spend their nights, all with an eye to witnessing that fleeting moment that marks the passage from life to death. Although this novella is usually read as evidence of Casey's obsession with death (the most original essay in *Memorias de una isla* meditates on José Martí's suicidal impulses), the simulator's choice of male subjects for his observations suggests that more than morbidity may be in play here.[28] In the typical episode, the narrator spots a possible "case" and tries to befriend him with gifts and other attentions. Once he succeeds in getting "as close as possible" to his subject (*Notas*, 186), he behaves like a jealous lover, fending off anybody who tries to come between them. As he puts it, "¿a qué dejar que otros vinieran torpemente a estropear nuestros últimos instantes juntos?" [Why should I let others spoil our last moments together?] (*Notas*, 211). Before he is able to achieve his goal, though, a female character, usually the man's wife, interposes herself. Confronted by the "immense body" (*Notas*, 195), "wounding voice" (*Notas*, 200), or "scrutinizing glance" (*Notas*, 207) of these women, the narrator retreats. When one of them accuses him of having murdered her husband, he is incarcerated.

Unfolding as a succession of triangles involving the narrator, another man, and the woman that comes between them, the novella records the narrator's unacknowledged fascination with male bodies. Showing off his sharp clinical eye, he fills his prison notebooks with physiological descriptions that prefigure the anatomy lesson of "Piazza Margana." The novella contains two separate acts of simulation: the pretense that the narrator is interested in the welfare of his subjects; and the cloaking of desire as morbidity. If "El regreso" turns on a pun on "ingles," "Notas de un simulador" exploits the ambiguity of the word "morbo," which in Spanish can mean both "morbidness" and "lust." When the narrator is accused of "homicide," the accusation is slanderous, but the prefix hints at the underlying truth. Like "El regreso," "Notas de un simulador" ends with a punishment whose real cause Casey leaves unnamed.

"Piazza Margana" is "Notas de un simulador" without the simulation. The fundamental difference is topographic. In the novella, the narrator is on the outside looking in; in the story, he is looking in from the inside. The first words of "Piazza Margana," "I have now entered your bloodstream," make up for all the failed entries into houses and hospitals of the novella. Unlike the *simulador,* the narrator of "Piazza Margana" has the freest, most unfettered access to his beloved's body. No womanly barriers block his way, no sexual inhibitions disguise his motivation. As he says, echoing Dante, "How shall I begin? With love! How else? Let love guide my exploration, my fabulous trip, the trip no man has taken before; let it be torch and compass to help me find my bearings" (189). Looking back to Cuba, "Notas de un simulador" evokes a world whose repressiveness induces the protagonist to equivocate and eventually deprives him of his freedom. By contrast, and as if to exorcise Cuban ghosts, "Piazza Margana" turns Gianni's foreign body into a venue liberated from political or sexual constraints. The torch that Casey carries for and into Gianni magnifies and replaces the matchbox of the simulator.

I don't think that Casey could have written "Notas de un simulador" and "El regreso" in English, or "Piazza Margana" in Spanish—not because of anything inherent in the languages, but because of his relations with them. George Steiner suggests that for a writer such as Oscar Wilde bilingualism may be, in Steiner's phrase, an "expressive enactment of sexual duality."[29] Although the connection between language choice and sexual identity is surely more complicated than this, he is right in pointing to their imbrication. For Casey, duality manifests itself as duplicity. The hispanophone stories, some of which involve heterosexual liaisons, insinuate his "intimate truth" only by falling back on screens and equivocations. Since Spanish is the language of the heterosexual norm, a tongue that ties, these stories speak intimately by intimation, never by assertion. But English gives voice to the love that dares not speak its Spanish name. In the closet of Casey's hispanophone fiction hangs a sign: *Se habla español.* In the paradoxically open spaces of Gianni's insides, one hears the rustle of English syllables.

Foremost among the barriers that come between Casey and his intimate truth is his mother's tongue, monumentalized in the "humid walls" of the jail cell from which the simulator writes (*Notas,* 226). If this enclosure is a womb, it also resembles the "black box" of modern grammarians, which contains the rules for the generation of allowable utterances. Inside Casey's Spanish "black box" is a prohibition, or, better, an interdict: You shall not know your father. But unknowing his father required him to repress his sexuality and fulminate against himself. The result, as in "El regreso," is dismemberment, or, as in "Notas de un simulador," imprisonment. Once distanced from Cuba, emotionally and politically, Casey was able to remember himself, to restore the fatherly tongue that his mother's country had mutilated. Unlike Havana, Casey's Rome was a refuge rather than a jail: not from the body, as in Santayana, but from all those forces that repress it. (In Santayana's closet the sign says: "English Only.")

For this reason, Casey's admirably mongrel English, which has a decidedly "foreign" and even "Spanish" feel, differs starkly from Santayana's marmoreal prose. In "Piazza Margana" Casey does not recoil from the "polyglot effect"; he cultivates it. The story's multilingualism shows up not only in quotations from Spanish and Italian, but in the proliferation of latinate nouns, most of them anatomical terms. A lover of Latin, if not a Latin lover, Casey delights in piling *latinajo* upon *latinajo* on his father's tongue: "The thalamus, the thalamus! Where is the thalamus after the horrors of the claustrum, the lunar light of the globus pallidus?" (190). Or: "I take to the depths: periosteum, outer table, diploe, inner table, sutures, calvaria (next to the dura, for warmth and compassion)" (190). Because these depths are not only physiological, the discoveries along the way are sometimes more than linguistic. The calvaria is the skull; but since "calvaria" is also the root of the Spanish *calvo*, Calvert, La Calvita, is making an onomastic pun; in fact, he's alluding to one of the many nicknames that he gave himself, Calvario. Not only does Casey lodge himself inside his beloved's organs, he inhabits their very names with a latinized, feminized variant of his own name. Is this change restorative or punitive? Is Casey giving his father his due, or is he once again punishing him (and thus himself)? Marshall McLuhan once remarked that a person's name is a blow from which he never recovers. In Casey's case, the blow left a permanent scar. He could no more obliterate his name than he could leave it alone.

The proliferation of words with Latin roots seeds "Piazza Morgana" with interlingual puns: The arbor vitae "ramifies"; the dura caresses "harshly"; the intestinal flora become "tiny monstrous flowers"; the nasal fossa turn into a "lively grave." This relentless punning differentiates Casey's two languages, since in his mother's tongue he does not allow himself such license. Contradicting the view of Spanish as a more "rhetorical" language than English, Casey's hispanophone prose relies on understatement and a deadpan tone, as in the last paragraph of "Notas de un simulador":

> El guardián acaba de entrar. Presiento que seremos amigos. Es lástima que tenga este oficio. Todo en él respira deseos de vivir. En él saludo a la vida. Pero nunca se sabe . . . (*Notas*, 228)

> [The guard has just come in. I sense that we'll be friends. It's too bad he has this job. Everything about him breathes desire to live. In him I salute life. But one never knows . . .]

Irrepressible in spite of repression, even in jail Casey's underground man fixes on a new object of desire. Placed one after the other like a row of dominoes, the five short declarative sentences come tumbling down with the final phrase—"But one never knows . . . "—which discloses what is *really* on the narrator's mind and unmasks his reticence as another imposture, one last act of *simulación*. The ellipsis with which he ends (and refuses to end) his story epitomizes Casey's stance as a hispanophone writer. His intimate truth is hidden in the elisions, in the silences between and after words and sentences. In Spanish, Casey often stutters. In English, the words come out in a flood.[30]

Let me now cite a brief passage from Casey's other English-language story, "The Walk." Also based on an autobiographical incident, "The Walk" describes the failed sexual initiation of an adolescent named Ciro. Pronounced in English, the protagonist's name already tells us what happens when his uncle takes him to a brothel—zero—for Ciro and the prostitute spend their hour together in small talk. But when he emerges from the bedroom, Ciro's uncle believes that the initiation into manhood has been accomplished, and his nephew does not correct the misimpression. (Already in Casey's literary debut, his fictional doubles are engaged in simulation.) What makes the story a little strange is that the oddly named Zenón may not be any more straight than his nephew. An outsider among his own relatives, he is a "half-accepted and colorless bachelor in a large family of solemn patriarchs" (2). In the light of Casey's later fiction, the bond between Zenón and Ciro, between the childless father and the fatherless son, is far more interesting than that between Ciro and the prostitute. As in "Notas de un simulador," the covert plot of "The Walk" outlines a triangle, the three vertices of which are Ciro, Zenón, and the prostitute who does not quite come between them.

"The Walk" exists in two versions. After writing the story in English, Casey translated it into Spanish and included it in his first volume of stories, *El regreso* (1962). In the original English, this is the narrator's description of the rumor that Ciro is going to a brothel for the first time:

> It transgressed the limits of the household, trickled down the inner court to the neighbors, flowed past the iron grates of the balconies overlooking the street and poured finally into the entire neighborhood. (2)

And this is Casey's translation:

> Aquello cruzaba los límites de la casa, atravesaba el patio para infiltrarse en el de los vecinos, salía por la baranda del balcón y trascendía a todo el vecindario. (*Notas*, 45)

The principal difference between the two sentences is that the translation all but eliminates the fluvial metaphor. In the place of "trickled . . . flowed . . . poured," Casey puts "atravesaba . . . salía . . . trascendía." In the passage from English to Spanish, from New York to Havana, the image of the spilling of the liquid, brimming with obvious sexual overtones, has evaporated. The one remaining hydraulic reference in the Spanish sentence is the infinitive "infiltrarse," but in Casey's English prose fluids do not have to filter in, because they pour out. And while the English text frames the event as a "transgression," the Spanish attenuates it to a mere "crossing." Even the use of the imperfect tense in Spanish blunts the impact of a flood that rises to a climactic outpouring.

The differences between these sentences illustrate the tension between Casey's father and mother tongues. Compared to his English, his Spanish is measured, restrained, affectless—in a word: *seco*. Another change in the story: In the English original, when Ciro goes into the bedroom with the young prostitute, a boy who works in the brothel breaks out into a fit of jealousy that the narrator calls a "torrent of words" (9). In the Spanish version, the boy's jealousy disappears, and with it the verbal torrent. This process of semantic dehydration reaches into the smallest stylistic details: In English, when Zenón shows up to take Ciro to the brothel, the nephew is "caught in the waves of cologne" that emanate from his uncle (4); in Spanish he only notices the "olor a colonia" (*Notas*, 47). In English the black attendant's high-pitched voice is a "thin stream of voice" (7); in Spanish it becomes "la voz atiplada" (*Notas*, 52). In English the attendant at the brothel "pours" beer into Ciro's glass (7, 8); in Spanish, the beer is not poured but "served" (*Notas*, 52, 53).

My point is that what Casey suppresses in "El paseo," the Spanish title of "The Walk," is what he gives vent to in "Piazza Margana," the account of a very different kind of *paseo*. Already in the first paragraph, the speaker of "Piazza Margana" inhabits a liquid world, a corporal geography of streams and eddies and channels and islands that reminds me, and that perhaps reminded Casey, of the Caribbean, the "mar" inside "Margana." Drifting down a large artery, Casey is dragged by the current; visiting the bladder, he almost gets flushed out; navigating the intestinal flora, he imagines that he is journeying to the sources of the Nile; when he says, "Let love guide my exploration," he floats on the tide of liquid consonants. In Spanish Casey reaches for dry land, for the stability, the sedentariness, that he associated with the words *bienestar* (well-being) and *sosiego* (calm, settledness). As he says in "El regreso," pondering the return to Cuba: "¿Y si regresara a los suyos, a amarlos a todos, a ser uno de ellos, a vivir aunque fuera entre los más pobres, entre aquéllos que a pesar de su pobreza parecían más tranquilos y contentos, tan sosegados. ¡Cómo le gustaba la palabra! Tan sosegados" [And if I were to return to my own kind, to love them all, to be one of them, to live even among the poorest of them, among those who in spite of their poverty seemed more peaceful and happy, so settled. How he loved that word! So settled] (*Notas*, 90). Stories like "Los visitantes" and "Mi tía Leocadia, el amor y el Paleolítico Inferior" register Casey's need for familial and communal connection; but the price of connection seems to be aridness, and the hydraulic energy incipient in "The Walk" and evident in "Piazza Margana" all but disappears from his Spanish-language writing. Loving everyone means desiring no one.

In "The Walk," when Ciro and the prostitute are making small talk, all thoughts of sex safely banished, the narrator remarks: "Ciro had a sensation of extreme well-being now. The beer had delivered him into a soft mellowness from which he had no desire to emerge" (10). In "El paseo," Casey translates "intense well-being" as "intenso bienestar" and "soft mellowness" as "suave placidez" (*Notas*, 55). The proximity of *bienestar* to softness and placidity hints at the asexuality of the young man's well-being. Ciro's "no desire to emerge" bespeaks a more general anaphrodisia, the opposite of the overflowing libido of "Piazza Margana," whose title not only evokes the sea but also the *gana*, or desire, that motivates the narrator. Margana: *mar de ganas*.

It is not true, as Cabrera Infante has said, that Casey's "Spanish is English by other means."[31] In English Casey is a different writer, and perhaps a different man, than he is in Spanish. That's why he said to Martínez Nadal, "en este caso particular el español no me servía" [in this particular case Spanish was of no use]. "Este caso particular" is also "este

Casey particular," the one who oozes, the one who gushes, the one who goes with the flow even if he risks drowning in the effluvia. Unlike Santayana, Casey does not avoid immersion; he thirsts for it. And if Spanish does not serve him (the literal translation of "no me servía"), it's because, for him, Spanish is not self-serving. In the diglossic world of Casey's fiction, Spanish is the language of family, of history, of the *sosiego* of social life and the *bienestar* of companionship; it is sociolect rather than idiolect, *idioma* rather than *lengua*. But since *sosiego* and *bienestar* carry a price, Spanish is also the language of normative heterosexuality and thus the medium for external and internal repression. At the end of "El regreso," when the moribund protagonist is dropped back off at the beach and crabs eat his eyes, *sosiego* turns into a cruel pun on *ciego*.

By contrast, English is the habitat for solitary self-assertion, a tongue bereft of community. Disinterring his father's tongue, Casey can speak without inhibitions. He can pour it on and flush it out, but he is only talking to himself. Even addressing Gianni, he is talking to himself. Although he claims over and over to have lost himself, to have lost his self, his individuality, inside his beloved, it's hard to imagine a more solipsistic performance than "Piazza Margana." From the beginning Casey insists on the first-person singular with self-serving fury: "I have now entered . . . I have gone beyond . . . I am here . . . I am not leaving." In the rest of the story, his "I" will recur countless times—another difference from his Spanish-language fiction, whose antiheroes typically crave effacement. Even when Casey momentarily switches into Italian, the language that he shared with Gianni, he cries out: "Sono io, sono io." Only when he lapses into Spanish, as happens at the end of the first paragraph, do Gianni and he become a "we": "Envejeceremos juntos, dijiste" [We will grow old together, you said]. But together, *juntos,* is what Gianni and Casey were not. In spite of his assertions and exertions, there is no companionship here, no merging of identities, no meeting of body or mind, but only an isolated "I" straining after an inaccessible "you." Perhaps for the first and only time, in "Piazza Margana" Casey used the medium of fiction to achieve an outcome that had eluded him in real life. Masking painful distance with outrageous intimacy, "Gianni, Gianni," the title of the novel he destroyed, is not an address but an incantation.

The English language, rather than Gianni's body, is Casey's "private claim," his "heritage," his "fief." Although the paternal legacy is no more than words, it gives the son a place from which to speak. No longer a resident of Havana or even of Rome, La Calvita becomes a citizen of the state of bliss, a homeland-for-one that exists only within his lush and lovely English prose. In *Aprecio y defensa del lenguaje,* Salinas quotes Karl

Vossler's indictment of those who forsake their native language: "The man who denies or gives up this last refuge and sally-port of his home sentiments, is without honor; he is dead to the community in which he received his first experience of human language."[32] "Piazza Margana" points out what can be gained by lifting anchor and setting out upon the open sea: freedom. "My freedom of choice and sojourn knows no limit. I have attained what no political or social system could ever dream of attaining: I am free, totally free inside you, forever free from all fears and cares. No exit permit, no entry permit, no passport, no borders, no visa, no carta d'identità, no nothing!" (189). I read this statement as a linguistic loyalty oath. If Casey is utterly free, it's because his is a freedom in utterance; if he can come and go as he pleases, it's because the only borders that limit him are those of the page; and if he needs no ID card, it's because he's in the act of writing his own. As Casey's own "poem to a body," "Piazza Margana" is performative rather than constative; his bliss arises from verbal rather than physical possession. The only body in the story is the fluent flesh of his father's tongue.

Emerson, who was never an exile, once declared: "Utterance is place enough." Like many of Emerson's aphorisms, this one isn't really true, though it's true enough. When he has no other place to live, a writer can live in the writing; when he has nobody's body to settle into, he can always settle into his words. But such a residence is makeshift and temporary, as Casey well knew. "I am here to stay" (86, 190), he repeats with the nervousness of a man who knows that he is in transit. "I can choose to settle on the right nipple" (189), he asserts with the willfulness of the helpless. "I am not leaving" (193), he reassures himself as he thinks of the barbiturates in his drawer. In the end all that La Calvita could do was curl up for a little while inside his father's tongue, there to dream, and write, of paradise.

Chapter 5

Remembering Things Past in Translation

El estudio propio de la literatura no es la obra sino el escritor.
[The proper object of literary study is not the work but the writer.]

—*Guillermo Cabrera Infante*

Of all the varieties of translation, perhaps none is more faithless than self-translation. Although the technical challenges are the same, it adds a dimension of personal and creative reassessment missing from second-party translations. The author who translates his or her own work knows it too well, rather than well enough. Unlike the typical translator, the autologous translator works not only with the finished product; present at the creation, he remembers the gestation of the work—the false starts, the dead ends, the changes of direction, all of the decisions and accidents that shaped the finished product. Equally important, biscriptive writers have a unique, *untranslatable* relation with each of their languages. Calvert Casey was able to recast "The Walk" as "El paseo," but what he could not do was translate into one language his relation with the other, which is why the two versions of the story differ in small but meaningful ways. In a truly multilingual writer, the translation of a tongue tie gets caught up in another tongue tie. Were Casey to have delved into "his" Spanish in "his" English, the tone and content of the remarks about Spanish would have been skewed by his relation to English. To examine his tongue ties without distortion, he would have had to resort to a "neutral" language, one divested of affect, one that—in Santayana's terms—would be no more than an instrument. But is there such a thing?

These complications tend to transform self-translation into a sophisticated form of second guessing. George Steiner points out in *After Babel* that strong writers don't often make good translators; this is even more true when strong writers attempt to translate themselves, for then they find it even harder to adopt the passive, absorbent posture required, at least initially, of an effective translator. No writer wants to play second banana to another writer, and least of all to himself. As if the web of tongue ties were not obstacle enough, the temptation to tinker, to amend, to get it right or righter the second time around, will tend to alienate the self-translated work from its original. The revisions may improve the original, may damage it, or may produce a version so unlike it that comparison is all but impossible. But only rarely will the two versions coincide. When Guillermo Cabrera Infante states that the "authority" of his translations stems from the fact that he is the author of the originals, he is making plain the hubris that, almost inevitably, infuses self-translation.[1] His arrogance—his "authoritarianism"—already comes to the fore in the English title of one of his novels, *Infante's Inferno,* whose possessive advertises the author's proprietary rights. Explaining his role in the English translation, Cabrera Infante says: "I took command of the book, as Dante would say, *da capo.*"[2] In spite of its brilliance, or perhaps because of it, *Infante's Inferno* is much more, and considerably less, than a translation of *La Habana para un Infante difunto.*

In this and the following chapter I want to study the psychological and literary implications of autologous translation apropos of two biscriptive Spanish American writers, Cabrera Infante and the Chilean novelist María Luisa Bombal. As we shall see, their relation to the English language differs from that of the other anglophone writers I have discussed thus far. Unlike Casey, who recast "The Walk" into what he considered his mother tongue, Cabrera Infante and Bombal translate from their first into their second or (in the case of Bombal) third languages. But unlike Santayana, whose English was also unmaternal, neither Cabrera Infante nor Bombal had family ties to the English language or grew up speaking it. For both it was a classroom language that, only in adulthood and for reasons they could not have anticipated, became a literary medium. In Cabrera Infante and Bombal, self-translation is not regress but egress; it does not map out an unlikely homecoming, as it did for Casey, or remap their family constellations, as it did for Santayana; rather, it gives them an opportunity to start afresh, to refashion themselves as people and artists.

Born in Cuba in 1929, Guillermo Cabrera Infante is widely regarded as the most accomplished "ambilingual" (to use Steven Kellman's term for biscriptive writers)[3] among contemporary Spanish American authors. Like Casey, Cabrera Infante was a strong supporter of the Cuban Revolution who eventually became disenchanted with the totalitarian turn of the Castro regime. Leaving Cuba in 1965, he lived in Spain for a few months and then moved to London, where he has resided ever since. As notorious for his playful, punning style as for his staunch anti-Castro politics, Cabrera Infante achieved renown with the publication of *Tres tristes tigres* (1967), a sprawling Joycean evocation of 1950s Havana nightlife that instantly became one of the centerpieces of the Latin American literary "boom." *Tres tristes tigres* was followed by *Vista del amanecer en el trópico* (1974), vignettes retracing the history of Cuba; several volumes of essays and divertimentos—*O* (1975), *Exorcismos de esti(l)o* (1976), *Arcadia todas las noches* (1978); and his much-awaited second novel, *La Habana para un Infante difunto* (1979), a fictionalized account of the author's coming of age. Since then Cabrera Infante has published *Holy Smoke* (1985), an idiosyncratic cultural history of cigar-smoking; the polemical *Mea Cuba* (1992), a collection of political and literary pieces; and several anthologies of previously published fiction and nonfiction.[4] He has not published any new fiction in over two decades.

Although Cabrera Infante's interest in English was kindled by the Hollywood movies that he watched as a child (he claims to have seen his first movie, *The Four Horsemen of the Apocalypse*, when he was twenty-nine days old), he did not begin formal instruction in the language until the 1940s, when his family moved to Havana and his father enrolled him in night school. Dutifully attending classes for four years, he graduated in 1948 with a certificate in the teaching of English. During the next decade, he honed his knowledge of the language by translating articles from American newspapers and working as a proofreader for *The Havana Herald*, an English-language paper. He also read widely in contemporary American literature, particularly Hemingway and Faulkner, and as a resident of Havana, he was continuously exposed to English, the unofficial second language of the city, at the time teeming with American tourists and consumer products. An anglophile ever since his youth, Cabrera Infante noted but did not seem to resent the presence of English in Cuban Spanish. As he said years later, "I've always had a passion for English. Ever since I first found English hidden behind a screen as a child, its mystery fascinated me."[5]

After he settled in England in 1966, his passion turned into a livelihood. Almost as soon as he arrived, he began writing movie scripts in English, work that he found profitable but difficult. It was one thing to use English in jokes and wordplay, as he had been doing for years, and another to compose sentences and paragraphs, even in the restricted format of the movie script. Of the half-dozen scripts that he wrote in the sixties, two were made into moderately successful movies, *Wonderwall* (1968) and *Vanishing Point* (1971). A few years later, when *Tres tristes tigres* was being turned into *Three Trapped Tigers* (1971), Cabrera Infante felt comfortable enough in the language to collaborate with his translators. From then on, he would assume an increasingly active role in the translation into English of his books. In addition, he would occasionally write short pieces directly in English, such as "Bites from the Bearded Crocodile" (1981), an essay on Cuban political culture, or "The Phantom of the Essoldo" (1983), a short story. His career as an anglophone writer culminated in 1985 with the publication of *Holy Smoke*, his first book written directly in English and his last major original work.

Although discussion of Cabrera Infante's anglophone writing has naturally focused on *Holy Smoke*, I want to examine the translation of one of his lesser-known works, *Vista del amanecer en el trópico* (1974), which he labelled "a biography of Cuba, my island, my self."[6] *Vista del amanecer en el trópico* offers a special case among Cabrera Infante's books because it exists in three versions—the Spanish original and two somewhat different English translations. The first translation, done by Suzanne Jill Levine, was published by Harper and Row in 1978. Although Levine consulted with Cabrera Infante, he was not entirely happy with the results because he worried that in English the "deadpan écriture" of the original sounded too much like Hemingway.[7] Ten years later, when Faber and Faber brought out the book in England, Cabrera Infante kept the bulk of Levine's text but took advantage of the opportunity to introduce significant revisions. In its original version *Vista del amanecer en el trópico* consists of 101 vignettes that recount representative moments in the history of Cuba. Written in unembellished, unselfconscious prose, the book is unique among Cabrera Infante's works for its almost total lack of humor and wordplay. There is perhaps only one pun in the entire book, but it is a crucial one. One of the last vignettes transcribes the monologue of a rafter who has escaped from Cuba. After detailing the death by drowning of his companions on the raft, he concludes that he was fated to survive the ordeal to tell the story: "Alguien tenía que quedar para hacer el cuento. Y yo me metí en la cabeza que ese alguien era yo" [Someone had to remain behind to tell the story. And I got it into my head that that someone was me].[8] The rafter ends his monologue with a pointed question: "¿Ves?" [See?] (194). Drawing on the visual and cognitive senses of the verb "to see," the rafter is not only asking whether we "get it," whether we understand, but whether we can visualize the horrid scene he has just described. Echoing the "Vista" of the title, he verbalizes the question that Cabrera Infante has implicitly asked his readers throughout the narrative: Do we "see" his "view" of Cuba?

This question is different from that which Cabrera Infante's fiction usually asks. Unlike Joseph Conrad, who wanted to make us see, Cabrera

Infante typically tries to make us hear. In *Tres Tristes Tigres* and *La Habana para un Infante difunto,* the primary aesthetic organ is the ear, not the eye. It is not incidental that most of the events of his first novel occur at night, for this puts the emphasis on sounds rather than sights, and particularly on the conversations of the protagonists. In the note at the beginning of *Tres Tristes Tigres,* Cabrera Infante informs the reader that the book is written "en cubano," explaining that *cubano* is not a written language but an urban dialect, "el habla de los habaneros" [the speech of Havanans].[9] Both in *Tres tristes tigres* and *La Habana para un Infante difunto,* his literary idiom has its basis in forms of orality grounded in a specific time and place. But *Vista del amanecer en el trópico,* whose title was suggested by a postcard of Cuba, upholds the preeminence of the visual. Unlike *Tres tristes tigres,* it is not a "gallery of voices"[10] but a picture gallery or a photo album made up of "viewgnettes," as Cabrera Infante called the fragments that make up the book.[11] Many of these "viewgnettes" are inspired by photographs, engravings, illustrations, or maps; others are framed by visual cues such as "Ahí está" [There it is], "He aquí" [Behold], "Se ve" [One can see]. The epigraph of the book comes from one of Goya's *Caprichos.*

This uncharacteristic emphasis on the visual has its origins in the circumstances of the book's composition. Although some of the vignettes were written in Cuba, Cabrera Infante put the book together in 1973, after a period of deep personal crisis. Depressed over the suicide of several friends (among them Calvert Casey), and pushed beyond exhaustion by his work on the English translation of *Tres Tristes Tigres* and a script of Malcolm Lowry's *Under the Volcano,* in the summer of 1972 Cabrera Infante suffered a nervous breakdown. As he told Raymond Souza years later, "I ended up a classic vegetable. I had no visible reactions, neither ate nor relieved myself nor heard anything said to me."[12] Also suffering from delusions (he told his wife that he had discovered the solution to the world's problems in an episode of the TV series *McMillan and Wife*), he was hospitalized and subjected to drug and electroshock treatments. The treatments worked, and some weeks later he was released from the "posh loony bin"[13] where his wife had put him. In addition to advising him to avoid stress and overwork during his convalescence, his doctors had a rather unusual recommendation: He should also stay away from wordplay, because the dissociative impetus of punning might precipitate another mental breakdown.[14] Only a year earlier Cabrera Infante had finished collaborating with Suzanne Jill Levine on the translation of *Tres tristes tigres,* a process that he described as a "verbal delirium tremens."[15] Now he needed to get on the wagon and abstain from puns, "the wine of prose."[16]

Back home in his London apartment, he returned to the vignettes about Cuban history that he had been working on for years, some of which had been part of the first draft of *Tres tristes tigres* (whose original title was *Vista del amanecer en el trópico*). Shaping the project as a work of recovery, personal as well as historical, Cabrera Infante sets out to test and restore his powers of recall, often with the aid of photographs, history books, and other secondary sources. As Raymond Souza points out, among other things *Vista del amanecer en el trópico* is a memory exercise, Cabrera Infante's way of piecing together his shattered recollections of Cuban history.[17] At the same time, the book represents an act of verbal detergence, an attempt to cleanse his writing of the excesses of *Three Trapped Tigers* to achieve "la cordura de lo simple" [the sanity of the simple].[18] Even though by 1974 Cabrera Infante was an established writer, *Vista del amanecer en el trópico* is an inaugural book, as if its author were trying to learn to write again for the first time. When in the opening sentence he describes the birth of the island, one has the feeling he is also evoking his own psychological and creative rebirth. Never before, and never since, has Cabrera Infante written as plainly. The elision of names and dates notwithstanding, *Vista del amanecer en el trópico* is a far more accessible book than either *Tres tristes tigres* or *La Habana para un Infante difunto*, where the reader's attention wavers between the narrated events and the narrating voice; what we see always competes with what we hear. But in *Vista del amanecer en el trópico* the eye reigns supreme. At crucial moments in the narrative, the author even limits himself to deictic gestures, preferring indication to description. No language is entirely transparent, of course, but that of *Vista del amanecer en el trópico* allows the reader to see through to the referent more clearly than is usually the case in Cabrera Infante. The focus throughout is on the historical referent, not the verbal medium: "¿Ves?"

Fifteen years after the book's composition, when Cabrera Infante got the chance to "re-view" his book on the occasion of its publication in England, he could not resist the temptation to make changes. As he had done in 1978, when Levine was working on her translation, he suppressed some vignettes and added others, but he also tinkered with Levine's sentences, which tried to capture the impassive tone and plain prose of the original. Many of the stylistic revisions are insignificant. In some instances, he only clarifies or adds precision, as when "morning" replaces "day," or "sunrise" replaces "morning," or "rifles" replaces "weapons." In other instances, he interpolates visual details not present either in the Spanish original or in Levine's translation. In the 1978 version, the entrance of a Cuban general into Havana is a "moment of glory," to which the 1988 version adds, "with crowds surrounding him literally everywhere."[19] Some revisions make Levine's translation more idiomatic by purging traces of hispanicizing diction; he removes cognates ("comical Spanish accent" becomes "funny Spanish accent"), calques ("wounded to death," which translates "herido de muerte," becomes simply "shot dead"), and simplifies the language ("In this instance the technique" becomes "Now the ploy"). At times only euphony motivates the edit, as in the sentence, "Later the islands joined to form a great island, which soon became green where it wasn't golden or reddish"—whose last words Cabrera Infante changes to "where it wasn't reddish or brown," thereby ending the sentence with a stressed monosyllabic word.

This minor edit raises a larger issue, however. Levine's "golden or reddish" translates literally the "dorada o rojiza" of the original Spanish. By substituting "brown" for "golden" and inverting the order of the adjectives, Cabrera Infante improves the cadence of the translation but modifies the island's color scheme. Sacrificing sense to sound, he reverts to his usual practice of writing with his ear rather than his eye.[20] The revision is more properly a re-audition, a retuning of the prose to his ear for the rhythms of English: "audit" as much as "edit." This attention to style or expression at the expense of content will characterize his most substantial alterations to Levine's text. Carried to its logical conclusion, it will graft onto *Vista del amanecer en el trópico* an expressive resource alien to the original—wordplay.

One of the vignettes that appears for the first time in Levine's 1978 translation describes a failed coup against Fulgencio Batista's regime. I reproduce excerpts from the 1978 and 1988 versions of this vignette:

1978:
> They attacked the guards as soon as they got out of the cars, but in the attack plans they had forgotten to include the nearby Café Palacio Bar, where soldiers from the garrison would often drink and eat, and these now formed a devastating surprise rear guard. That was when the rest of the cars arrived. All the attackers carried only handguns. The van of the Fast Delivery Dry Cleaners, full of rifles and submachine guns, remained parked on a side street, waiting for the support group—which never arrived.[21]

1988:
> The guerillas fired at the palace guards even before they got out of the cars. But in the *plan de ataque* they had failed to include the café on the corner, where soldiers from the garrison would often eat and drink. Alerted by the shots they really became a devastating surprise rear guard: the surprisers taken by surprise. Fortunately (though they couldn't use that word) that was when the rest of the cars arrived.

> For their own protection, all the insurgents were armed only with handguns and a few hand grenades they could hide in their pockets. The van of the Fastaction Dry Cleaners ("We deliver"), full of M1 rifles and submachine guns and ammunition, remained parked on a side street of the palace, waiting for the support group to come. They never came. (90)

The augmentations made in 1988 fall into three categories. Some make the description more exact: "palace guards" replaces "guards"; "the café on the corner" replaces "the nearby Café Palacio Bar." Others provide motivation for behavior, as when the narrator explains that the Batista guards were alerted by the shots of the attackers, or that the attackers only carried small arms. The most glaring interpolations, though, occur on the plane of expression rather than of content. To Levine's translation Cabrera Infante adds an epigram ("the surprisers taken by surprise"), editorial comment ("Fortunately [though they couldn't use that word]"), and a pun ("We deliver"). Diverting the reader's attention from the tale to the telling, from the message to the medium, these changes put the narrator front and center. The epigram, which provides no new information about the assault, slights the bloodiness of the assault for the sake of the clever inversion. And his editorial comments nullify the reticence of the original, establishing the narrator's cognitive superiority over the guerillas. The disparity between tone and content increases in the second paragraph when the sign on the van changes from "Fast Delivery Dry Cleaners" to "Fastaction Dry Cleaners." Since the portmanteau "Fastaction" is possible only in English, the revision all but obliterates the original referent. "Fastaction" does not translate, it displaces—as does the pun on "deliver," another English-only product of the linguistic occasion rather than of the historical incident. As *View* fades into mirage, the island drifts away and the vignettes start to turn into *exorcismos de estilo,* Cabrera Infante's punning name for his genre of phonic and graphic wordplay.

The next vignette recounts the escape from jail of one of the attackers. After describing the prisoners' uniform—"blue trousers and blue shirt and blue cap"—Cabrera Infante adds to the 1988 version that the prisoners looked like "demons in denim" (93). Then he comments on the simple escape plan:

1974:
   Pero no hubo plan maestro, ni mapas de fuga, ni complot y fue así de fácil. (138)

1978:

But there was no master plan, no escape maps or plots, and it was just as easy as that. (89)

1988:
But there was no master plan, no escape maps or plots. In one word, no maze—though it was of course amazing. (94)

The puns on "demon"/"denim" and "maze"/"amazing" are not only incongruous but discordant. The quiet ending of the Spanish original and the 1978 translation matches the plainness of the diction to the simplicity of the event—"y fue así de fácil" / "and it was just as easy as that." Once again calling attention to the narrator, the pun on amazing, which Cabrera Infante does not tire of making in his English writing, ruins the effect.

This type of change in tone and phrasing occurs repeatedly in the 1988 translation. A nattily dressed member of Machado's dreaded secret police is said to be "dressed to kill" (55). Because he is wearing a white linen suit, this man, who is black, is a "black in white" (55). A guerilla fighter who in the 1978 translation is "a bullfighter scarred with wounds" (119) becomes, in 1988, "a bullfighter scarred but not scared" (129). In the Spanish original, a politician who hurts his right hand by shaking it so often remarks that his hand was "enferma de popularidad" (77); Levine translates the phrase as "a casualty of popularity" (47); Cabrera Infante retranslates it as "a casualty in the war of hands" and adds that the politician came to regard the outstretched hands of his supporters as "a new enemy weapon in friendly hands" (47). The 1988 translation even puts in the mouth of Batista, a man not known for his wit, a pun on Ides of March (*Idus/idos*, 68) that Cabrera Infante has exploited on other occasions. A vignette added in 1988 concludes: "Never trust a cop who banters. Remember that a joke is closer to a yoke than you think" (113). As the bantering cop finds his match in the bantering narrator, the "deadpan écriture" that distinguished the Spanish text gives way to "vintage" Cabrera Infante.

These changes, of which many other examples could be cited, spoil the book. Puns intensify, they raise discourse to a febrile pitch, they make us laugh or groan. But the distinctiveness of *Vista del amanecer en el trópico* resides in the contrast between the narrator's impassiveness and the mostly horrid events he narrates. Artfully monotone, deftly understated, the language of the book has few highs and lows, few moments when the reader's attention is diverted from the view to the window or the window pane. Only at the end, when the narrative perspective abruptly switches to the first person and one hears the voice of three survivors of the Castro regime, does the tale share the spotlight with the teller. But the effect is dramatic rather than merely histrionic. Reading the rafter's account, one realizes that he talks in the first person because he speaks for the author, another survivor of the Revolution. The question that closes the monologue—"¿Ves?"—also asks whether the reader understands that the anonymous rafter is the author's *porte parole,* that his desire to leave a record is what motivates not only this vignette but the entire book.

These nuances disappear from the 1988 version, since the interpolations foreground the act of narration from the first. A pun not only shifts a reader's or listener's attention from the message to the medium; it also calls attention to the punster, for wordplay is exhibitionistic, self-indulgent. When he was writing *Vista del amanecer en el trópico,* Cabrera Infante allowed himself to be effaced. Trying to control his mood swings, he put together an even-tempered book, one that stares at the world impassively, almost numbly. Years later, in a much better mood, he couldn't resist the temptation to play.

To play, that is, or to cover up, for it could be that Cabrera Infante's revisions arise from a lack of confidence in his material. Comparing the three versions, one sometimes gets the impression that the author of the 1988 version does not trust his subject, that he fears that, absent verbal pyrotechnics, the "biography of Cuba" may not hold the reader's attention. Rather than trusting the muted drama of the vignettes, he falls back on stylistic embellishments. Here are the three versions of the last sentence of the opening vignette:

1974:
    Ahí está la isla, todavía surgiendo de entre el océano y el golfo: ahí está . . .

1978:
    There's the island, still coming out between the ocean and the gulf, there it is . . .

1988:
    There's the island, still coming out between the sea and the gulf, garlanded by keys and cays and fastened by the stream to the ocean. There it is . . .

The 1988 interpolation—"garlanded . . . ocean"—blunts the impact of the repetition that begins and ends the sentence. This clause is itself a "garland," a verbal ornament that adds nothing of substance. "Garland" puns on "land" and echoes "island;" "keys" and "cays" are redundant variants of the same word, the Spanish *cayo.* Rather than letting us see, they make us hear. And because one thinks of things that fasten as stationary, the image of the endlessly moving stream as a clasp also hampers rather than aids visualization. Moreover, by saving the word "ocean" for one of the poles of the metaphor, Cabrera Infante is forced to alter the original to say that the island rises between "the sea and the gulf," which is imprecise, since the gulf is also a "sea" and in English the Atlantic is always an "ocean." In a vignette about the Cuban liberator Antonio Maceo, the 1988 version adds the phrase I have put in italics: "He finished his letter with a personal remark *like a flourish of his pen*" (41). The simile is itself a flourish, another small garland. These flowers of rhetoric introduce into the book a playful metalinguistic consciousness inconsistent with the original. Whereas the Spanish of *Vista del amanecer en el trópico* was restorative, the English of the 1988 revisions is mostly recreational; it does little to sharpen the view.

Now contrast the different versions of the first sentence of the book:

1974:
Las islas surgieron del océano, primero como islotes aislados, luego los cayos se hicieron montañas y las aguas bajas, valles.

1978:
The islands came out of the ocean as isolated isles, then the keys became mountains and the shallows, valleys.

1988:
The island came out of the sea like a Venus land: out of the foam constantly beautiful. But there were more islands. In the beginning they were solitary isles really. Then the isles turned into mountains and the shallows in between became valleys.

It's not clear what Cabrera Infante gains by splitting one flowing sentence into four choppy ones, or by inserting a mythological allusion, or by belaboring the echoes of Genesis with the phrase "In the beginning." And the "really" that ends the third sentence really limps. Again, the purpose of these changes seems to be to spruce up the description, but in light of what is to follow, nicknaming Cuba a "Venus land" is hugely inappropriate. The personification runs counter to the crucial distinction between Cuba as geography and as history, between the unnamed island in the stream and the country whose tragic history he goes on to reconstruct.

The 1988 *View of Dawn in the Tropics* is not the only one of Cabrera Infante's English translations in which flourishes trump content. Something similar happens with his first book, *Así en la paz como en la guerra*

(1960), a collection of stories and vignettes that reflect Cuba's political turmoil in the 1950s. As he has apropos of *Vista del amanecer en el trópico*, Cabrera Infante has expressed mixed feelings about this book because, in style and structure, it too reveals the imprint of Hemingway's *In Our Time*.[22] When the book finally appeared in English as *Writes of Passage* (1993), some of the original stories—particularly those that Cabrera Infante translated himself—were almost unrecognizable, not because the plots had been changed but because they had been buried under layers of wordplay and metafictional musings. One egregious example is the translation of "Un nido de gorriones en un toldo" ["A Nest of Sparrows on the Awning"], an unpretentious story written in 1955 about the protagonist's concern for the sparrows that have made their nest on his American neighbor's awning. In Spanish, the story's point and poignancy derive from the implied parallel between the sparrows' chicks, which the protagonist tries to protect, and the American couple's teenage niece, whom he tries to seduce. But in Cabrera Infante's anglophone version, the human interest takes a backseat to the narrator's ruminations on the act of translation, which include the quotation of several long passages on the translation of puns from Louis B. Solomon's *Semantics and Common Sense* (1966), the book that he is reading when his wife comes to tell him about the nest of sparrows. Given that the story is explicitly set in Havana in the mid-1950s, fully a decade before Solomon's book was published, the anachronism injects into the story an account of its translation many years later. Not unexpectedly, Cabrera Infante's English title—"Nest, Door, Neighbours"—leaves out the sparrows, which are central to the story, to make a pun.[23]

Somewhat the same thing happens in the one piece of fiction that Cabrera Infante has written directly in English, "The Phantom of the Essoldo," an almost unintelligible pastiche of snippets from movies, clever repartees with ghosts, and self-reflexive asides.[24] The narration itself, about an outing to the movies during which the narrator and his wife get scammed by a couple of young women, takes a backseat to the digressions that occupy most of the text. In the "Prologue for English readers" from *Writes of Passage,* Cabrera Infante avers that "form is all and that everything that is not form is bad form. But sometimes content seeps through like a leak."[25] Sadly, this sounds like a writer who has run out of things to say, or who worries that what he has to say will not interest anyone. And at least in "The Phantom of the Essoldo," he very nearly satisfies his desire for leak-proof formalism. Would he have adopted this Mallarmean pose in a "Prologue for *Cuban* Readers"? The author's note to *Tres tristes tigres* propounds a mimetic rather than a hermetic aesthetics; the events in the novel, he says, are "taken from reality," and his aim has been to "capture" and "reconstruct" Havana speech.[26] Although *Tres tristes tigres* or *La Habana para un Infante difunto* also indulge in verbal humor and playful digressions, I cannot think of a nontrivial sense in which they could be said to be "all form."

There is more to this than Cabrera Infante's anxiety of influence or his fear of irrelevance, for even in *Holy Smoke,* a nonfiction book clearly not derivative of Hemingway, he relies relentlessly on puns and smart-alecky asides. Cabrera Infante's escape into form may also betray his lack of investment in the English language as *idioma,* as *habla,* as the speech of a community. No society speaks in puns, for community depends on communication, and punning hampers communication by making meaning ambiguous. When Cabrera Infante states that *Tres tristes tigres* is written "in Cuban," he roots his language in a place, ties his tongue to an *idioma* that tempers his flights of fancy. His Spanish acquires its distinctive voice not from word games, but from a Cernudan *acorde* between mouth and ear, between inner and outer sounds, between the words with which Cabrera Infante talks to himself and those he hears around him. And it does not matter whether the ambient sounds are real or imagined, whether he is actually listening, as he did when he lived in Havana, or only remembering what he heard.

Not so with English. Neither a *lengua* nor an *idioma,* unmoored from history and enervated by the author's disconnection from any anglophone community, Cabrera Infante's English is disembodied and groundless. Hence the odd anachronisms, the erasure of referentiality, and the sometimes disconcerting mix of British and American idioms. One of the highpoints of *Tres tristes tigres* is the section entitled "Ella cantaba boleros," which tells the story of Estrella Rodríguez, a larger-than-life bolero singer. The narrator of this section is the character nicknamed Códac, a photographer, who explains how he got to know La Estrella:

> Yo soy fotógrafo y mi trabajo por esa época era de tiraplanchas de los cantantes y la gente de la farándula y la vida nocturna, y yo andaba siempre por los cabarets y nite-clubs y eso, haciendo fotografías.[27]

This is the English translation:

> I am a press photographer and my work at that time involved taking shots of singers and people of the *farándula,* which means not only show business but limelights and nightlife as well. So I spent all my time in

cabarets, nightclubs, strip joints, bars, *barras, boîtes,* dives, saloons, *cantinas, cuevas, caves,* or caves.[28]

In Spanish, the oral quality of Códac's monologue is conveyed not only by the string of "ands," but by the tag "y eso," a colloquial "etcetera" or "and so on" that illustrates perfectly Cabrera Infante's flawless ear for Cuban speech patterns. In the English translation both mannerisms disappear. By splitting the sentence in two, he trims the "ands"; in place of the colloquial "y eso," he concocts a redundant multilingual enumeration without basis in the original. (Among the novel's tigers, Códac, an image man, is the least given to wordplay.) Instead of discovering or underscoring shades of meaning and intention in the original, as good translations do, the fanfare of puns and alliterations drowns out Códac's voice. In English, Códac just sounds like Cabrera Infante. What would have been wrong with a more literal rendering of the sentence?

> I'm a photographer and my job at that time was getting shots of singers and people in show business and in the night life, and I was always in cabarets and night-clubs and so on, taking pictures.

It may be heretical to say this, but Cabrera Infante does his best writing when he bites his tongue, when he cuts down on his witticisms, as in "Ella cantaba boleros" or *Vista del amanecer en el trópico.* But he rarely shows this restraint in English, no matter how inappropriate the punning. He has bragged that *Three Trapped Tigers* is fifty pages longer than the original—"all of them full of puns!"[29] The small excerpt quoted above suggests that the translation's gain may be the novel's loss.

In a review of *Holy Smoke* published in *The New Yorker,* John Updike charges Cabrera Infante with lack of "tact," which Updike defines as "the tension and economy that enforce themselves when method and material are in close touch."[30] For Updike's method and material I would substitute Santayana's instrument and source. Tact is contact. When Cabrera Infante writes in English, his instrument is estranged from his source—be it the world he evokes or the world he inhabits. In Spanish his most outrageous or whimsical word games never lose touch with Cuban speech; in English he can be just as inventive, but—like the description of Códac's bar-hopping—it's an unsituated, unmotivated inventiveness, puns without point and alliterations without music. As a collection of speech-habits detached from a speech-world, English is for Cabrera Infante what Santayana only claimed that it was for him, an instrument rather than a source. Regina Janes gets it right when she says that Cabrera Infante feels no responsibility to English.[31] His English is irresponsible because it does not respond to a community or even to the writer's idea of himself. Cabrera Infante flirts with English, but he does not surrender to it, he does not let the language understand him. Writing in English in England, he is more of an exile than when he writes in Spanish in England. "The Phantom of the Essoldo" begins: "The L in London is for labyrinth: the city is indeed an enormous maze of names. Let me amaze you utterly, foreign visitor."[32] Addressing the reader, Cabrera Infante portrays himself, a foreigner in London though not exactly a visitor. And he also gives his impression of the English language, a maze of names. Since he has never felt at home in England, since his familiarity with its language has never ripened into a tongue tie, he compensates by molding a prose so dense and labored that it lapses into a "write of passage," a monument to virtuosity and unhousedness.

A few years ago he was asked whether he was ever planning to write another novel. He replied that he was, since he still had unused memories of Cuba. Even though Cabrera Infante has lived much longer in London than he ever did in Havana, the world of his fiction remains circum-scribed to decades-old memories of another country. In none of his many interviews has he ever suggested that the "British" half of his life could provide material for his novels. But this may explain why he has not published a novel in over twenty years—the storehouse of memories may be all but depleted—and why his English-language writing has not achieved real depth or distinction. For Cabrera Infante to acquire a voice in English, his switch in language would have to be accompanied by a degree of psychic or emotional relocation. He would need not only to look back, but to look around. Nabokov wrote *Lolita,* Casey wrote "Piazza Margana"—both are clearly the work of exiles, both evince the "xenity" characteristic of such literature, but both also enact, in however oblique a way, their authors' decision to assume new writerly identities. Other than the screenplays that he churns out for the money (or so he says), Cabrera Infante has shown little interest in writing anything but what Casey called, with remarkable prescience, "texts exclusively about Havana melancholies."[33] Though understandable in human terms, his insistence on nostalgia, his exclusionary definition of what it means to be an exiled writer, and more particularly an exiled Cuban writer, has made his English a museum piece rather than a living tongue.

In 1967 Cabrera Infante wrote the screenplay for *Wonderwall* (1968), a badly dated "psychedelic" movie (with music by George Harrison) about a bookish entomologist, Oscar Collins, who discovers a peephole through which he observes the seductive young woman who lives next door. As the film progresses, Oscar, now a full-time voyeur, opens larger and larger holes in the "wonderwall" of his apartment. By the end of the film, his beautiful next-door neighbor—Lolita as flower-child—has introduced Oscar not only to eroticism but to the world at large. The Nabokovian echoes of the protagonist's profession and fixation make it plausible that his surname alludes to the Collins English Dictionary, which Cabrera Infante sometimes quotes in his writings.[34] The protagonist's name may then summarize his initial means of access to the English language: Hollywood films and books. The "wonderwall" is not only a symbol of the disjunction between Oscar Collins and the outside world, but of the language barrier that Cabrera Infante was trying at the time to overcome. Whether he has actually overcome it is an open question. Nabokov once wrote, "I am as American as April in Arizona."[35] Such a wonderfully quirky sentence—just how "American" is April in Arizona?—could have been written only by someone equally at home and adrift in the English language. For his part, Cabrera Infante has said: "I am as English as the fish and chips I detest."[36] Unlike Nabokov, Cabrera Infante has never made his peace with exile. Although he navigates his adopted language masterfully, it does not connect him to the people or the country where he has now lived for most of his life. Rather than using English as a window, as he does with Spanish in *Vista del amanecer en el trópico*, he uses it to block the view. Cabrera Infante's English is a wonderwall without a peephole.

Chapter 6

Spanish Passion, English Peace

Translation is an activity, in no way unregulated, through which we are able to understand what our own language was unable to say.

—*Umberto Eco*

If Cabrera Infante is Latin America's most celebrated biscriptive writer, María Luisa Bombal (1910–1980) is one of the most neglected. Not that her work has been ignored, for even though she wrote very little—a handful of short stories and two novellas—her fiction has been the object of almost uninterrupted commentary ever since the publication of her first book in 1934. Usually regarded as Spanish America's most important female novelist, Bombal holds a secure place not only as one of the continent's first feminist voices but as a precursor to the magical realists of the 1960s and 1970s—"the mother of us all," as Carlos Fuentes once remarked.

Nonetheless, an important segment of Bombal's work remains largely unknown or unappreciated—her anglophone writings, which include self-translations of her two novellas, *La última niebla* (1934) and *La amortajada* (1938), published in English as *House of Mist* (1947) and *The Shrouded Woman* (1948). The disinterest in Bombal's career as an anglophone writer is surprising, given that her output in English is actually larger than that in Spanish, since she also wrote another novel (*The Foreign Minister*), a play (*Dolly Jeckyll and Mrs. Hyde*), and several TV and movie scripts. Moreover, Bombal's fame outside the Spanish-speaking world rests not on her Spanish novellas but on the English adaptations, since the translations of *La última niebla* into Portuguese, French, Swedish, Japanese, and other languages have used *House of Mist* rather than the Spanish original. And yet, because she changed the plot of *La última niebla* at the urging of her American agent, who wanted her to make the novel less ambiguous, *House of Mist* in particular is dismissed as Bombal's unfortunate attempt to pander to middle-brow American tastes. Her biographer, Ágata Gligo, finds the novel "disconcerting" because the plot has a logical explanation; Lucía Guerra-Cunningham, the editor of Bombal's *Obras completas,* brands *House of Mist* a "degraded ghost of the original"; Gloria Gálvez Lira, who thinks the English version "monotonous, boring and puerile," concludes that Bombal's decision to translate *La última niebla* was a "monumental mistake"; and Kimberly Nance regards the novel as a "blot on her record as a writer."[1]

Any book that elicits such contempt cannot be all bad. At least such a work, along with the attacks it has provoked, deserves a closer look. Interestingly, Bombal did not share the low opinion of *House of Mist,* for she regarded the novel as "algo lindo literariamente" [literarily well-done] (*OC,* 353) and "una joya como novela poética" [a jewel as a poetic novel] (*OC,* 345).[2] The difference stems in part from Bombal's fondness for old-fashioned melodrama, a genre that, until recently, has had few defenders among academic critics. In 1939, writing in *Sur,* Victoria Ocampo's influential journal, Bombal caused a stir with her lavish praise for the movie *Puerta cerrada* (1939), "a tremendous melodrama" (*OC,* 332). The review led Luis Saslavsky, at the time Argentina's leading director, to invite her to write the script for his next film. Bombal's initial idea was to bring Jorge Isaacs's romantic tear-jerker, *María* (1867), to the screen, but when she was told that an American film company already owned the film rights, she decided to write her own version, *La casa del recuerdo* (1940), whose heroine, the illegitimate daughter of an aristocrat, is (like María) separated from her beloved and eventually perishes of a mysterious illness.[3] A few years later, when she was recasting *La última niebla* as *House of Mist,* Bombal applied the lessons she had learned from *La casa del recuerdo* (which turned out to be a big hit), filling out the slight original with truculent scenes, surprising plot twists, and even a happy ending. If the purpose of these revisions was to make money, Bombal certainly succeeded, since Hal Wallis of Paramount Pictures bought the film rights for $125,000, a stunningly large sum for an unknown novelist from Chile. (By way of comparison, in 1940 Paramount bought the rights to Hemingway's *For Whom the Bell Tolls* for $136,000, at the time the largest price ever paid for the film rights to a book.)

House of Mist's English undoubtedly has also played a part in its poor reputation. As Roberto Ignacio Díaz points out in an important recent book, the deeply entrenched monolingual bias in Hispanic literary scholarship has led to the neglect of works not written in Spanish by Spanish American authors.[4] Marjorie Agosín, one of the most knowledgeable Bombal scholars, expresses the majority view when she asserts that "Bombal stops publishing officially in 1946 with *La historia de María Griselda,*"[5] as if *House of Mist,* which appeared the following year, were a phantom book, not part of Bombal's "official" curriculum. Lucía

Guerra-Cunningham begins her own monograph by declaring her intention to study the "total corpus" of Bombal's writing; yet she too does not consider the English-language writing.[6] Her edition of Bombal's misnamed *Obras completas* [Complete Works] excludes *House of Mist* in spite of the author's assertion that it is not merely a translation: "*House of Mist* no es *La última niebla*. Es una nueva novela que yo escribí en inglés (con la ayuda de mi marido para el inglés) basada sobre el *tema* de mi *Última niebla*" [*House of Mist* is not *La última niebla*. It's a new novel that I wrote in English (with my husband's help with English) based on the theme of *La última niebla*] (*OC,* 345). Bombal even wrote to Guerra-Cunningham: "Sobre *House of Mist*. Espero no hayan Uds. olvidado que es una nueva novela, versión en inglés (basada sobre mi novela en castellano *La última niebla*) y escrita directamente al inglés por mí" [About *House of Mist*. I hope you haven't forgotten that it's a new novel, an English version (based on my Spanish novel *La última niebla*) written directly in English by me] (*OC,* 374). This "forgetting" of the differences between the two novels has produced some curious critical comment. In a recent edition of *House of Mist,* Naomi Lindstrom discusses the novel in terms that apply rather to *La última niebla,* asserting that *House of Mist* offers "an often bitter novelistic assessment of the situation of women in the Chilean landed aristocracy," and that the protagonist "is acutely conscious of the repression she endures in her social role."[7] The reader who reads this will be puzzled by the romantic story that follows, which ends when the protagonist finds the happiness she has always longed for, "as is usual in old-time love stories."[8]

The underlying issue is that *House of Mist* does not fit Bombal's profile in Latin American letters as the hispanophone author of socially aware and formally innovative fictions. Closer to Knut Hamsun's *Victoria* than to Virginia Woolf's *A Room of One's Own, House of Mist* is neither an indictment of patriarchy nor a precocious anticipation of magical realism. Out of *La última niebla,* a prose poem about a nameless woman's misery, Bombal has spun what she called "a modern fairy tale" (*OC,* 345), "my Hans Christian Andersen story" (*OC,* 407). Conventional in structure and saccharine in sensibility, the novel offers an interpretation of *La última niebla* strikingly inconsistent with the standard readings of the Spanish original. To read *La última niebla* "after" *House of Mist* is an unsettling experience, for it makes one wonder how the author could have so badly misconstrued her own achievement. In this situation, it is understandable that critics would dismiss *House of Mist* as an anomaly, a lapse in creative imagination caused by the switch in languages and Bombal's ambition for commercial success.

I intend to take a different approach. Like Roberto Ignacio Díaz, I regard *House of Mist* as an important item in Bombal's curriculum. Unlike Díaz, however, I do not read the novel as "another foundational fiction" or "a meditation on the nation."[9] In my view, *House of Mist* has nothing to do with nation building and everything to do with life-writing. The novel's significance does not arise from its shadowy engagement with Latin American history, but from the role it played in the author's efforts to remake herself as woman and artist. In this respect *House of Mist* is Bombal's "Piazza Margana," though the two works could not be more different in style and content. Elizabeth Klosty Beaujour observes that "self-translation is frequently the rite of passage, the traditional, heroic psychic journey into the depths of the self."[10] In the last chapter we saw that for Cabrera Infante self-translation is not a journey into the self but a way of skating on its surface. As different as his English versions are from their Spanish originals, the changes are superficial, "writes" rather than rites of passage, linguistic diversions that avoid the often painful reassessments that self-translation tends to foster. Not so for Bombal, whose recreation of *La última niebla* as *House of Mist* signals her desire to begin afresh, personally as well as literarily. Although her English is no match for Cabrera Infante's, she takes more chances with it; she lets it lead her into emotionally uncharted territory. Derek Walcott writes: "To change your language, you must change your life." The converse can also be true: To change your life, you must change your language. For Bombal, who always saw her books in personal terms— "mi obra, que después de todo es mi persona" [my work, which after all is my person] (*OC*, 342)—the change in literary medium gave her the opportunity to write herself into a new life.

In an influential early essay about *La última niebla*, Cedomil Goic argued that the book's originality resides in its collapse of the distinction between the objective and the subjective, a hallmark of the classical novel.[11] Like the protagonist, Bombal's reader is hard-pressed to tell reality from dream, fact from fantasy. Because the world of the narration is coextensive with the narrator's somnambulistic consciousness, it is not even possible to determine whether her blissful one-night stand, the pivotal episode in her account, actually happened: The man of her dreams may have only been a man in her dreams. She says: "La neblina, esfumando los ángulos, tamizando los ruidos, ha comunicado a la ciudad la tibia intimidad de un cuarto cerrado" [Blurring contours, muting sounds, the fog has given the city the lukewarm intimacy of a closed room] (*OC*, 65). Since all of the events in the novel are shrouded in fog, a "closed room" describes not only the city but the narrative itself. Hermetic and ungrounded, *La última niebla* offers no independent perspective from which to assess the protagonist's experiences. As Goic mentions, the narrator-protagonist exercises little control over the narrated world.[12] She sees but lacks the ability to understand what she has seen, and her story unfolds as a succession of tableaux whose logical and chronological connections remain obscure. Significantly, when she attempts to write down her experiences, and perhaps by so doing make them intelligible, she fails: "Escribo y rompo" [I write and I tear up] (*OC*, 71).

In *House of Mist* the fog is a stage rather than a state. Unlike her hispanophone double, Helga gains in knowledge and maturity as the novel advances, eventually discovering that her adulterous tryst was no more than a champagne-induced fantasy. Trying to figure out what really happened that night, she says to her maid: "But Amanda, how could you see all that through the mist?" Amanda, playing Sancho Panza to her mistress's Quijote, replies, "What mist?" (*HM*, 151). Gone is the vagueness of *La última niebla*, replaced by a contoured narrative that guides the protagonist, as in the classical novel, from illusion to reality. In *House of Mist*, characters have names and biographies, family relationships are clearly delineated, and the narration is divided into parts and subdivided into chapters. The action begins in the fall when the mist moves in and ends in the spring when the mist dissipates. Instead of the hazy mental stream of *La última niebla*, Bombal contrives a complicated machinery of causes and effects set in motion by a well-developed, if somewhat heavy-handed, sense of narrative timing. While *La última niebla* is a puzzle without a solution— mist and mystery rolled into one—*House of Mist* is a "mystery" in the literary sense, a suspenseful story that delays rather than withholds the answers to its enigmas.

Explaining the differences between the two books, Bombal stated that *La última niebla* represents "un tema tomado desde adentro y tratado en prosa, casi como un poema. Tomar este mismo tema desde afuera me tentó, como un desafío intelectual, y lo hice desarrollándolo con toda la técnica que requiere la novela" [a theme taken from the inside and treated in prose, almost like a poem. Taking this same theme from the outside tempted me as an intellectual challenge, and I did it developing it with all of the technique required by a novel] (*OC*, 407). According to Bombal, the difference between novel and poem depends on point of view; but since both *House of Mist* and *La última niebla* are narrated by the protagonist, the distinction between "inside" and "outside" is not that between a first and a third person narration, as her statement might lead one to believe, but between two modes of self-writing. *La última niebla* begins:

El vendaval de la noche anterior había remojado las tejas de la vieja casa de campo. Cuando llegamos, la lluvia goteaba en todos los cuartos. (*OC,* 55)

[The previous night's storm had drenched the roof tiles of the old country house. When we arrived, rain was leaking into every room.]

Compare this to the opening of Helga's account:

The story I am about to tell is the story of my life. It begins where other stories usually end; I mean, it begins with a wedding, a really strange wedding, my own. (*HM,* 3)

In *La última niebla* we find ourselves inside the "house"—narration as well as abode—from the outset. In *House of Mist* Helga begins with a brief introduction that separates her roles as narrator and protagonist. Because the woman who tells the story is older and wiser than the woman who lived it, she has the ability to summarize and evaluate. As narrator, Helga stands outside the mist, allowing the reader to witness her evolution from the person she was to the person she is. The exteriority of *House of Mist* is internal to the narrative voice. (Even Helga's disclosure of her name in the course of the narrative indicates exteriority, her ability to look at herself as an other.) What Bombal expresses as a difference in location—"outside" versus "inside"—arises from the separation between the "now" of the act of narration and the "then" of the narrated events. In *La última niebla* the predominance of the present tense, into which the narrative lapses as soon as the protagonist enters the house, makes it impossible for her to establish distance from the events she reports. Her narrative is not discovery but reportage.

Granted the benefit of hindsight, Helga will often interrupt her account to tie up loose ends or alert her reader to the significance of some forthcoming event. This is how she introduces the account of the ball from which she supposedly ran away with David Landa:

Here begins the account of one of the most extraordinary experiences any woman has ever lived through.

Everything I have written up to now which may have seemed trivial and unimportant to the reader was nevertheless a necessary foundation for the episodes that are to follow.

If the simple story I am relating now had been written as a novel, and if I had to choose a title for every one of the chapters, I would have named this one THE BALL, further trying in a subtle way to warn my reader of the importance of each one of the details, even those which in themselves seem altogether insignificant. (*HM,* 102)

Intrusive as they are, these interpolations make evident the narrator's lucidity and control. As character, Helga spends most of the novel in a fog, like her Spanish-language counterpart; but the same cannot be said of Helga as narrator. When the time comes to explain what really occurred that night, she will preface the scene by suggesting another title, "The Ball in Reverse" (*HM,* 223). Fast-forwarding and flashing-back at will, Helga orchestrates each scene to peak the reader's interest. Contrast this to the last sentence of *La última niebla:* "Alrededor de nosotros, la niebla presta a las cosas un carácter de inmovilidad definitiva" [All around us, the fog gives things the appearance of definitive immobility] (*OC,* 95). As an inert depiction of inertertness, *La última niebla* lacks the forward impetus of narrative; the only actor is the ubiquitous mist, perhaps the true protagonist of the novella. The narrator's last words reprise her description of a female corpse she had seen earlier: "Y ahora hela aquí, aprisionada, inmóvil, en ese largo estuche de madera, en cuya tapa han encajado un vidrio para que sus conocidos puedan contemplar su postrera expresión" [And now here she is, imprisoned, immobile, inside that long wooden box with a glass top so that her acquaintances can contemplate her last expression] (*OC,* 58). The "reversals" of *House of Mist* have no place in *La última niebla,* whose title conveys the same sense of finality as the phrase "postrera expresión." Closed room or see-through casket, this novella portrays its narrator in fixed, motionless poses, as a living corpse.

Helga's ability to stand outside herself finds a parallel in Bombal's exteriority to her own fiction. Unlike *La última niebla,* which plunges the reader directly into the story, Helga's account is preceded by a brief "Prologue":

> I wish to inform the reader that even though this is a mystery, it is a mystery without murder. He will not find here any corpse, any detective; he will not even find a murder trial, for the simple reason there will be no murderer. There will be no murderer and no murder, yet there will be crime.
> And there will be fear.
> Those for whom fear has an attraction; those who are interested in the mysterious life people live in their dreams during sleep; those who believe that the dead are not really dead; those who are afraid of the fog and of their own hearts . . . they will perhaps enjoy going back to the early days of this century and entering into the strange house of mist that a young

woman, very much like other young women, built for herself at the southern end of South America.

The first voice the reader hears is not the character's but the author's, who situates the novel in relation to two genres familiar to American readers, the detective story and the gothic romance.[13] Bombal makes clear that, however exotic the locale—the original book jacket showed a castle shrouded in fog—the story itself will not be unfamiliar; even the protagonist, whatever her nationality, is "very much like other young women." Enticing the reader to enter the "strange house of mist," the prologue establishes that the author writes, and we read, from outside the mist. This demarcation contains the mist, as it were, ensuring that neither reader nor author will be immobilized by it. Rather than merging the poles of the objective and the subjective, Bombal sets them apart.

At the end of the novel, after Helga's story has played out, Bombal once again enters the text by injecting a geographical notation—"Captain's Cottage, Rockport, Maine." If the Prologue is the front frame, this signature is the back frame, for in addition to indicating where the book was written, it takes author and reader out of the realm of fiction and back to the Rockport-solid outside world. As the "strange house of mist" is replaced by a real cottage, the redundantly remote "southern end of South America" gives way to the northeastern tip of the United States. Unlike *La última niebla, House of Mist* posits a life outside the mist, outside the text, for the author and her readers.

Bombal's wholesale revision of *La última niebla* cannot be adequately explained as her misguided attempt to write a best-seller any more than Salinas's *El contemplado* can be explained as an homage to the sea of San Juan. Although money was undoubtedly an incentive, the composition of *House of Mist* also subserved other needs, for it helped Bombal take distance from the turbulent events fictionalized in *La última niebla*. The English language played no small part in this process, for it seconded emotional distance with linguistic separation. Revisiting her life in English, Bombal saw herself in ways unavailable to her in Spanish, as if her mother tongue was part of the fog that beclouded her vision. In such circumstances, the distance between source and medium proved empowering rather than disabling.

Bombal wrote *La última niebla* in Buenos Aires in 1933, where she had moved to get over Eulogio Sánchez, a married man with whom she had an affair that ended with her suicide attempt in his apartment. In Argentina she befriended many of the leading literary lights of the day, including Jorge Luis Borges and Pablo Neruda, at whose kitchen table she wrote the novella. Greeted by glowing reviews from Amado Alonso, Hernán Díaz Arrieta, Ricardo Latcham, and other respected critics, *La última niebla* made Bombal something of a celebrity, her appeal enhanced by her youth, liveliness, and good looks. Still in love with Eulogio Sánchez, her "black angel,"[14] in 1935 she married Jorge Larcos, an openly homosexual painter with whom she had been friends for several years; but Larcos's lifestyle left him little time for his wife, and they separated two years later. She followed her fictional debut with her second novella, *La amortajada* (1938), the monologue of a dead woman who reviews her life during her funeral, which cemented Bombal's reputation as one of Latin America's most original young novelists.

In 1941, back in Chile after an absence of almost ten years, and not having had any contact with Eulogio Sánchez during that time, she ran into him, apparently by chance, as he was leaving an office building in Santiago. Following him down the street, she pulled out a gun from her purse and shot him in the back three times. (It was not only in her fiction that Bombal displayed a flair for the melodramatic.) Sánchez was seriously wounded and she was tried for attempted murder. Eventually acquitted on the grounds of temporary insanity, she left Chile and came to the United States, living first in Washington, D.C., and then New York, where she held several jobs, among them dubbing Hollywood movies into Spanish (she was Judy Garland's voice in the Spanish version of *The Clock*). Early in 1944, a wealthy Chilean acquaintance invited Bombal to his annual ball, which he had moved from Paris to the Waldorf Astoria Hotel in New York City because of the war. Cinderella-like, Bombal borrowed a dress from a friend. At the ball she met a distinguished, white-haired French-born aristocrat, Count Raphael de Saint-Phalle, whose formerly wealthy family had founded the Banque de Saint-Phalle. A widower with several grown children, "Fal" was twenty-five years older than Bombal, an age difference that made him remind her of her father. But unlike her father, who died of a heart ailment when Bombal was nine years old, Fal was strong and healthy, "un viejo macanudo, fuerte como un roble" [a formidable old man, strong like an oak].[15] After a brief courtship, Fal and María Luisa were married on April 1, 1944. Their only child, Brigitte, was born later that year.

Bombal spent the first couple of years of her marriage, perhaps the happiest period of her life, transforming *La última niebla* into *House of Mist*. As she admitted, her first novel had been inspired by her disastrous affair with Eulogio Sánchez: "Mi primera experiencia amorosa fue bastante espantosa, yo lo puse a él como marido, la novela tiene una base autobiográfica bastante trágica y desagradable. [. . .] La novela está basada en mi primer amor, que terminó a balazo limpio" [My first amorous experience was pretty horrendous, I made him the husband; the novel has a fairly tragic and unpleasant autobiographical basis. (...) The novel is based on my first love, which ended with bullets flying] (*OC*, 336). After Bombal's marriage to the fatherly Saint-Phalle, the turmoil of the previous decade seemed to be behind her. She had a young daughter, had settled into the conventional marriage she had always desired, and her well-connected husband knew people in the publishing industry who expressed interest in her work.

House of Mist not only reflects but is part of these changes for the better in Bombal's life. She once said of her English-language writing: "Al editar mis obras en inglés les hice agregados con el fin de decir muchas cosas que antes no había tenido la madurez de decir" [When I published my works in English I made additions with the purpose of saying things that before I didn't have the maturity to say](*OC*, 401). The exteriority of *House of Mist*, its "objective" treatment of the same subject matter as *La última niebla*, is one of those additions that reflect the author's increased maturity, her new-found balance between personal continuity and emotional renewal. In "Piazza Margana" Calvert Casey states, "It is only here that I can be myself," where "here" refers as much to the English language as to his lover Gianni's body.[16] Writing in English was equally valuable to Bombal, but for a different reason; it gave her the opportunity to *not* be herself, to deal with her past in a detached and analytical way. I do not think that Bombal was deeply invested in English, her third language. At home, she spoke French with her husband and Spanish with her daughter. English was a literary medium, not a maternal or conjugal tongue. But because she never developed strong ties to the language, because it was neither *lengua* nor *idioma*, it allowed her to come to terms with her past without becoming absorbed by it, as she had been for many years. Echoing the title of her Argentine movie script, *House of Mist* is a "house of memories," but one that the author can enter and leave. When Bombal looks back on her life from the vantage point of English, she does not try to negate time and distance. Unlike Cabrera Infante's *Holy Smoke* or *Infante's Inferno*, *House of Mist* is not nostalgic. Helga's story pushes the past into the present, not the present into the past.

In a 1952 letter, Bombal discussed her career as a multilingual writer:

Mi destino (literario) siempre ha sido muy raro, complicado, y difícil, y distinto, casi diría anormal. Comencé escribiendo en francés, que yo consideraba mi idioma, el medio de expresión que había conquistado. Las circunstancias hacen que yo deba volver a Sudamérica y mi carrera, mi expresión debió ser en español. Ahora, las circunstancias me empujaron a este país que ha pasado a ser mi país (mi marido es francés-americano, mi hija americana) y resulta pues que me he visto obligada a expresarme en inglés. Tercera etapa, la más difícil y dolorosa, "la prueba de fuego," diría yo. (*OC*, 345)

[My (literary) destiny has always been very strange, complicated, and difficult, and different, I would almost say abnormal. I began writing in French [Bombal went to school in France], which I considered my language, the medium of expression I had mastered. Circumstances made me return to South America and my career, my writing, had to be in Spanish. Now, circumstances have driven me to this country that has become my country (my husband is French-American, my daughter, American) and it turns out that I have been forced to express myself in English. The third stage, the most difficult and painful, the "trial by fire," I would say.]

Because Bombal's career as an anglophone writer has not stirred much interest, I have not been able to find any information on her acquisition of English, a language she must have learned as a child in Viña del Mar, a city that had a large English-speaking population. In 1939, when she first visited New York City as the Chilean delegate to a PEN Congress (the same one that Salinas attended), she spoke English well enough to interview American writers and make friends with Sherwood Anderson, who took her sightseeing in Manhattan. But adopting a new literary medium was surely no easier for her than for Cabrera Infante, who also began writing in English in his thirties. Even in Spanish Bombal worked very slowly; switching to a new language must have seemed to her a nearly unsurmountable ordeal, the "trial by fire," as she said.

Indeed, it is remarkable that she wrote as *much* as she did in English. *House of Mist*, for one, is longer and structurally more complex than *La última niebla*. Whatever help Saint-Phalle gave her with the language (but *his* mother tongue was French), the novel required an act of imaginative construction unprecedented in her work. Rather than dipping into the mental stream of characters much like herself, as she had done in her Spanish novellas, in *House of Mist* she created a fictional world with a large cast of characters, concrete physical settings, and a conventional plot. Devoid of the stifling hermeticism of *La última niebla*, *House of Mist* is accessible, extroverted, like her narrator.

Critics of *La última niebla* have written extensively about Bombal's style, the painstaking care she lavished on every word, every sentence. But even as it makes for memorable prose, this emphasis on expression reinforces the narrative's morose, cloistered ambience. Although *La última niebla*'s protagonist does not seem aware of the act of narration in which she is embarked, her delectation in the words with which she records her feelings and experiences is evident on every page. Helga's English, by contrast, is vehicular, not literary. Less artful but more communicative, she narrates thinking of the message rather than the medium. Bombal once said that, writing in English, she never experienced the "intimate pleasure" (*goce íntimo*) that Spanish gave her (*OC*, 317). Strange as it sounds, this is what *House of Mist* has going for it, its author's inability to enjoy herself, which made possible (in fact, inevitable) a narrative turned outward toward the world, be it that of the reader or that of the characters. In the 1960s Bombal tried to translate *House of Mist* "back" into her mother tongue under the title of "Embrujo" [Bewitchment]. It is not surprising that she failed; her poetic Spanish was not up to her pedestrian English.

Like *La última niebla*, *House of Mist* contains much that is autobiographical. Helga's physique—slight, with dark hair and dark eyes—is reminiscent of the author's, as is Helga's loss of her father from a heart ailment when she was a young child. The Andersen fairy tales that Helga's mother reads to her daughter (from which Helga's name is taken) are the same ones that Bombal's mother read to María Luisa. Helga's mother's surname, Hansen, may allude to Bombal's favorite author, Knut Hamsun. When Helga and Daniel travel to the city, they plan to stay at the "Hotel Astoria," whose name alludes to the New York City hotel where Bombal met Saint-Phalle. Although she moves the locale, she also includes in the novel a fancy ball to which Helga, like Bombal, wears a borrowed dress. Even Helga's getting "absolutely drunk" during that evening (*HM*, 147) evokes Bombal's life-long struggles with alcoholism. And what Helga says about the fictional ball—that it changed her life—applies equally to the impact of the Waldorf-Astoria ball on Bombal's own life.

Some of the revisions clearly aim to distance Bombal from her past. She leaves out of *House of Mist* the character of Regina, Daniel's sister-in-law, who in *La última niebla* tries to kill herself in her lover's home, as Bombal herself had done.[17] Regina is replaced by Mariana, Daniel's sister, who, like Bombal, is married to a French Count, Guy de Nevers (to whom she is not faithful!). And Mariana's name inverts that of *La amortajada*'s protagonist, Ana María, as if the corpse in that novel had been given a new lease on life. But the most telling hint of Bombal's intention to break with her past occurs in the prologue when she states that her book, a "mystery without murder," will not include a corpse, a murder trial, or a murderer. As Roberto Ignacio Díaz shrewdly notes, this passage is a thinly veiled reference to the darkest incident in Bombal's life, her attempted murder of Eulogio Sánchez.[18] Díaz goes on to argue that since the novel's American readers would not have picked up on this, *House of Mist* presupposes a hispanophone reader who would grasp this and other autobiographical clues.[19] Although I agree that the novel includes allusions unintelligible to an American audience, in practical terms the implied hispanophone reader can be no one other than Bombal herself. Using the prologue to confess and exorcise the violent end to her relationship with Eulogio Sánchez, Bombal tells herself that the woman who writes *House of Mist* is a different person from the one who, only four or five years earlier, had tried to murder her lover.

In this light, Helga's discovery that her extramarital affair with David Landa was illusory is yet another act of autobiographical revisionism: "Yes, my flight with Landa was nothing more than a dream! And that other house built by my subconscious self in a night of madness and memories, desires, and mist, was now going back, and crumbling down again into the mist" (*HM*, 244). Significantly, *House of Mist* not only reveals the affair to have been a dream, but it omits the description of the protagonist's night of lovemaking, the most sexually explicit scene written by a Spanish American woman novelist up to that time. Whether prompted by delicacy for Saint-Phalle's feelings, or by her knowledge that such a scene could never be filmed, or by the impossibility of writing about pleasure in a pleasureless tongue, this deletion further disassociates Bombal from the stormy relationship with Sánchez. Reviewed from the perspective of her new life with Saint-Phalle, those episodes may well have seemed like a dream. When Helga states that the story of her life begins where others end, with a wedding, she is speaking for her creator.

The last few chapters of *House of Mist* complete Bombal's rite of fictional passage. After Helga's affair with Landa has been explained away, one more mystery remains, her vivid memory of the house where she and Landa had their imagined tryst. As it happens, Helga's aunt Adelaida has just died and left her house to Helga. When Daniel takes her there, Helga recognizes it as the house in the dream. She doesn't want to go in, but Daniel insists, uttering a sentence that could summarize the whole novel, "You shouldn't be afraid of memories" (*HM*, 235). The moment Helga sets foot in the house memories flood back upon her, for this is none other than her childhood home, the "old house" where she spent her first blissful years with her parents—a house of pleasure indeed, but of the innocent pleasures of a five-year-old child.

Several times in her account Helga mentions that throughout her life she has often dreamed of a flowering tree, a dream that fills her with "great contentment, deep calm, and profound joy" (*HM*, 136). As the

novel ends, she discovers that very tree in the patio of her childhood home.

> "Look, Helga, isn't this the tree of your dreams?"
> I raised my eyes and remained speechless, overwhelmed.
> For, oh miracle! it was my tree! this gigantic mimosa, standing there in
> the midst of crumbling walls, still shedding its perfume on this Spring day
> in Ebba Hansen's patio!
> Yes, it was the Tree of Happiness, this blossoming golden tree,
> swarming with bees, under which Daniel was now enticing me with a
> tender mocking smile while whispering to me, as is usual at the end of all
> old-time love stories:
> "I LOVE YOU."

The novel's conclusion stages one last reversal: As Helga's affair vanishes
into a dream, the tree of her dreams becomes a reality. And it is her real
husband, not her imaginary lover, who has led her to her dream house.
This "miracle" is made possible by one further revision to *La última
niebla,* Daniel's fairy-tale transformation from toad to prince, from
sullen tyrant to loving husband, a transformation that Helga also terms a
"miracle" (*HM,* 181). This change, perhaps Bombal's most unsettling
departure from *La última niebla,* grows out of the conflation in his
character of Eulogio and Fal. Five years older than Helga (as Eulogio was
five years older than Bombal), the "reformed" Daniel differs from his
namesake in *La última niebla* in that he comes to treat his wife with the
solicitude and patience of a kindly father. In Helga's dreams, he even
addresses her as "my child" (*HM,* 51). Using Casey's terminology, one
can say that Bombal's Helga (and Helga's Bombal) exchange "bliss" for
"bienestar," except that here the language values are reversed, since the
locus of well-being is an anglophone fiction. No less regressive than
"Piazza Margana," *House of Mist* takes Bombal back to an Edenic garden
whose Tree of Happiness, the flowering mimosa, serves as the emblem of
emotional rebirth and candid affection (*mimosa* comes from *mimar,* to
pamper). During her murder trial, Bombal explained her failure to find a
suitable companion in this way: "Yo buscaba paz, no pasión. Necesitaba
un cariño que me descansara" [I was looking for peace, not passion. I
needed restful affection].[20] This is what Helga finds in Daniel, and what
María Luisa believed she had found in Fal, to whom *House of Mist* is
dedicated.
Like Calvert Casey, but unlike Cabrera Infante, in English Bombal is a
different writer, and perhaps a different woman, than she is in Spanish. In
a novel so centrally concerned with the issue of fidelity, her forceful

misprision of *La última niebla* cannot but appear like an adulteration. *House of Mist* is indeed a "strange" translation, to use the adjective that Helga repeats like a mantra; but translation, when used as a vehicle for self-invention, is necessarily a strange and estranging enterprise. If the novel seems anomalous, it's because our notions about Bombal's career are based on half a life. Reading *House of Mist* should be no more disconcerting than finding out that María Luisa Bombal's daughter, Brigitte de Saint-Phalle, is a biostatistician who lives in California.

It is condescending to say, as Gloria Gálvez Lira does, that Bombal belongs in the world of dreams and should have stayed there.[21] Although I understand the objections to *House of Mist,* I am impressed by her ability to transform herself and her writing, to take apart *La última niebla* and rebuild it into a different kind of narrative altogether. From the perspective of a modernist aesthetics that values texture over spectacle, *House of Mist* is unsatisfying; and its occasionally lyrical, sometimes awkward and often exclamatory English lacks the subtlety and elegance of Bombal's Spanish. But a writer's best book is not necessarily her most meaningful. Bombal's "I" differs from her "yo" in ways that exceed, and supersede, aesthetic appraisal.

Life rarely imitates old-time love stories, however. Unlike Helga and Daniel, Bombal and Saint-Phalle did not live happily ever after. Even though she said that Fal was the only man who ever made her feel loved, the marriage did not live up to its early promise. As the years went by, Bombal felt increasingly out of place among Saint-Phalle's friends, mostly retired bankers and transplanted European aristocrats. The couple was beset by recurring money problems, and her career as an English-language author foundered. In spite of several tries, Paramount could not come up with an acceptable script for *House of Mist.*[22] *The Shrouded Woman,* a more conventional translation that augmented the original without taking substantial liberties with it, received mixed reviews and did not sell as well. Bombal then spent several years working on *The Foreign Minister,* a long novel completed in 1954 based on the life of the Czech patriot Jan Masaryk, whom she had met in New York; but she couldn't find a publisher, a circumstance that she attributed to the tense political climate of the era. She also tried her hand at plays and TV scripts, though without success. The older she got, the more depressed she became, the more she drank, and the less she saw Brigitte, a "career girl" for whom Bombal would have preferred the life of a housewife (*OC,* 349). After Saint-Phalle's death in 1969, Bombal returned to Chile, living meagerly and in obscurity until her own death in 1980. She left all her unpublished manuscripts, including *The Foreign Minister* and the rest of her English-language writings, to Brigitte, who has shown no interest in retrieving them. To this day they languish in a bank vault somewhere in Santiago de Chile, at the southern end of South America.

Chapter 7

Words That Smell Like Home

Hey, I just do Spanish, I don't explain it.

—*Judith Ortiz Cofer*

Given the number and size of the Spanish-speaking communities of the United States, it is perhaps surprising that what has come to be known as "Latino literature," the imaginative writing by and about Hispanics in this country, exists almost entirely in English. As the monolingual expression of a largely bilingual population, Latino literature detaches culture from language, celebrating the former even as it silences the latter. Even the English of Latino writers, with some exceptions, bears little resemblance to the hybrid sounds and rhythms of the barrios where many of them grew up. What happened to the Garcia girls has also happened to the writers: They have lost their accents. For every Latino writer like Gloria Anzaldúa and Roberto Fernández, who endeavor to reproduce the actual speech, the *idioma*, of a particular group of Latinos, there are several like Cristina Garcia and Julia Alvarez, who translate it into something like George Santayana's Received Standard English.

A principal reason for this is that, by and large, Latino writers do not write for a Latino audience. All those descriptions of foreign foods and ethnic rituals that fill the pages of ethnic novels make clear that the presumed reader is someone who has never dined on *mofongo* or disemboweled a papier-maché donkey. Like other crossover products, Latino literature baits the reader with the lure of the exotic, promising safe, uncompromising access to an unfamiliar world. In this respect, *House of Mist* is "latino." If the original cover of the novel opened the door to a faraway castle, that of Cristina Garcia's *Dreaming in Cuban* (1992), already a classic of the genre, simulates a box of cigars whose seal announces, in English, "Exported from Havana," and, in Spanish, "De Cuba." Figuratively skirting the U.S. embargo on Cuban products, which had been stiffened the very year that the novel was published, *Dreaming in Cuban* trades on the discreet charm of the illicit; enjoying a 200-page whiff of Cuban culture is as simple as tearing the imaginary seal and opening the book-box. Although predicated of the Cuban American protagonist, the title is really addressed to Garcia's non-Cuban readers, who can dream in Cuban merely by reading the novel.

Similarly, Esmeralda Santiago's memoir, *When I Was Puerto Rican* (1993), opens with a prologue entitled "How to Eat a Guava." Puerto Ricans or their Newyorican cousins do not need to learn this skill; but Santiago is not writing for them. One can go through the memoir and find conversation after conversation whose real interlocutor is not the young Esmeralda but the non-Hispanic reader. "What are those, mami?" she asks her mother, pointing to a ribbon-like appendage hanging from a bamboo stem. Thereupon follows a lengthy question-and-answer session on the confection of pig sausages, in the course of which Esmeralda's mother explains what's inside a *morcilla*: "Mostly blood. Some people call it blood pudding."[1] But the people who use this term are the non-Hispanic Americans reading the memoir, since in Spanish *morcillas* are called *morcillas*.

Perhaps more than other types of serious writing, Latino literature caters to the limitations of its audience, which expects that the author and her stand-ins will act as cultural tour guides. If the name of Cristina Garcia's protagonist is the doubly architectonic Pilar Puente, it's not only because she is the support of the story, but because she builds bridges to Cuba for the reader. Like other ethnic writing, Latino literature is bound to a pedagogical imperative that requires it not only to distract, entertain, elevate, but also teach; it must be *útil* as well as *dulce (de guayaba)*. And what does Latino literature teach? For the most part, what its readers already know, or think they know, about Latinos, Latinas, and Latin Americans: that they are slightly wacky, somewhat mysterious, very sensuous, and definitively spiritual. Julia Alvarez illustrates her admiration for a "compañero writer" with this anecdote: "I remember discovering Gabriel García Márquez and giving the novel to my father. He just couldn't put it down, and I told him, Papi, this is called magical realism. He said, what do you mean—this is the way we think!"[2] Since Alvarez includes herself in the "we," she partakes of magical-realist thinking. Yet, since she also can translate her father as saying, "what do you mean—this is the way we think," rather than whatever he originally said, Alvarez may think like a Dominican, but she thinks about thinking like a plain old American. The intercultural bridge is built on anglophone words, that "snowy, blond, blue-eyed, gum-chewing English" that she elsewhere derides.[3]

This is not to say that most Latino writers can choose whether to write in English or Spanish. For many, Spanish is their "heritage language," a tongue learned in childhood and then forgotten or abandoned. Although Alvarez was born in New York City, she did not move permanently to the United States from the Dominican Republic until she was ten years old. Other Latino writers, who were born in this country and raised in English-speaking households, have much less reason to write in Spanish. But even those who are bilingual tend to prefer English as a literary medium, in part because of the paucity of publishing outlets in the Unites States for Spanish-language books. In the last decade the ranks of crossover writers have even swelled with bilingual Latin Americans who have switched to English, apparently not for complicated personal reasons (like Calvert Casey), but in search of larger audiences. Some recent Latin American novels—Carlos Fuentes's *Gringo viejo* (1986) comes to mind—read as if they had been written to be translated. Like that of *House of Mist*, the prose of *Gringo viejo* carries a foretaste of the English-language movie script it was destined to become.

Because of these personal, cultural, and commercial circumstances, the Spanish language plays an increasingly ornamental role in Latino writing. Rather than a medium for literary expression, it has become a token of cultural filiation, like wearing dashikis or dousing your children with violet water. Said differently: Spanish figures in Latino literature as a connotative language, a "secondary signifying system" that establishes the book's or author's membership in Latino or Latin American culture.[4] In this respect, the function of Spanish in John Sayles's *Gusanos* differs little from that in Cristina Garcia's *Dreaming in Cuban*, even though Garcia is Cuban American and Sayles is not. In these books Hispanicisms are invariably set in italics, which produces instant xenity even as it reinforces the English-language norm, and they sometimes remain untranslated, for their specific meaning is less relevant than their ability to connote "Cuban-ness" or "Puertorican-ness" or "Latino-ness." Screaming at her errant husband, Esmeralda's mother asks, "Do those *hijas de la gran puta* know you have children in this Godforsaken hellhole?" (24). So long as the English-speaking reader understands that "hijas de la gran puta" is some sort of invective, it doesn't matter what the phrase means. Indeed, the odd juxtaposition of Spanish and English profanities within the same utterance makes this another of those virtual sentences addressed as much to the readers of the memoir as to one of its protagonists. The Spanish language has no expletives that correspond to "Godforsaken hellhole," an eminently un-Spanish turn of phrase whose component words all have Anglo-Saxon roots. The italicized expletive signifies that Esmeralda's mother, unlike her daughter, is still Puerto Rican; the second one reassures the reader by bringing her speech back to the American vernacular that is the narrative's dominant idiom. Inter-posed between the Spanish and English phrases are the "children," among them Esmeralda, who bridge the linguistic and cultural divide.

As Ernst Rudin has shown, Hispanicisms in Latino literature fall within specific semantic categories—proper names; place names; terms of endearment; babytalk; the vocabulary of music, food, and sex; idioms and proverbs; and interjections, curses, and prayers.[5] If someone were to attempt to learn Spanish from Latino literature, he'd be able to do little else but cuss, pray, make love, and order lunch. Dictated less by the needs of the story than by the desire to give non-Hispanic readers a taste of the foreign flavors they came for, Latino literature's Hispanicisms turn many of these works into formula fiction, novels and memoirs written *for* rather than written *by*. In "The Task of the Translator," Walter Benjamin states that "no poem is intended for the reader, no picture for the beholder, no symphony for the listener."[6] But Benjamin never read *When I Was Puerto Rican*—or my own *Next Year in Cuba,* for that matter.

Nonetheless, the incidence of Spanish in Latino literature is not always or only opportunistic. The connotative use of Spanish can express a writer's awareness of the literary marketplace, but also his or her emotional ties to the language. What is seductively exotic for the reader may be nostalgically familiar for the author. If the anglophone reader gets a *frisson* from all those italicized words, a Latino author may derive a different kind of pleasure from words that take her back to her home culture, "words that smell like your house."[7] Take the opening stanza of "Dulzura," by Sandra Cisneros, whom I've just quoted:

> Make love to me in Spanish.
> Not with that other tongue.
> I want you *juntito a mí,*
> tender like the language
> crooned to babies.
> I want to be that
> lullabied, *mi bien
> querido,* that loved.[8]

With that other tongue, or *in* that other tongue? One preposition evokes the organ, the other the language. Switching between them, the speaker calls attention to her ties to Spanish, a tongue made for touching, emotionally and erotically. Although the Spanish phrases in this stanza fall into predictable categories, they reveal important things about the speaker—her lover's gender, for one, since only in Spanish is the lover identified as male: *juntito a mí.* The Spanish phrases also point to the dilemma that lies at the heart of the poem. Visualizing being loved in Spanish, the speaker portrays herself as the passive recipient of affection, as lullabied baby; but it is in English, "that other tongue," that she asks to be treated in this way. By reverting to Spanish, she alienates herself from her medium. However much the speaker may miss the soothing sounds of Spanish, it seems that she has no other option, as writer and perhaps also as woman, but English.

But if the languages of affection and poetry are incompatible, every tender poem will be riven in half, as this one is. Indeed, after the first stanza, "Dulzura" abandons Spanish altogether, a tacit confirmation that babytalk is unsuitable for poetry, or even for adult communication. Like Casey's, the unbalanced bilingualism of "Dulzura" is a symptom of internal dissension, of the speaker's inability to meld *lengua, idioma,* and *lenguaje.* Consisting of bits of *lengua* and fragments of *idioma,* the poem's residual Spanish evokes a language that is no more available to the speaker than the security she felt as a baby.

In another poem, "You Bring Out the Mexican In Me," Cisneros lists her Mexican traits, from "the *mariachi* trumpets of the blood" to "*barbacoa taquitos* on Sunday."[9] But when she translates the poem's title as "Me sacas lo mexicano en mi," a jarringly unidiomatic sentence, she demonstrates that she may have kept the music and flavor of Mexico, but she has lost most of its *idioma.* In "Dulzura," the speaker's demand that her lover pronounce her name in Spanish, "the way it's supposed to be said," perhaps involves doing something she herself is no longer capable of—hence the anxious, hectoring tone of the poem's conclusion. Cisneros's untranslated Spanish title makes clear the rift between tongue ties and linguistic competence. Like many other Latinos, the speaker of "Dulzura"—a word whose warm, cooing sound disappears in the squeaky sibilance of "sweetness"—feels torn between languages that fulfill different but equally crucial functions. What is more important, the ability to say "I want" or the comforting sensation of being swaddled in one's mother tongue? In the best of all possible word-worlds, both needs would be answered by a single tongue, by one native language, but that is not the world that many bilinguals inhabit.

The work of Richard Rodriguez, perhaps the most widely known and controversial figure in Latino letters, illustrates in a powerful way the tensions glimpsed in Cisneros's poems. In the two decades since its publication, Rodriguez's autobiography, *Hunger of Memory* (1982), has become a fixture in course syllabi and ethnic anthologies. The object of many scathing attacks as well as much fulsome praise, Rodriguez's small volume has been considered a paralyzing exercise in self-hatred as well as an eloquent meditation on the risks and rewards of assimilation. When I teach this book, which I often do, I'm always struck by the vehemence of students' reactions. A few years ago, the final paper of one Mexican American student took the form of a letter, in Spanish, to Rodriguez. After upbraiding him for his opposition to affirmative action, she ended with the following admonition: "Señor Rodríguez, quiero darle un consejo: *get a life!*" Of course, Rodriguez would reply that writing *Hunger of Memory* was his way of getting a life, an instrument for self-invention. As De Man put it years ago, in autobiography the figure determines the referent as much as the referent determines the figure.[10] Whatever we may think of Rodriguez's views on affirmative action or bilingual education, they emerge from the vexed compositional stance that underlies them, a stance determined by the linked issues of sexual and linguistic identity. To evaluate Rodriguez's mixed feelings about Mexico, we have to read what he says—and what he omits to say—about the intrication of gender roles and cultural stereotypes. Before we can understand his opposition to bilingual education, we need to grasp the inner dynamic of his relations with Spanish, his deliberately forsaken mother tongue.

Let me begin with the following proposition: *Hunger of Memory* is the public confession of a man who does not believe in public confessions. Postulating the existence of a gap between inner and outer selves, between private experience and public expression, traditional autobiography assumes that it is not only possible but desirable to bridge that gap. Although Rodriguez buys into the first of these assumptions, he has grave reservations about the second. Early in the book he reminds us that from the time he was a child, he was taught that it is wrong to give public expression to private experience. From the Baltimore Catechism he memorized in parochial school he learned that the sacrament of confession required a secretive oral transaction between priest and sinner. As the nuns said, only the Protestants bare their souls in public. Add to this his parents' disapproval of the smallest acts of public disclosure, and young Richard grows up in the habit of witholding even the most innocuous bit of personal information. When he is asked by a fourth-grade teacher to write about his family, he produces a "contrivance," a "fictionalized account" that bears little resemblance to his actual life.[11] As the mature Rodriguez mentions, disclosures like these—disclosures about the author's reluctance to disclose—make him a most unlikely candidate for autobiographer. No wonder, then, that his story culminates in a chapter entitled "Mr. Secrets."

Rodriguez believes that this moniker, which he earns by refusing to tell his mother about his writing, no longer applies to him. He tells us about his habits of privacy to impress upon us the vast differences between the taciturn boy he was—"I kept so much, so often, to myself" (51)—and the self-disclosing man he has become. By writing publicly about his life, Mr. Secrets has become a tattletale, a metamorphosis with profound personal and cultural implications, for it not only breaks with his family's code of secrecy, but violates the Mexican ethic of reserve or *formalidad*: "Writing these pages, admitting my embarrassment or my guilt, admitting my sexual anxieties and my physical insecurity, I have not been able to forget that I am not being *formal*" (130). In a book full of painful epiphanies, one of the most uncomfortable is the author's lingering awareness that the act of recollection constitutes a betrayal. He cannot remember his childhood without at the same time remembering that he is violating his family's trust, a guilt-ridden admission of *informalidad* that confirms that he is indeed engaged in revealing "what is most personal" (187). As he puts it, "There was a time in my life when it would never have occurred to me to make a confession like this one" (109).

If we now turn to the book's opening paragraph, it does read somewhat like a confession: "I have taken Caliban's advice. I have stolen their books. I will have some run of this isle" (3). But the admission of having broken the seventh commandment turns out to be equivocal, for the fact is that Richard doesn't steal books, he borrows them from the Sacramento Public Library or the British Museum. If we read these sentences in the backlight of the rest of the book, it is difficult to understand what sin Rodriguez is owning up to. Moreover, the invocation of Caliban as the author's brutish muse clashes with the book's style, tone, and content. After all, whereas Caliban curses Prospero, Rodriguez offers benedictions to the American way, and his refined, self-conscious prose is anything but calibanesque.[12] A few pages into the prologue Rodriguez himself will switch allegiances by labelling his narrative "Ariel's song," an identification reinforced by the title of the first chapter, "Aria." Rodriguez may behave like Caliban, but he writes with Ariel-like grace.

These ambiguities complicate the author's confessional gestures, for they turn his account into something other than an informal act of self-disclosure. In fact *Hunger of Memory* is an extraordinarily reticent autobiography, a book of revelations that often reads like a mystery story. Even at his most personal, at his most confessional, Rodriguez is nothing if not *formal,* a word whose variants recur throughout the book. He asserts, for example, that autobiography's goal is "to form new versions of oneself" (190), that the purpose of education is "radical self-reformation" (67), that he was taught that a man should be "feo, fuerte y formal" [ugly, strong, and formal] (128). Since there is little in *Hunger of Memory* that could be termed misshapen or unformed, monstrous Caliban, the "freckled whelp" of Shakespeare's play, could never be Rodriguez's muse. As Ramón Saldívar has pointed out, each of the chapters is a set piece, a carefully crafted tableau that organizes different aspects of the author's life around a central theme: "Complexion," "Credo," "Profession."[13] Rather than narrating his life experiences, Rodriguez distills them, reduces them to abstractions. This generalizing impulse extends even to the people in his life, who are seldom identified by a proper name; instead, they are referred to according to their relationship with the author: "my brother," "my sister," "my editor," "the person who knows me best." Even his parents do not escape anonymity, for not once does Rodriguez provide their given names. In fact, the only important cognomen in the whole book is the author's, a situation that, while not unique in autobiographical writing, is certainly unusual.

As the metaphorical "hunger" of the title makes clear, Rodriguez's autobiography moves relentlessly from the concrete to the abstract, from the individual to the categorical. Rather than giving narrative shape to his life, Rodriguez elects a coherence based on the subordination of incident to theme. Rather than telling stories, he offers illustrations; instead of dwelling on details, he jumps to conclusions. His overriding criterion is intelligibility, an essayist's virtue, rather than narrative interest, the storyteller's goal. His justification for this approach is that since he is writing an account of his education, of his self-reformation, the book should reflect the outcome of the process—his ability to abstract from experience:

> My need to think so much and so abstractly about my parents and our relationship was in itself an indication of my long education. My father and mother did not pass their time thinking about the cultural meanings of their experience. It was I who described their daily lives with airy ideas. And yet, *positively*. The ability to consider experience so abstractly allowed me to shape into desire what otherwise would have remained indefinite, meaningless longing. (72)

As I read this passage, I want to ask what it means to "shape into desire." Desire can be expressed, repressed, sublimated; it can attach to specific objects or float free. But how does one shape, that is, mold or *form* something into desire? Modern wisdom has it the other way around: We don't shape our desires; they shape us, mostly in ways of which we are not even aware. The notion of shaping desire verges on the solecistic, but not any more so than the title of the chapter in which this passage appears, "The Achievement of Desire." If one reads "achievement" in its primitive sense, the achievement of desire is synonymous with its termination. When Rodriguez conjugates desire, its libidinal grounding gets lost in abstraction. He treats desire much as he treats hunger, as a figure, a rhetorical and intellectual entity. Although he asserts that he is "engaged in writing graffiti" (187), the coarse, elemental scribblings that one finds in bathroom stalls have nothing to do with *Hunger of Memory*'s genteel formulations. Perhaps Caliban could write graffiti, but I doubt that he would know how to shape or achieve desire. In fact, by describing his abstractions as "airy ideas," Rodriguez once again allies himself with Ariel, which suggests that the distinction between shaped desires and indefinite longings recovers that between tame Ariel and unruly Caliban. If so, the underlying subject of Rodriguez's narrative is his gradual de-Calibanization.

In a fine essay about *Hunger of Memory*, Paul John Eakin has called attention to the presence of two voices in this book, one narrative and the other expository.[14] For Eakin these voices reflect the split in Rodriguez's authorial persona between the essayist and the storyteller, and he points out that most of the chapters in the book were originally written as opinion pieces for various newspapers and magazines. What I would add to Eakin's insight is that the two voices are not only distinct but, to some extent, dissonant. Although Rodriguez's deftness makes their mingling seem harmonious, the expository voice acts to mute or drown out the narrative voice. Rather than two voices singing in concert, the book offers an active and a passive voice: the active voice of the essayist, the passive voice of the autobiographer. Rodriguez admits as much when he describes his book as "essays impersonating an autobiography" (7). Asked by his editor to write the book "in stories," Rodriguez demurs, asserting that his "most real life" lies in his controversial views on such issues as bilingualism and affirmative action (7).

I would also suggest that the two voices that Eakin hears could well be, at bottom, the shaped voice of desire and the indefinite voice of longing—Ariel's song and Caliban's gabble.[15] And what may be happening in Rodriguez's memoir is what often happens elsewhere: Conscious assessments suppress recalcitrant urges. Much closer to the Santayana of *Persons and Places* than to the Casey of "Piazza Margana," Rodriguez shapes in order to sublimate. It is telling that he never relates an incident whose meaning he does not understand. He assures us that he is revealing "what is most personal," and yet what is most personal is often what is most puzzling. But there is little room for puzzlement in *Hunger of Memory*. Every fragment of narrative, every anecdote or story is firmly embedded within an expository context that determines its significance. Rodriguez gives his readers less a life than a vita, a conspectus of emblematic incidents and achievements carefully arranged by heading. As a result, we come to the end of the book without knowing very much about large areas of his life. Particularly in the later chapters, he devotes as much space to thinking about autobiography as he does to writing one. Rather than an emperor without clothes, Rodriguez is a well-dressed strip-tease artist, but one who insists on his nakedness so often that after a while we begin to believe him.

Since Rodriguez offers his story as a "parable" about the consequences, good and bad, of leaving home, references to the house where he grew up frame his account. If the first chapter opens by evoking the day when he first left his home to go to elementary school, the last chapter concludes by showing the grown-up Rodriguez leaving his childhood home again after a Christmas dinner. Between these two scenes, almost any time that his parents' house is mentioned Rodriguez includes a reference to the screen door at its entrance. Underscoring the isolation of his family, he explains: "Outside the house was public society; inside the house was private. Just opening or closing the screen door behind me was an important experience" (16–17). And: "Until I was six years old I remained in a magical realm of sound. I didn't need to remember that realm because it was present to me. But then the screen door shut behind me as I left home for school. At last I began my movement toward words" (39). The memory of the door even accompanies him to the British Museum, where many years later he researches his dissertation on Renaissance pastoral. Hearing some Spaniards whispering to each other in Spanish, he has a flashback: "Their sounds seemed ghostly voices recalling my life. Yearning became preoccupation then. Boyhood memories beckoned, flooded my mind. (Laughing intimate voices. Bounding up the front steps of the porch. A sudden embrace inside the door)" (71).

Whatever this door may have looked like in reality, in his recollections Rodriguez imagines it as a protective barrier: opaque rather than transparent, occlusive rather than permeable. If his childhood home is a world apart, a Spanish-language fortress, that door is the bulwark that keeps intruders away. These associations become stronger when the screen door is contrasted to another door in the book. Speaking of his boyhood friendships with non-Mexican children, Rodriguez relates: "In those years I was exposed to the sliding-glass-door informality of middle-class California family life. Ringing the doorbell of a friend's house, I would hear someone inside yell out, 'Come on in, Richie; door's not locked'" (179). Unlike the screen door, which separates, this door connects. If the screen door is a buffer, the sliding-glass door is a bridge. If one encloses, the other exposes. In the typical middle-class American household—let's not forget that Rodriguez writes as "a middle-class American man" (3)—the transition from inside to outside, from private to public, from the family circle to the social sphere, is gradual rather than abrupt. Middle-class Americans "yell out" from inside their homes. Instead of two separate worlds, there is one continuous, uniform space.

The recurrence in this context of the key notion of informality suggests that Rodriguez's education can be summarized as the passage from working-class Mexican formality to middle-class American informality, an evolution that the narrative images as the replacement of a screen door with a sliding-glass door. And since Catholic confession takes place behind a screen—typically a screen with a sliding cover—the image of the sliding-glass door also implies a departure from the confessional model. Speaking to a non-Hispanic audience a couple of years after the publication of *Hunger of Memory*, Rodriguez described his life as a move "out of my house and over to yours."[16] The architectural imagery in the book bears out this assertion.

The difficulty is that Rodriguez's implicit identification of *Hunger of Memory* with glass rather than screen, with openness rather than enclosure, with yelling out rather than keeping in, runs counter to our experience of the book. It is hard to see *Hunger of Memory* as an autobiographical correlate of "sliding-glass-door informality." Even the syntax of this phrase, with its string of modifiers linked by hyphens, clashes with Rodriguez's usual diction, which segments rather than joins. Writers have their favorite punctuation marks. Hemingway loved his commas; Milan Kundera has spoken of his affection for the semicolon; the Cuban poet José Kozer cannot versify without parentheses. Nothing if not punctilious, Rodriguez favors the period. He interposes them between adjectives—"Eccentric woman. Soft. Hard." (36); uses them to split appositions—"A woman of Mexico. The woman in long black dresses that reached down to her shoes" (36); puts them in the way of infinitives and conjunctions—"Dark-skinned. To be seen at a Belgravia dinner party. Or New York" (3). There is no "sliding" in Rodriguez's prose; each chapter, each paragraph, each sentence, appears as a discrete, free-standing unit, a cameo or miniature. What Casey's *simulador* says about himself—"Mi aliento literario es corto, desigual" [My literary breath is short, uneven][17]—applies to Rodriguez, whose prose is also short-winded, pause-pregnant, concise to the point of constriction. At times, the halting rhythm gives the impression of great effort, as the periods between words punctuate the slow pace of composition: "A college essay took me several nights to prepare. Suddenly everything I wrote seemed in need of revision. I became a self-conscious writer. A stylist" (182). At other times, the impression is that the periods serve to button-up uncomfortable feelings, as when he relates an encounter with Mexican construction workers: "The dark sweating faces turned toward me as I spoke. They stopped their work to hear me. Each nodded in response. I stood there. I wanted to say something more" (135). In the anglophone Rodriguez as in the hispanophone Casey, parataxis bespeaks repression. Life is full of ifs, ands, and buts.

Since Rodriguez has asserted that "autobiography is the genre of the discontinuous life,"[18] it is not surprising that he should write discontinuous, paratactic prose. The style is the man, or at least the mannerism. And there is much in this book that speaks of discontinuity: between Spanish and English, between parents and children, between home and school, between longing and desire, between the young Ricardo and the adult Richard. My point, however, is that the book's diction is far removed from the agglutinative impetus of an expression like "sliding-glass-door informality," where the words come together, syntactically and typographically, as they do also in the prepositional phrase that completes the thought—"of middle-class California family life." Diction like this is quite rare in *Hunger of Memory,* for instead of a life on the hyphen, Rodriguez draws a portrait in pieces, a mosaic of frozen, fragmentary poses.

Composed in the image and likeness of the house and the family and the culture that the author has supposedly outgrown, his autobiography is more screen than glass. As Tomás Rivera suggested years ago, there are moments when *Hunger of Memory* reads like a crabbed and crabby postscript to Octavio Paz's *El laberinto de la soledad* (1950), a book whose influence Rodriguez has acknowledged.[19] What Paz did for (or to) the *pachuco,* the zoot-suited teenager of the barrio, Rodriguez does for (or to) the *pocho,* his assimilated cousin from the suburbs. In spite of the author's claims to the contrary, *Hunger of Memory* is a profoundly "Mexican" performance, another *máscara mexicana,* at least according to Paz's notions of *mexicanidad.* In this context, Rodriguez's characterization of his memoir as "essays impersonating an autobiography" takes on added meaning, as does his self-portrait as a "great mimic" (67). Paz writes, "el mexicano se me aparece como un ser que se encierra y se preserva: máscara el rostro y máscara la sonrisa [...] Entre la realidad y su persona establece una muralla, no por invisible menos infranqueable" [the Mexican appears to me as a being who encloses and withholds himself: his face a mask, his smile a mask. (...) Between reality and his person he erects a wall, no less impassable for being invisible] (29). These sentences also describe the protagonist of *Hunger of Memory,* who may be much less of a *pocho* than he thinks. One man's wall is another man's screen door.

The question now is: If *Hunger of Memory* turns out to be a wall of words, an artfully reticulated screen, what lies behind it? Half of the answer has to do with Rodriguez's homosexuality, which he hardly mentions. Limiting himself to a couple of brief, equivocal references to his "sexual anxieties" (30), Rodriguez writes as if issues of sexuality had played no part in making him the man he has become. Yet one suspects that his reticence on this score may reflect not that there is little to be said, but that there is too much; and some of the difficulties with *Hunger of Memory,* one reason why it has seemed such a elusive book, is that Rodriguez attributes to class or race or culture conflicts and insecurities that have rather—or also—to do with sexuality.[20] The second half of the answer, not unrelated to the first, is that what lies behind the screen door is the Spanish language, that "magical realm of sound" that Rodriguez and his siblings inhabited until they started school. Although Rodriguez places the theme of language at the center of his autobiography, the abstractness of his formulation once again diverts attention from the concrete circumstances. When he states that "language has been the great subject of my life" (7), the singular subject masks the plural reality of his upbringing, the fact that until he was six years old he spoke only Spanish. It is not language in the abstract but his intense ties to two specific languages, Spanish and English, that may be the great (if unacknowledged) subject of his life. Nonetheless, the mask is the message: What lies behind the screen door is what always lay behind the screen door, those "ghostly" hispanophone voices that he hears even in so improbable a setting as the "reading room" of the British Museum.

Although the number of Spanish words in *Hunger of Memory* is minimal, the book as a whole is haunted by Spanish—not by Spanish words exactly, not by a language in the usual sense of the term, but by something less formed, less formal. He remembers: "Family language: my family's sounds. Voices singing and sighing, rising, straining, then surging, teeming with pleasure that burst syllables into fragments of laughter" (17). As syllables shatter into laughter, Spanish becomes an euphoric, logoclastic phonation that is both more and less than a language. It is more than a language because it serves as the channel for intimacy; it is less than a language because this channel cannot be used for articulate communication. For Rodriguez, Spanish is rich in significance but poor in signification. As *lengua* rather than *idioma* or *lenguaje,* the meaning of its utterances matters less than the connotation of their sound: "My parents would say something to me and I would feel embraced by the sounds of their words. Those sounds said: *I am speaking with ease in Spanish. I am addressing you in words I never use with* los gringos. *I recognize you as someone special, close, like no one outside. You belong with us. In the family*" (16). About his grandmother he remarks, "The words she spoke were almost irrelevant to that fact—the sounds she made" (37).

When Rodriguez characterizes Spanish, he invariably resorts to a musical vocabulary. In the banter with his siblings, "a word like *sí* would become, in several notes, able to convey added measures of feeling" (18; in Spanish *si* is a note on the musical scale). His own Spanish name consists of "three notes, *Ri-car-do*" (21; "do," of course, is another note). Recalling his father's arrival from work in the evenings, he writes: "I remember many nights when my father would come back from work, and I'd hear him call out to my mother in Spanish, sounding relieved. In Spanish he'd sound light and free notes he could never manage in English" (18). In this resonant household, even the screen door has a "clicking tongue" (17). In a more radical way than any other writer I have discussed, Rodriguez strips Spanish of everything but its voice print, its physical reality as a distinctive orchestration of sounds, what he calls "intimate utterance" (36). Even more than Cisneros, he turns Spanish into baby-talk or "motherese," caressing coos and gurgles that have not yet evolved into intelligible speech. Evoking his and his siblings language play, he employs an image that conjures up the picture of a child at his mother's breast: "Tongues explored the edges of words, especially the fat vowels" (18). Later, he refers to the "hiccuping sounds" of his broken Spanish; when he is forced to speak it to Mexican relatives, he "coughs up" a "warm silvery sound" (28). In English, Rodriguez is an articulate artist; in Spanish, a hiccuping baby. As he mentions, it is only when the screen door shuts behind him that he begins his movement toward words.

Since the opposite of wordless sounds is soundless words, Rodriguez's view of Spanish cannot be divorced from the primacy he gives to the written over the spoken word. The distinction between Spanish and English folds into the contrast between speech and writing: words first, English only.[21] In his daily anglophone life, he explains, "I rush past the sounds of voices attending only to the words addressed to me. Voices seem planed to an even surface of sound. A business associate speaks in a deep baritone, but I pass through the timbre to attend to his words" (33). When Rodriguez speaks of Spanish, he musicalizes; when he speaks of English, he becomes tone deaf. Could it be that he secretly loathes the sounds of English as much as he loves those of Spanish? If he actually let

himself listen to English, would he (like Cernuda) hear only noise—
ruido, ruido, ruido? Writing *Variaciones sobre tema mexicano,* Cernuda
enclosed himself a noise-proof Spanish music room. But Rodriguez lacks
this option. Like a man who tries to hear by putting on earplugs, he
chooses a medium for recollection, English, that silences some of his
most indispensable memories, the sounds of his mother tongue. Although
maybe the truth is that he cultivates deafness because he knows that he
cannot hear. If self-writing is a way of dressing wounds, the hurt that
Rodriguez dresses and redresses is a wound of language. His English
prose is a silent screen, a technique of *simulación* that mutes a certain
kind of inarticulateness, Rodriguez's inability to speak what he calls,
tragically echoing Santayana, "su *proprio* idioma" (29; my italics).[22] This
unsatisfied hunger underlies his attachment to Italian opera and the
Roman mass. His description of "old Spanish words" as "tender accents
of sound" (24) translates the title of an aria in Bellini's *I Puritani.* As
"blank envelopes of sound" that echo Spanish words (98–99), the Latin
liturgy also serves as a surrogate mother tongue.

But it would be too simple to say that *Hunger of Memory* is Rodriguez's valedictory to Spanish, a "work of mourning." Grieving for the
loss of one language in another is tricky, because the act of mourning is
implicated in the death. By grieving for Spanish in English, Rodriguez
works through the extinction of his mother tongue in the language that
extinguished it. In this situation, the gestures of mourning turn against
the mourner. Since the loss is self-inflicted, Rodriguez cannot grieve
without self-reproach, which turns lament into torment and mourning
into melancholy. After all, Spanish has died only *in him*; what has
become extinct is not the language but his ability to use it. Of the two
tongues within Rodriguez's mother tongue, the dead one is the child's,
not the mother's. This is what the images of coughing up or vomiting
suggest, that Spanish has spoiled inside him. His second book, *Days of
Obligation* (1992), begins: "I am on my knees, my mouth over the
mouth of the toilet, waiting to heave. It comes up with a bark. All the
badly pronounced Spanish words I have forced myself to sound during
the day, bits and pieces of Mexico spew from my mouth, warm, half-
understood, nostalgic reds and greens dangle from the long strands of
saliva."[23]

In a essay written in the mid-seventies, Rodriguez explained his
relation with Spanish:

> Coming from a home in which mostly Spanish was spoken, I had to decide
> to forget Spanish when I began my education. To succeed in the class-
> room, I needed psychologically to sever my ties with Spanish. Spanish

represented an alternate culture as well as another language—and the basis of my deepest sense of relationship to my family. Although I recently taught myself to read Spanish, the language that I see on the printed page is not quite the language I heard in my youth. That other Spanish, the spoken Spanish of my family, I remember with nostalgia and guilt. [. . .] Yet, having lost the ability to speak Spanish, I never forgot it so totally that I could not understand it. Hearing Spanish spoken on the street reminded me of the community I once felt a part of, and still cared deeply about. I never forgot Spanish so thoroughly, in other words, as to move outside the range of its nostalgic pull. Such moments of guilt and nostalgia were, however, just that—momentary. They punctuated the history of my otherwise successful progress from *barrio* to classroom.[24]

Throwing up is also momentary, but it may be a symptom of chronic disease. What Rodriguez describes here, in prose more transparent than any in *Hunger of Memory,* is the knot of a tongue tie. He says that as a young man he "had to decide to forget Spanish." But how does one decide to forget something? A decision to forget is as unnatural, and perhaps as unrealizable, as a decision to desire. When Rodriguez refers in the last sentence to his "otherwise successful progress," the qualifier undercuts the assertion, for the extirpation of one's native tongue makes an otherwise successful education very nearly a failure. Not because of some vague, sentimental attachment to one's "roots," but because of the profound and necessarily inexpressible damage to the men and women who suffer this loss. The conquest of English cannot console us for the loss of Spanish. In some ways, it makes it worse. Early in his life Rodriguez decided that the convenience of English-only was preferable to paradoxes of a bilingual self. But when these paradoxes speak one's intimate truth, as they do in "Dulzura," convenience can spawn deeper and more intractable dilemmas.

For Rodriguez, the logical follow-up to the regurgitation of Spanish was the ingestion of English: "I represent someone who has swallowed English and now claims it as *my language,* your books as *my books.*"[25] But *Hunger of Memory* suggests that English was hard to swallow, for Rodriguez writes neither easily nor with ease. However polished, his prose is all burps and stutters. Perhaps Rodriguez is afraid that if he were to remove the caesuras, unstop the end-stops, only foulness would spew out. But who knows? Were Richard to eroticize his language as Casey did in "Piazza Margana," were he to make his mother tongue the organ he makes love in and with, Ariel's song might begin to sound like Caliban's gabble, and be all the richer for it.

Discussing his passion for opera, Rodriguez states: "At one moment the song simply 'says' something. At another moment the voice stretches out the words—the heart cannot contain!—and the voice moves toward pure sound. Words take flight" (38). Like an aria, *Hunger of Memory* says many things, but it also contains—and fails to contain—the far cry of Spanish vocables, the *ay* inside the aria. Rodriguez responds to the loss of Spanish sounds by seeking shelter in English words (the original title of the book was "Toward Words"). But his autobiography is valuable not only because of his way with words, but because of the muffled music in the spaces between them. Rodriguez abandons his mother tongue, but he cannot escape her. He escapes his mother tongue, but he cannot abandon her. Every word in his memoir spells out his hunger for a sweetness that can only be had in *dulzura*.

Like Richard Rodriguez, Judith Ortiz Cofer spoke Spanish before she spoke English. The author of several volumes of poetry, as well as of a semi-autobiographical novel (*The Line of the Sun*, 1989) and a memoir (*Silent Dancing*, 1990), Ortiz Cofer was born in Puerto Rico but raised in Paterson, New Jersey. Like Rodriguez, once she began school in the United States her second language gradually replaced her first, and now Ortiz Cofer writes only in English. Her first book of poems, *Reaching for the Mainland* (1987), concludes with a poem entitled "Lesson One: I Would Sing":

> In Spanish, "cantaría" means I would sing,
> "Cantaría bajo de la luna,"
> I would sing under the moon.
> "Cantaría cerca de tu tumba,"
> By your grave I would sing,
> "Cantaría de una vida perdida,"
> Of a wasted life I would sing,
> If I may, if I could, I would sing.
> In Spanish the conditional
> is the tense of dreamers,
> of philosophers, fools, drunkards,
> of widows, new mothers, small children,
> of old people, cripples, saints, and poets.
> It is the grammar of expectation and
> the formula for hope; "Cantaría, amaría, viviría,"
> Please repeat after me.[26]

There are two poems inside this poem; both are dirges, but one is a Spanish song, while the other one is a Spanish lesson. The Spanish song sings of the death of a loved one; the Spanish lesson teaches that such singing is impossible. Why? Because the language of song has itself been lost. None of the three Spanish phrases in the poem can stand by itself. Each is half an utterance—a "then-clause" without the requisite "if-clause." The missing antecedent does appear in the poem, and Ortiz Cofer places it right in the middle of it, but in English: "If I may, if I could, I would sing." The switch in languages justifies the negation implicit in the conditional tense: The speaker cannot sing because she lacks the words to accompany her song. The poem's center, structurally as well as emotionally, is the middle clause of line eight, "if I could."

Coming at the end of a collection whose title alludes to crossing over from the island to the mainland, existentially and literarily, "Lesson One" illustrates the difficulties of language mourning. That the implied setting for the poem is a classroom indicates that Spanish, once the speaker's mother tongue, is now a foreign language. In this hypothetical class—hypothetical like a conditional sentence—the speaker plays the part of both instructor and student, for rather than speaking to an imaginary audience, she is talking to herself. The split into Spanish teacher and American student suggests a more profound division into "Spanish" and "American" selves. The song within the lesson does name an addressee, the *tú* next to whose grave she would sing. But as the recapitulation of the penultimate verse makes clear, that *tú* is Ortiz Cofer herself: She would sing, she would love, she would live—if only she could. As in *Hunger of Memory,* the object of mourning is not external to the mourner. Lamenting the extinction of her mother tongue, the mourner mourns for a part of herself. Cofer mourns for Ortiz. It is by the grave of her own Spanish-speaking self that she would sing.

I don't personalize the poem out of a whim. In *Woman in Front of the Sun* (2000), Ortiz Cofer, a professor of English at the University of Georgia, relates the reaction of her students when they first walk into her classroom:

> The fact that English is my second language does not seem to matter beyond the first few lectures, when the students sometimes look askance at one another, perhaps wondering whether they have walked into the wrong classroom and at any moment this obviously "Spanish" professor will ask them to start conjugating regular and irregular verbs. They can't possibly know this about me: in my classes, everyone is safe from Spanish grammar recitation. Because almost all of my formal education has been in English, I avoid all possible risk of falling into a discussion of the uses of the conditional or the merits of the subjunctive tense in the Spanish language: Hey, I just *do* Spanish, I don't explain it.[27]

What Ortiz Cofer avoids in real life is what she fantasizes about in "Lesson One": a discussion of the uses of the conditional and the merits of the subjunctive. The witticism at the end, meant to release tension, only underscores her anxiety about her lack of fluency in Spanish. By the end of the passage, Ortiz Cofer has put herself in the position of her students, for she also fears that she is going to be quizzed about her Spanish skills. The comeback that she only "does" Spanish is a meaningless laugh line, especially for a writer as subtle as Ortiz Cofer. Since a crucial component of our self-image is the idea we have of ourselves as language users, one of the most disabling forms of self-doubt arises from the conviction that we cannot speak our native language well enough. When the young Rodriguez gets a summer job that requires him to speak with Mexican *braceros,* he confesses: "As I started to speak, I was afraid with my old fear that I would be unable to pronounce the Spanish words" (264). In my own classes, where grammar recitation is not unknown, I have witnessed this fear many times in students of Hispanic background. I have seen how they squirm and look away when you call on them, when they think you think they should speak like natives. I have often squirmed and looked away myself, feeling that no matter how good my Spanish may be, it is just not good enough, not what it should be for someone born and raised in a Spanish-speaking country: If I may, if I could, *I* would sing.

Once these feelings of lingual inadequacy take hold, they are difficult to eradicate. The last line of "Lesson One"—"Please repeat after me"— hints that the work of language mourning never ends. Longing for Spanish in Spanish is a form of having, as in Cernuda's "Retrato de poeta." But longing for Spanish in a different tongue deepens the loss. Rodriguez tries to escape this cycle by silencing both his mother and his other tongue, but he does not succeed, not only because his enterprise is psychically destructive—muteness mutilates—but because muteness speaks volumes, among them *Hunger of Memory.* The only release from death is resurrection. Those of us of who fret about the passing of our mother tongue have one escape: bringing her back to life. It's not easy, but tongues are organs that regenerate, and what we take for death is often only dormancy. If you miss it, you haven't lost it. If you genuinely feel its absence, it's still with you. Supply the missing condition and finish the sentence. After "Lesson One" comes "Lesson Two," which drills the present indicative: *Canto, amo, vivo, hablo.*

Please repeat after me.

Epilogue

I'm Cuban—What's *Your* Excuse?

In one of my favorites *I Love Lucy* episodes, Lucy hires a language tutor to help her Cuban husband improve his English pronunciation. The stuffy, bow-tied Mr. Livermore, delightfully played by Hans Conreid, speaks English with an outrageously affected British accent. During the first lesson, Mr. Livermore instructs his class (which also includes Lucy, Fred, and Ethel) on the correct pronunciation of the English vowels. Lucy, Fred, and Ethel imitate Livermore's fastidious enunciation well enough, but Ricky pronounces the vowels in Spanish. Livermore cannot believe his ears. He goes through the vowels again, accompanying himself with hand gestures to emphasize their open or closed sounds, and asks Ricky to repeat after him. Ricky does no better the second time—"ah," "eh," "ee," "oh," "oo." Stunned, Livermore asks, "Mr. Ricardo, wherever did you acquire that odd pronunciation?" Ricky replies, "I'm Cuban, what's *your* excuse?"

I'm Cuban too, and that's *my* excuse—both for my accent and for this book. I set out to study other bilinguals' tongue ties to gain insight into mine. It was not until halfway through the book, however, that I realized that its real subject was not "language loyalty" (as I had originally framed the topic), but the impact of the English language on the lives and careers of Spanish, Spanish American, and Latino writers in whom I saw bits and pieces of myself. From Santayana to Ortiz Cofer, all the writers I have discussed claim Spanish as their mother tongue; and all had their lives changed by the entrance or intrusion of the English language, which nudged, rubbed against, and in some instances shoved aside their mother tongue.

This pattern holds true for me, as it does for millions of other U.S. Hispanics with different backgrounds from mine. Although I did not move to the United States until I was almost an adolescent, I cannot remember a time before I knew English. When I was growing up in Havana, my mother wielded her knowledge of English as a weapon against strangers, in-laws, and even my father, who understood the language well enough but never spoke it. In the car, at the beach, or over the dinner table, she would often address me and my brothers and sister in English. I must have answered back in Spanish, because I can't remember actually uttering a complete English sentence until I was in sixth grade in an American elementary school. I do remember sitting in the living room of our Cuban house, getting lessons in pronunciation from *my* English tutor, *tía* Mary, who spoke even better English than my mother. Rather than the vowels, it was the contraction "didn't" that stumped me. The way I pronounced it, the second "d" was either too strong—"diddint"—or not strong enough—"dint." To this day I'm not sure I've mastered that slippery consonant.

After we settled in Miami, the American vernacular gradually, almost imperceptibly, crept up on my *idioma cubano,* even though I still spoke Spanish most of the time. I used English to communicate with teachers and American classmates, but in my family and among my friends Spanish prevailed, particularly since we were all planning to return to Cuba at any moment. Although I'm sure that all through high school I remained Spanish-dominant, I never thought of my command of English as deficient, perhaps because I lived among other Cuban exiles. A few years later, I was very puzzled when I got back my first assignment in a creative writing class and the instructor wrote that although he didn't like my story, "at least your English is good." It had never occurred to me that it wouldn't be. What Mr. Genaro probably intended as a compliment, and what others may interpret as an insult, I took as a weird, off-the-wall remark.

For most of my adult life, the language I have felt uneasy about has been Spanish, not English; my mother tongue, not my second language. Even though I'm not certain when this unease began, by the time I was in graduate school I felt more comfortable in classes where the professors were not Spaniards or Latin Americans, and any time I had a choice I would write term papers in English. The paradox—but perhaps it's not a paradox but a consequence—is that I was preparing myself to make a living as a professor of Spanish, which I have done now for nearly twenty-five years. To justify why I wrote in English, I cited careerist reasons; but I have always known that my avoidance of Spanish did not have to do solely with professional ambition. I teach in Spanish, sometimes publish poetry in Spanish, and have written a fair amount of literary criticism in Spanish; yet I have always thought of myself as an anglophone writer. Although I still speak English with a Cuban accent (more or less noticeable depending on my stress level), I'm relieved to be judged by my English rather than by my Spanish sentences. Not necessarily because I "do" English better, but because I don't take personally ungrammaticalities and infelicities in English. To the Mr. Livermores in my life I can always reply, "I'm Cuban, what's *your* excuse?"

I cannot dispose of criticisms of my Spanish so lightly. Since I insist I'm still Cuban, even after all these years, I should speak and write it like a native. According to E. M. Cioran, only in our mother tongue do we have a right to make mistakes. But for people who tie their identity to their nationality, as exiles often do, and who then tie their nationality to their speech, as exiles also do, their mother tongue is the only language in which they cannot afford to make mistakes. If I'm speaking Spanish and I hear myself fumbling for words, I get embarrassed. Every time I commit an anglicism, I cringe. Criticize my English, and your words will never hurt me. Criticize my Spanish, and you're attacking *me,* my deepest convictions and theories about myself.

As I have gotten older, I have become more willing to admit to mother-tongue anxiety. I understand better its causes and occasions, and my lingual superego treats me less harshly than it used to. At the same time, I have also become more aware of my need for Spanish. Not for the Spanish that I speak in the classroom or that I use to talk to my mother every Sunday, but for a deeper, more personal Spanish, a tongue that is mine alone. A few years ago, when I turned fifty, my American life wasn't going all that well. I decided that it wasn't too late to reach out and back to my mother tongue. After all, though I may not recall it, there *was* a period in my life before I knew English. Even my anglophile Cuban mother lullabies and prays only in Spanish. Before I learned to speak, my ear was tuned to the scale of Spanish vowels. As in Cisneros's "Dulzura," inside my bilingual adult self there was a monolingual baby crying to get out. So I wrote a little book in Spanish, about Spanish, a combination language proficiency test and belated love poem.

I have never written more easily, or with more ease. Every word seemed newly minted—and newly minted for me. Those I liked best did not have English cognates *(pericia, destierro, retruécano)* or the cognates were unexpected or misleading *(fracaso, vilo, recuerdo);* but there were none I didn't like. Just putting accents was a thrill, generating an *ñ* an occasion for celebration (in spite of the many-stroked tilde). Every time I got lost inside those expansive periods of Spanish sentences, I relished the adventure. Somehow I always found my way out. I know what Bombal meant when she said that in English she never experienced the *goce íntimo* that Spanish gave her. (Somewhere between "joy" and "bliss," *goce* is another of those words without a good English equivalent.) In English I write silently, hearing the words only in my head. Composing *Cincuenta lecciones de exilio y desexilio* (2000), my Spanish book, I found myself sounding out each word, reciting each sentence as I wrote or rewrote it. The pleasure was lingual rather than merely linguistic. It did not only arise from the act of composition, from the sensation of obstacles overcome, of intention realized as meaning. What I felt was something like the Cernudan *acorde* between mouth and ear. Rather than manipulating a language, I was using my tongue. If I wrote "exilio," the word came alive in the saying. If I rewrote "país," each letter was poised for vocalization. In Spanish vowels are *vocales,* words are *voces.* I felt so comfortable in my mother tongue, so surprisingly at home in my home, that I wondered how I could have spent all those years in another dwelling. Compared to Spanish, English offered bare accommodations, little more than four walls and a roof over my head. But Spanish was my homestead, somewhere I could settle for life. I swore to myself that I had written my last English sentence.

Evidently, I did not live up to my loyalty oath. After finishing *Cincuenta lecciones de exilio y desexilio,* I rewrote another book, *Life on the Hyphen,* in Spanish, a therapeutic self-translation not unlike Bombal's, but soon afterward I began to miss English. I began to miss words like "miss." I began to miss words like "word," so different from the Spanish *palabra,* which in English is simply palaver. Just as it hadn't been enough to speak Spanish with my mother and my students, it wasn't enough to speak English with my wife and my children. If I needed Spanish, I needed English no less. Although the needs came from different places, they were equally urgent, equally defining. Spanish-only, English-always: That was (and is) my impossible program of unilingual education.

It was at this point that I became interested in how others had dealt with similar issues. Reading Santayana and company, I've learned two lessons. The first is that there is no model, no rule, no syntax, for the relation between Spanish and English or (more generally) between a first and a second language; the same tongues tie different speakers differently. Spanish is the language of the soul no more than English is that of the wallet. Perceptions of difference emerge from personal history, not linguistic theory. For Santayana, English was renunciation; for Casey, bliss. For Salinas, Spanish was renunciation; for Cernuda, bliss. The second lesson is that a bilingual's languages are not interchangeable. Whatever the outcome of the debate about the location of speech centers in the bilingual brain, it's clear to me that in the true (I could say "chronic") bilingual, languages occupy distinct psychic slots and serve separate affective agendas. Even Cabrera Infante, who intends his English as Spanish by other means (as he wrongly said about Casey), is not the same writer in English. The person I am closest to is an American woman; the person who had the biggest impact on my life, and to whom

I was never close, was a Cuban man. The language of my inner discourse, the taunts and endearments I whisper only to myself, is shaped by these and other logo-erotic entanglements. While I talk to myself both in Spanish and English, when I hear Spanish voices in my head, they are usually male; when I hear English voices, they are usually female. Like these voices, my languages are gendered—not intrinsically but circumstantially. English is a loving and accessible she-tongue; Spanish, a distant but beloved he-tongue. Although I understand the current focus on the cultural and political dimensions of bilingualism, before it becomes a political, social, or even linguistic issue, bilingualism is a private affair, intimate theater.

Speaking about this book with friends, I have told them that its subject is "el lío de la lengua." As a literal translation of "Tongue Ties," "El lío de la lengua" almost works. *Lío* comes from *liar*, which means to tie; literally, a *lío* is a bundle, and I have been writing about how Spanish and English bundle together. But colloquially a *lío* is something else—a "mess," a "dilemma," a "problem." (Hence Emilio Díaz Valcárcel's memorable Spanglish version of Hamlet's question: "Sel o no sel, *that* is the lío.") When I think about the issue of bilingualism in Spanish, my questions turn into quandaries, tongue ties are reworded as lingual *líos*. But this accords with my sense that of the two languages, Spanish is the hard and hazardous one, the tongue that knots my tongue. I can translate from English to Spanish and from Spanish to English. What I cannot do is translate to one language the affect of the other.

Back to *I Love Lucy*. After a few more funny scenes, Lucy's plan to improve Ricky's English comes to an unexpected conclusion: Instead of correcting Ricky's pronunciation, Mr. Livermore ends up speaking English with a Cuban accent. "It was a battle of the accents," Lucy says, "and Mr. Livermore lost." I cherish the clarity of this dénouement, Ricky's triumph as well as Lucy's gracefulness in defeat. But when the struggle is internal, when Ricky and Mr. Livermore inhabit the same body, it's not easy to declare winners and losers. Every writer in this book is both victim and victor in his or her battle of the accents. When they lose, they get lucky. When they win, they have already lost. Bilingual blues equals bilingual bliss.

Notes

INTRODUCTION

1. Ivan Turgenev and Ludwig Pietsch, *Briefe aus den jahren 1864–1883*, ed. Alfred Doren (Berlin: Im Propyläen Verlag, 1923), 147.
2. Uriel Weinreich, *Languages in Contact* (New York: Publications of the Linguistic Circle of New York, Number 1, 1953); see also Joshua A. Fishman, *Language Loyalty in the United States* (The Hague: Mouton, 1966).
3. On the connection between language and nationalism, see Leonard Forster, *The Poet's Tongues: Multilingualism in Literature* (London: Cambridge University Press, 1970) and Benedict Anderson, *Imagined Communities* (London: Verso, 1991). It is well to remember that language loyalty occurs also in non-Western cultures. In *Passions of the Tongue: Language Devotion in Tamil India* (Berkeley: University of California Press, 1997), Sumathi Ramaswamy studies this phenomenon apropos of Tamil, a Dravidian language spoken by several million people in India.
4. See Andrée Tabouret-Keller, "Language and Identity," in *The Handbook of Sociolinguistics*, ed. Florian Coulmas (Oxford: Blackwell, 1997), 315–326; also R. B. Page and Andrée Tabouret-Keller, *Acts of Identity: Creole-based Approaches to Language and Ethnicity* (Cambridge: Cambridge University Press, 1985).
5. Henry James, *The American Scene* (Bloomington: Indiana University Press, 1968), 85.
6. Jacqueline Amati-Mehler, Simona Argentieri, and Jorge Canestri, *The Babel of the Unconscious*, trans. Jill Whitelaw-Cucco (1990; Madison, CT: International Universities Press, 1993), 139, 153.
7. George Fletcher, *Loyalty: An Essay on the Morality of Relationships* (New York: Oxford University Press, 1993), 8.
8. Gloria Anzaldúa, *Borderlands: The New Mestiza*, 2d. ed. (San Francisco: Aunt Lute Books, 1999), 81.
9. I do not know of any writers, with the possible exception of Calvert Casey, whose first language was English and who wrote in Spanish. The language migration seems always to flow from Spanish to English. I will have more to say about this when I discuss U.S. Latino writing in the last chapter.
10. James Clifford, *Routes* (Cambridge: Harvard University Press, 1997), 264.

11. On this point, see Elizabeth Klosty Beaujour, *Alien Tongues: Bilingual Russian Writers of the "First" Emigration* (Ithaca: Cornell University Press, 1989), 37–51.
12. Steven Kellman, *The Translingual Imagination* (Lincoln: University of Nebraska Press, 2000), viii.
13. M. Grammont, as quoted in François Grosjean, *Life with Two Languages* (Cambridge: Harvard University Press, 1982), 142.
14. This distinction was introduced to differentiate between simultaneous and successive language acquisition. A polylingual is someone who acquires more than one language very early in life; by contrast, a polyglot learns other languages only after a first language has been firmly imprinted. See Grosjean, *Life with Two Languages*, 179–198; and Amati-Mehler, Argentieri, and Canestri, *The Babel of the Unconscious*, 45.
15. Jane Miller, "Writing in a Second Language," *Raritan* (summer 1982): 115.
16. George Steiner, *After Babel: Aspects of Language and Translation*, 3rd. ed. (Oxford: Oxford University Press), 120; see also Steiner, *Errata: An Examined Life* (New Haven: Yale University Press, 1997), 87–114.
17. Amati-Mehler, Argentieri, and Canestri, *The Babel of the Unconscious*, 101.
18. The phrase, transcribed as "Mod hed god hep," appears in the *Cancionero de Baena*, a collection of several hundred poems by diverse authors compiled by Juan Alfonso de Baena around 1445. In the poem, which commemorates the birth of John II of Castile, his mother (Catherine of Lancaster) calls out for divine help in her native tongue while in the throes of childbirth. Also containing phrases in Latin and Arabic, the stanza in which Catherine's plea appears is notable for its multilingualism:

    En boses mas baxas le oy decir:
    "¡Salue, Regina! ¡Saluadme, Señora!"
    e a las de vezes me paresçie oyr:
    Mod hed god hep, alumbradm'agora."
    E a guisa de dueña que deuota ora:
    "¡Quam bonus Deus!," le oy rezar,
    e oyle a manera de apiadar:
    "Çayha bical habin al cabila mora."

    See *Cancionero de Juan Alfonso de Baena*, ed. José María Azaceta (Madrid: Consejo Superior de Investigaciones Científicas, 1966), 413; also Emilio Lorenzo, *Anglicismos hispánicos* (Madrid: Gredos, 1996), 9.
19. James Bossard, "The Bilingual as a Person," *American Sociological Review*, 10, no. 6 (1945): 699–709.
20. Paul Christophersen, *Bilingualism* (London: Methuen, 1948), 9–10. Compare Claudio Guillén's observation: "In the literary field, international relations often mean relations that a writer maintains with himself" (*The Challenge of Comparative Literature,* trans. Cola Franzen [Cambridge, MA: Harvard University Press, 1993], 260).

21. Cherríe Moraga, *Loving in the War Years*, 2d. ed. (San Francisco: South End Press, 2000), 54.

22. María Luisa Bombal, *Obras completas,* ed. Lucía Guerra (Buenos Aires: Editorial Andrés Bello, 1996), 317.

23. Judith Ortiz Cofer, *Woman in Front of the Sun* (Athens: University of Georgia Press, 2000), 29.

24. Rosario Ferré, "Writing in Between," *Hopscotch* 1, no. 1 (1997): 109.

25. I am paraphrasing. Canetti wrote: "Of all the words in all languages I know, the greatest concentration is in the English word *I*" (*The Human Province,* trans. Joachim Neugroschel [New York: Seabury, 1978]), 36.

26. Jacques Derrida, *Monolingualism of the Other*, trans. Patrick Mensah (Stanford: Stanford University Press, 1998), 28–29.

27. Edward Sapir, "The Status of Linguistics as a Science" (1929), in *The Selected Writings of Edward Sapir in Language, Culture and Personality*, ed. D. G. Mandelbaum (Berkeley: University of California Press, 1949), 162.

28. Benjamin Whorf, *Language, Thought, and Reality*, ed. J. B. Carroll (Cambridge, MA: MIT Press, 1956), 213. For recent assessments of the Sapir-Whorf hypothesis, see John A. Lucy, *Language Diversity and Thought: A Reformulation of the Linguistic Relativity Hypothesis* (Cambridge: Cambridge University Press, 1992); and John J. Gumperz and Stephen C. Levinson, eds., *Rethinking Linguistic Relativity* (Cambridge: Cambridge University Press, 1996).

29. Steiner, *After Babel*, 381–382.

30. George Santayana, *The Sense of Beauty* (1896; New York: Dover, 1955), 104. I take the Bianciotti quotation from Amati-Mehler, Argentieri, and Canestri, *The Babel of the Unconscious,* 194.

31. Popularized by John Ferguson in the 1950s, the term "diglossia" originally referred to two dialects of the same language. Joshua Fishman extended the notion to apply to different languages rather than to varieties of the same language. The bibliography on diglossia is extensive; see Mauro Fernández, *Diglossia: A Comprehensive Bibliography, 1960–1990* (Amsterdam: J. Benjamins, 1993). For the so-called "Fishman extension," see Joshua Fishman, "Bilingualism with and without Diglossia; Diglossia with and without Bilingualism," *Journal of Social Issues* 23, no. 2 (1967): 29–38.

32. Edmundo Desnoes, "Nacer en español," in *An Other Tongue*, ed. Alfred Arteaga (Durham: Duke University Press, 1994), 271.

33. Cristobal de Villalón, *Antología de elogios de la lengua española,* ed. Germán Bleiberg (Madrid: Ediciones Cultura Hispánica, 1951), 37. Villalón, a humanist poet and grammarian, died around 1559.

34. Juan Ramón Jiménez, *Guerra en España (1936–1953)*(Barcelona: Seix Barral, 1985), 59.

35. Pedro Salinas, *Cartas de viaje: 1912–1951*, ed. Enric Bou (Valencia: Pre-Textos, 1996), 77.

168   ❖   TONGUE TIES

36. Charles Simic, *The Uncertain Certainty* (Ann Arbor: University of Michigan Press, 1985), 118.
37. Juan Marinello, *Ensayos* (La Habana: Editorial Arte y Literatura, 1977), 48. The quotations come from the essay "Americanismo y cubanismo literarios" (1932).
38. Jiménez, *Guerra en España*, 62
39. Walter Ong, *Interfaces of the Word: Studies in the Evolution of Consciousness and Culture* (Ithaca: Cornell University Press, 1977), 140.
40. Pedro Salinas, *Poesías Completas* (Barcelona: Barral, 1975), 644.
41. Juan de Valdés, *Diálogo de la lengua*, ed. Oreste Macrí (Barcelona: Planeta, 1986), 8.
42. Rubén Darío, *Los raros* (1896; Mexico City: Universidad Autónoma Metropolitana, 1985), 21. Darío goes on to say that New Yorkers do not speak but "scream, moo, below, howl" (23). See Roberto Ignacio Díaz, *Unhomely Rooms: Foreign Tongues and Spanish American Literature* (Lewisburg: Bucknell University Press, 2002), 73–74.
43. Joseph Brodsky, "The Condition We Call Exile," in *Altogether Elsewhere*, ed. Marc Robinson (Boston: Faber and Faber, 1994), 3–11.
44. George Santayana, *Scepticism and Animal Faith* (1923; New York: Dover, 1955), 252.

Chapter 1

1. Concha Zardoya, "Poesía y estilo de George Santayana," *Cuadernos Americanos* 49 (January–February 1950): 131. See also: Concha Zardoya, "Santayana y España," *Insula* 83 (November 1952): 1, 4, 8; Ramón Sender, "Santayana y los castellanos interiores," in *Unamuno, Valle Inclán, Baroja y Santayana* (Mexico City: Ediciones de Andrea, 1955), 137–170; Carlos M. Fernández Shaw, "El españolismo de George Santayana," *Revista de Estudios Políticos* 140 (March–April 1965): 541–59; Carlos Clavería, "España en la obra de Santayana," *Filología moderna* 4, no. 13 (October 1963): 1–28; Guillermo de Torre, "Santayana, el desasido," *Revista Hispánica Moderna* 34, no. 1–2 (January–April 1968): 446–452; Enrique Zuleta Álvarez, "Santayana en Hispanoamérica," *Revista de Occidente* 79 (Diciembre 1987): 9–25); and *Santayana Abroad: The Reception of Santayana's Philosophy in Europe, Latin America, Africa, and Asia*, ed. David Wapinsky and Zechariah Switzky (New York: Publications Philanthropica for Public Libraries, 1993).
2. Sender, "Santayana," 142.
3. Pedro Salinas and Jorge Guillén, *Correspondencia (1923–1951)*, ed. Andrés Soria Olmedo (Barcelona: Tusquets, 1992), 586–587. A few years later, Guillén would commemorate the occasion with a poem describing the

philosopher as "español de raíz, inglés de idioma." In "Al margen de Santayana," in *Aire nuestro* (Milan: Pesce D'Oro, 1968), 1179.

4. From the Preface to his *Poems* (New York: Charles Scribner's Sons, 1923), vii-viii.

5. George Santayana, *Persons and Places: Fragments of Autobiography*, ed. William G. Holzberger and Herman J. Saatkamp, Jr. (Cambridge: MIT Press, 1986), 282. Other page references to this edition (*PP*) will be included in the text. Santayana's autobiography was originally published in three separate volumes: *Persons and Places* (1944), *The Middle Span* (1945), and *My Host the World* (1953). It had been his intention to gather the three volumes under the title of the first, as in the MIT edition.

6. George Santayana to Henry Ward Abbot, May 20, 1887. In *The Letters of George Santayana, Book One, [1868]-1909*, ed. William G. Holzberger (Cambridge, MA: MIT Press, 2001), 75.

7. The phrase is Baker Bromwell's, in "Santayana, the Man and the Philosopher," in *The Philosophy of George Santayana*, ed. Paul Arthur Schilpp (1940; New York: Tudor, 1951), 49. On this point see also Michael Hodges and John Lachs, *Thinking in the Ruins: Wittgenstein and Santayana on Contingency* (Nashville: Vanderbilt University Press, 2000), 63, 87–89.

8. Timothy Sprigge, *Santayana: An Examination of his Philosophy*, rev. ed. (London: Routledge, 1995), 220.

9. *The Letters of George Santayana*, ed. Daniel Cory (New York: Charles Scribner's Sons, 1955), 430.

10. George Santayana, "Apologia pro mente sua," in *The Philosophy of George Santayana*, ed. Paul Arthur Schilpp (1940; New York: Tudor, 1951), 599.

11. George Santayana, *Reason in Art*, vol. 4 of *The Life of Reason or The Phases of Human Progress* (New York: Charles Scribner's Sons, 1905), 85. Other references to this edition (*RA*) will be included in the text.

12. I take the term "xenity" from John Taylor, "On the Ledge: Joseph Brodsky in English," *Michigan Quarterly Review* 40, no. 3 (summer 2001): 594–603.

13. George Santayana to Henry Ward Abbot, May 20, 1887. In *The Letters of George Santayana, Book One, [1868]-1909*, ed. William G. Holzberger, 74.

14. Since Santayana's letters to his father have not survived, it is impossible to gauge the extent of his difficulties with Spanish when he was a young man. Agustín Santayana repeatedly assures his son that his deficiencies are not serious and would disappear once he took up residence in Spain. As he writes on one occasion, "Yo no creo que te resulte ningún inconveniente de no hablar con toda facilidad y fluencia el castellano durante algún tiempo. Y es lo más natural que te suceda mientras estás hablando casi siempre en inglés. [. . .] En fin, esto que me dices que te preocupa mucho es lo que, en mi sentir, debe preocuparte menos" [I don't think that not speaking Spanish completely fluently and easily will be an inconvenience. It's the

most natural thing since now you almost always speak in English. (. . .) In sum, what worries you the most is what, in my view, should worry you the least]. Letter of July 4, 1985, George Santayana Papers, Rare Book and Manuscript Library, Columbia University.

15. George Santayana, *The Last Puritan*, ed. William G. Holzberger and Herman J. Saatkamp, Jr. (1935; Cambridge, MA: MIT Press, 1995), 6. Other page references to this edition (*LP*) will be included in the text.

16. *The Letters of George Santayana*, ed. Cory, 62.

17. *The Letters of George Santayana, Book One, [1868]-1909*, ed. William G. Holzberger, 75; Santayana, *Persons and Places*, 201.

18. Letter of December 16, 1879. The George Santayana Collection, Butler Library, Columbia University.

19. Daniel Cory, *Santayana: The Later Years* (New York: George Braziller, 1963), 210.

20. Elias Canetti, *The Tongue Set Free*, trans. Joachim Neugroschel (New York: Seabury, 1979), 70.

21. Reproduced in J. M. Alonso Gamo, *Un español en el mundo: Santayana* (Madrid: Ediciones de Cultura Hispánica, 1966). In his superb biography, John McCormick states that Santayana's "command of Spanish was such that he would meticulously correct accent marks, diction, and style in the Spanish works he often read" (*George Santayana* [New York: Alfred A. Knopf, 1987], 4); but to judge by this writing sample, as well as by the mistakes in the Spanish words that Santayana occasionally put into his books, his command of Spanish was not very good. In *Persons and Places*, speaking of his difficulties in communicating with his father, Santayana states that his "powers of expression in Spanish were limited, for I had read, and even now have read, hardly any Spanish books" (199). He makes similar statements elsewhere. Santayana's comments about Spanish literature are limited to a few references to *Don Quijote*, which he read as a child but never re-read, and to other classics such as Calderón's *La vida es sueño* and Zorilla's *Don Juan Tenorio*.

22. Although Santayana's father had dropped the commonplace "Ruiz" for the elegant "Santayana," his full name was Agustín Ruiz de Santayana.

23. George Santayana, *The Philosophy of George Santayana: Selections*, ed. Irwin Edman (New York: Charles Scribner's Sons, 1936), 4–5. This essay originally appeared in *Contemporary American Philosophy: Personal Statements*, ed. George P. Adams and William Montague, (New York: Macmillan, 1930), 2: 239–257.

24. *The Letters of George Santayana*, ed. Cory, 380.

25. George Santayana, *The Sense of Beauty* (1896; New York: Dover, 1955), 104. In "The Task of the Translator" (1923), Walter Benjamin makes the same point with the same example: "The words *Brot* and *pain* 'intend' the same object, but the modes of this intention are not the same. It is owing to these modes that the word *Brot* means something different to a German

than the word *pain* to a Frenchman, that these words are not interchange-
able for them, that, in fact, they strive to exclude each other." In *Theories of
Translation*, ed. Rainer Schulte and John Biguenet (Chicago: University of
Chicago Press, 1992), 75.

26. In George Santayana, *Dominations and Powers* (1950; New Brunswick,
New Jersey: Transaction, 1995), 142.

27. George Santayana, *Interpretations of Poetry and Religion* (New York:
Charles Scribner's Sons, 1900), 256. Ortega, who had read Santayana,
used a similar image to describe the "intranscendence" of vanguard art,
which makes the reader focus on the window pane rather than on the
garden beyond it; see *La deshumanización del arte* (1925), in *Obras
completas* (Madrid: Revista de Occidente, 1957), 3: 357–58. I discuss the
significance of this passage in my *Idle Fictions: The Hispanic Vanguard
Novel, 1926–1934* (Durham: Duke University Press, 1992), chap. 3.

28. George Santayana, *Realms of Being*, vol. 14 of *The Works of George
Santayana*, Triton Edition (New York: Charles Scribner's Sons,
1932), 109–110.

29. A new volume of unpublished poems, *The Poet's Testament*, appeared a
year after his death, but most of the poems had been written fifty years
earlier.

30. George Santayana, "Apologia pro mente sua," in *The Philosophy of George
Santayana*, ed. Paul Arthur Schilpp (1940; New York: Tudor, 1951), 598.

31. From the author's preface to *Poems* (New York: Charles Scribner's Sons,
1923), a selection from Santayana's earlier volumes.

32. *The Letters of George Santayana*, ed. Cory, 200.

33. Aware of his weakness for metaphor, Santayana wrote on the margin of the
manuscript of *Persons and Places*, "Away with metaphors!"

34. George Santayana, *The Idler and His Works*, ed. Daniel Cory (New York:
George Braziller, 1957), 4.

35. In "Apologia pro mente sua," a response to criticisms of his work, he
concedes, "it is as an American writer that I must be counted, if I am
counted at all"—but immediately adds that in his heart he remains a
"Castilian mystic" (*The Philosophy of George Santayana*, ed. Schilpp, 603).

36. Late in his life, talking about A. E. Housman, Santayana said: "I suppose
Housman was really what people nowadays call 'homosexual.' [. . .] I think
I must have been that way in my Harvard days—although I was uncon-
scious of it at the time" (Daniel Cory, *Santayana: The Later Years: A
Portrait with Letters* [New York: Braziller, 1963], 40). On Santayana's
homosexuality see McCormick, *George Santayana*, 49–52; Robert K.
Martin, *The Homosexual Tradition in American Poetry* (Austin: University
of Texas Press, 1979); Ross Posnock, "Genteel Androgyny: Santayana,
Henry James, Howard Sturgis," *Raritan* 10, no. 3 (winter 1991): 58–78;
Irving Singer, *George Santayana, Literary Philosopher* (New Haven: Yale
University Press, 2000), 57–63.

37. George Santayana, *Soliloquies in England* (1922; Ann Arbor: University of Michigan Press, 1967), 4.

38. Cioran, *De l'inconvénient d'être né* (Paris: Gallimard, 1973), 49. On the autobiographical basis of *The Last Puritan,* see McCormick, *George Santayana,* and H. T. Kirby-Smith, *A Philosophical Novelist: George Santayana and "The Last Puritan"* (Carbondale: Southern Illinois University Press, 1997). In the preface to *The Last Puritan,* Santayana describes Oliver as "a stage-presentation of myself" (3).

39. Santayana, *Dominations and Powers,* 142.

40. George Santayana, *Platonism and the Spiritual Life* (New York: Charles Scribner's Sons, 1927), 36.

41. "In man spirit is not a mere truant, as it seems to be in the lark, but is a faithful chronicler of labour and wisdom. Man is hard-pressed; long truancies would be fatal to him. He is tempted to indulge in them—witness his languages and pyramids and mythologies" (Santayana, *Soliloquies in England,* 111).

42. Letter to Charles Scribner's Sons, October 30, 1901 (*The Letters of George Santayana, Book One, [1868]-1909,* ed. William G. Holzberger, 241). But the removal of "George" from the spine of his books also highlighted the author's heterolingualism, the fact that a "G. Santayana" wrote books in English.

43. Umberto Eco, *The Search for the Perfect Language,* trans. James Fentress (Cambridge, MA: Blackwell, 1997).

44. Explaining the evolution from vegetable to animal life, Santayana writes: "Meantime the organs of fertility, which were the flowers, sunning themselves wide open and lolling in delicious innocence, are now tucked away obscurely in the hind quarters, to be seen and thought of as little as possible. This disgrace lies heavy upon them, prompting them to sullen discontent and insidious plots and terrible rebellions" ("The Philosophy of Travel," in *Altogether Elsewhere: Writers on Exile,* ed. Marc Robinson [Boston: Faber and Faber, 1994], 42).

45. Santayana, *The Complete Poems of George Santayana,* ed. William G. Holzberger (Lewiston: Bucknell University Press, 1979), 127.

46. Santayana, *The Complete Poems of George Santayana,* 250

CHAPTER 2

1. George Santayana, *The Letters of George Santayana,* ed. Daniel Cory (New York: Charles Scribner's Sons, 1955), 319.

2. Juan Ramón Jiménez, *Guerra en España (1936–1953),* ed. Ángel Crespo (Barcelona: Seix Barral, 1985), 64. See also José María Naharro Calderón, *Entre el exilio y el interior: El "entresiglo" y Juan Ramón Jiménez* (Barcelona: Anthropos, 1994), 303–306.

3. José Gaos, "La adaptación de un español a la sociedad hispanoamericana," *Revista de Occidente* 38 (May 1966): 168–178.

4. Pedro Salinas and Jorge Guillén, *Correspondencia (1923–1951)*, ed. Andrés Soria Olmedo (Valencia: Tusquets, 1992), 314.

5. Pedro Salinas, *Ensayos completos*, ed. Solita Salinas de Marichal (Madrid: Taurus, 1983), 3: 421. This essay was first published in the inaugural issue of *Asomante*, the Puerto Rican literary journal that Salinas helped to found.

6. Pedro Salinas, *Aprecio y defensa del lenguaje* (1944; San Juan: Editorial de la Universidad de Puerto Rico, 1995). Other page numbers refer to this edition.

7. Pedro Salinas and Jorge Guillén, *Correspondencia*, 325, 328, 330.

8. On Panhispanism, see Frederick Pike, *Hispanismo. 1896–1936: Spanish Conservatives and Liberals and Their Relations with Spanish America* (South Bend: University of Notre Dame Press, 1971); also my *The Cuban Condition: Translation and Identity in Modern Cuban Literature* (Cambridge: Cambridge University Press, 1989), chap. 2.

9. Salinas, *Cartas de viaje (1912–1951)*, ed. Enric Bou (Valencia: Pre-Textos, 1996), 161.

10. Claudio Guillén, "Pedro Salinas y las palabras," *La Torre* 3, no. 10 (abril-junio 1989): 350.

11. Juan Marichal, *Tres voces de Pedro Salinas* (Madrid: Taller de Ediciones, 1976), 75.

12. Pedro Salinas, *El defensor*, ed. Juan Marichal (1948; Madrid: Alianza, 1967), 118.

13. Salinas, *Cartas de viaje*, 172.

14. Pedro Salinas, "Defensa de la carta misiva y de la correspondencia epistolar," in Salinas, *El defensor*, 19–20.

15. Salinas's description of the business man: "[el] príncipe de los ocupados, [el] *busiest among men*, [el] *busi ness man*" (*El defensor*, 123). As Salinas surely knew, at around the same time that he was inveighing against advertising, Leo Spitzer, his colleague at Hopkins, was brilliantly demonstrating just how "poetic" a Sunkist orange juice ad could be. See Spitzer's "American Advertising Explained as Popular Art," in *A Method of Interpreting Literature* (Northhampton: Smith College, 1948), 102–149. In a footnote, Spitzer takes issue with *Aprecio y defensa del lenguaje*, pointing out that "art can arise within the realm of the utilitarian" (133).

16. At one of few formal occasions when Salinas talked about his own poetry, during a lecture at Wellesley in 1947, this was the poem that he selected for explication; see "Deuda de un poeta," in *Ensayos completos*, 3: 434–447.

17. Pedro Salinas, *Poesías completas*, ed. Soledad Salinas de Marichal, 2d. ed. (Barcelona: Barral, 1975), 720. Page numbers accompanying quotations from Salinas's poetry refer to this edition.

18. Salinas, *El defensor*, 20.

19. Letter of July 22, 1939; as quoted in Jean Cross Newman, *Pedro Salinas and His Circumstance* (San Juan: Inter American University, 1983), 178.

20. Pedro Salinas, *Reality and the Poet in Spanish Poetry*, trans. Edith Fishtine Helman (Baltimore: Johns Hopkins University Press, 1966), 3.

21. Before Whitmore passed away in 1981, she left 355 letters by Salinas as well as many manuscript poems and other memorabilia to the Harvard Library, with the provision that these materials would not become available for twenty years (Katherine Prue [Reding] Whitmore, Pedro Salinas Papers, Houghton Library, Harvard University, bMS Span 107). Finally available, the correspondence makes clear that Whitmore was indeed the inspiration for *La voz a ti debida*. A selection of Salinas's letters to Whitmore has been published as *Cartas a Katherine Whitmore: El epistolario secreto del gran poeta de amor*, ed. Enric Bou (Barcelona: Tusquets, 2002). Since this compilation only includes about half of the letters, I will cite the Salinas Papers unless the particular letter is included in Bou's collection. All quotes from the Salinas Papers are used by permission of the Houghton Library, Harvard University. For more details on the correspondence, see Bou's introduction and Ruth Katz Crispin, "'Qué verdad revelada!': The Poet and the Absent Beloved of Pedro Salinas's *La voz a ti debida, Razón de amor and Largo lamento*," *Revista Hispánica Moderna* 54 (2001): 108–125.

22. The dissertation was published in English as *The Generation of 1898 in Spain as Seen Through Its Fictional Hero* (Northhampton: Smith College Studies in Modern Languages, 1936). Whitmore is also the author of *The Handbook of Intermediate Spanish* (New York: Norton, 1942), with which Salinas helped her.

23. Salinas, *Cartas de viaje*, 60.

24. Salinas, *Cartas a Katherine Whitmore*, 289.

25. Salinas, *Cartas a Katherine Whitmore*, 333. Letter of November 27, 1938.

26. Salinas, *Cartas a Katherine Whitmore*, 289. Letter of November 27, 1938.

27. Letters to Katherine Prue (Reding) Whitmore, Folder 164, Salinas Papers.

28. Salinas, *Cartas a Katherine Whitmore*, 368.

29. Letters to Katherine Prue (Reding) Whitmore, Folder 137, March 27, 1936, Salinas Papers. The "K" and "P" stand for Katherine and Pedro.

30. "'¿Que tal, 'buena mujer burguesa,' como tú te bautizas a ti misma en tu epístola? Burguesa? No habíamos quedado en que eras una Musa? Has dimitido de ese alto cargo? Por eso será que ya hace tiempo que un cierto poeta que conozco como a mis entretelas, calla, y deja las cuartillas en blanco. ¿Será porque la Musa se le ha casado? Es posible ser Musa y casada? O se ha tomado simplemente unas vacaciones, y es *la Muse en vacances?*" [How are you, 'good bourgeois woman,' as you call yourself in your epistle? Bourgeois? Hadn't we decided that you were a Muse? Have you resigned from that high post? That must be why for some time now a certain poet that I know as well as I know myself has grown silent, and leaves the sheets of paper blank. Could it be that his Muse has married? Is it posible to be a Muse and be married? Or has she simply taken some time off, and is *la Muse en vacances?*] (Salinas, *Cartas a Katherine Whitmore*, 349).

31. Letters to Katherine Prue (Reding) Whitmore, Folder 159, February 1, 1940, Salinas Papers.

32. Salinas and Guillén, *Correspondencia*, 290.

33. As quoted in Newman, *Pedro Salinas and His Circumstance*, 210. The speech was delivered in May 1939.

34. Letters to Katherine Prue (Reding) Whitmore, Folder 35, January 27, 1933, Salinas Papers.

35. Salinas intends "anglicano" not as "Anglican" but in the old Spanish sense of "English," for which see Emilio Lorenzo, *Anglicismos hispánicos* (Madrid: Gredos, 1996), 13.

36. Letters to Katherine Prue (Reding) Whitmore, Folder 143, June 28, 1936, Salinas Papers.

37. Letters to Katherine Prue (Reding) Whitmore, Folder 35, January 27, 1933, Salinas Papers (original in English).

38. "La consecuencia a que llego es que yo no hablaba con estos individuos. Yo hablaba con su idioma, hablaba con algo que no es de ellos, que han heredado sin querer, que fue de sus padres y de los míos, y que está por encima de los individuos. Hablaba yo con la lengua española, con una abstracción, momentáneamente personificada en estos dos tipos. Hablaba, quizá, conmigo mismo" [The conclusion I reach is that I was not talking with those individuals. I was talking with their language, I was talking with something that doesn't belong to them, that they have unwillingly inherited, that belonged to their parents and to mine, and that transcends individuals. I was talking with the Spanish tongue, with an abstraction, momentarily personified in those two men. I was talking, perhaps, with myself] (Salinas, *Cartas de viaje*, 161).

39. Salinas quotes Whitmore's phrase in one his letters, where he mentions her complaints and responds to them. Her letters to him have not survived (apparently). Letters to Katherine Prue (Reding) Whitmore, Folder 166, May 17 [1934?], Salinas Papers.

40. Pedro Salinas, *El Contemplado. Todo más claro y otros poemas,* ed. Francisco Javier Díez de Revenga (Madrid: Castalia, 1996), 28.

41. Letters to Katherine Prue (Reding) Whitmore, Folder 133, March 19, 1936, Salinas Papers.

42. Salinas, *Cartas a Katherine Whitmore*, 309.

43. Gustavo Correa, "*El Contemplado*," in *Pedro Salinas,* ed. Andrew P. Debicki (Madrid: Taurus, 1976), 143.

44. Robert Havard, "The reality of words in the poetry of Pedro Salinas," *Bulletin of Hispanic Studies* 51 (1974): 44.

45. The epigraph is taken from Shelley's *Epipsychidion,* an allegorical account of Shelley's adulterous love affair with Emilia Viviani. Many years earlier, Salinas had mentioned this poem (but not this line) several times in letters to Margarita, at the time his fiancée. In Pedro Salinas, *Cartas de amor a Margarita (1912–1915),* ed. Solita Salinas de Marichal (Madrid: Alianza, 1984), 47, 64.

46. Leo Spitzer, "El conceptismo interior de Pedro Salinas" (1941), in *Lingüística e historia literaria* (Madrid: Gredos, 1961), 199.

47. Pedro Salinas, *Reality and Poet in Spanish Poetry,* trans. Edith Fishtine Helman (1940; Baltimore: Johns Hopkins University Press, 1966), 4.

48. Receiving a telegram from her, Salinas comments, "la palabra más bonita de todas las del telegrama, la más adorable, la *palabra* por excelencia: Katherine" [the most beautiful word in the telegram, the most adorable,

the *word* par excellence: Katherine] (Letter of November 7, 1932; *Cartas a Katherine Whitmore*, 88). It is worth remarking that Salinas's aversion to telegraphy took some time in developing. During the 1930s he exchanged telegrams with Whitmore and availed himself without compunction of the "barbaric laconism" that he later condemned. The entire text of one of his messages: "ALWAYS YOU. PEDRO."

49. Jacques Derrida, *Monolingualism of the Other; or, The Prosthesis of Origin*, trans. Patrick Mensah (1996; Stanford: Stanford University Press, 1998), 81.

50. Compare these lines from *La voz a ti debida*: "No sirves para amada; / tú siempre ganarás, / queriendo, al que te quiera. / Amante, amada no" [You won't do as a loved one; / you will always win, / loving, over whoever loves you. / Lover, not loved one] (275).

51. Salinas, *Poesías Completas*, 664. The poem is part of *Todo más claro* (1949). In a perceptive analysis of "Verbo," Vicente Lloréns notes that this poem reflects Salinas's anxiety about his mother tongue, an anxiety no less real for remaining unexpressed: "De uno u otro modo, el exiliado vive con la preocupación del idioma. Y aunque no la manifieste, se revela en lo que escribe, a veces inesperadamente, casi sin querer" [In one way or another, the exile lives with the worry about his language. And even if he doesn't admit it, it shows in what he writes, at times unexpectedly, almost unwillingly]. Vicente Lloréns, "El desterrado y su lengua: Sobre un poema de Salinas," in *Literatura, historia, política* (Madrid: Revista de Occidente, 1967), 37.

52. In *Cartas de amor a Margarita (1912–1915)*, Salinas writes: "Margarita, Margarita, bendita seas, dulce nombre" (65). He also composed a poem to her that began, "Antes de hablarte el alma dice siempre / tu nombre, dulce nombre" [Before speaking to you my soul always says / your name, sweet name] (142).

53. There are hardly any elements of imagery or phrasing in *El Contemplado* that do not have a precedent or *presagio* in the trilogy; even the term "contemplado" and the notion of "theme and variations" already occur in the trilogy in a context reminiscent of the later book. *Largo lamento* includes a poem entitled "Adiós con variaciones." "Suicidio hacia arriba," from *Razón de amor*, includes the lines: "Flotantes, boca arriba, / en alta mar, los dos. En el gran horizonte, solo, nadie, / nadie que mire al cielo, / nadie / a quien pueda él mirar, sino estos cuatro ojos únicos, / cuatro, por donde al mundo / le llega el necesario / don de ser contemplado" [Floating, on our backs, / in the open sea, the two of us. On the great horizon, alone, nobody, / nobody to look at the sky, / nobody / for the sky to look at, except these four eyes only, / four, from which the world / receives the necessary gift / of being contemplated] (440). One of Salinas's letters to Whitmore after her marriage includes a passage that also contains the germinal idea of *El Contemplado*: "Sufro, resignado, con cierto reflexivo contento, ese rebrotar del amor de antes. Nada de desesperación, ni de esperanza, tampoco. Algo como una contemplación profunda y vagamente triste, de la misma clase que se tiene a la orilla del mar, cuando lo miramos mucho, minutos y minutos, como a algo prodigioso que nos posee, pero

que nunca poseeremos. [. . .] Hasta que comprendemos que no se puede estar siempre así y nos levantamos, para volver . . . ¿adónde? Y se queda allí, lo contemplado, hermosamente inaccesible, solo consigo mismo" [I suffer with resignation, with a kind of reflective contentment, the rebirth of the old love. No hopelessness, but no hope either. Something like the deep and vaguely sad contemplativeness that one feels by the sea, when we look at it for a long time, minutes and minutes, like some prodigious thing that possesses us but that we will never possess. (. . .) Until we understand that we can't be there forever and we get up to return . . . where? And it stays there, what we have contemplated, beautifully inaccessible, alone with itself]. Letters to Katherine Prue (Reding) Whitmore, Folder 145, Letter of May 1940, Salinas Papers.

54. Note appended to letter of November 30, 1935; Letters to Katherine Prue (Reding) Whitmore, Folder 129, Salinas Papers.

55. Whitmore quotes a line from *La voz a ti debida* in which Salinas explains why he was not able to leave Margarita and start a new life with her. A Spanish translation of Whitmore's memoir appears in Salinas, *Cartas a Katherine Whitmore*, 377–384. The English original has not yet been published.

CHAPTER 3

1. Max Aub, *La poesía española contemporánea* (Mexico City: Imprenta Universitaria, 1954), 175.

2. For Salinas's "La nieve (Pensamientos de Thanksgiving day, para mi amada)," which formed part of a letter to Whitmore, see Pedro Salinas, *Cartas a Katherine Whitmore*, ed. Enric Bou (Barcelona: Tusquets, 2002), 292–294.

3. In the biographical essay "Historial de un libro" (1958), Cernuda says that he met Salvador in 1951, but the prologue of *Variaciones sobre tema mexicano*, written in the fall of 1950, already alludes to him. For "Historial de un libro," see Luis Cernuda, *Prosa I*, ed. Derek Harris and Luis Maristany (Madrid: Ediciones Siruela, 1994), 625–661.

4. I will be quoting Cernuda's poems, including *Variaciones sobre tema mexicano*, from *Poesía completa*, 3d. ed., ed. Derek Harris and Luis Maristany (Madrid: Ediciones Siruela, 1999). Page numbers will refer to this edition. Information about the dating of the poems is taken from Maristany and Harris's annotations.

5. "Palabras ante una lectura" (1935), in Cernuda, *Prosa I*, 602.

6. "El acorde" is Cernuda's clearest statement of the "mystical" ecstasy that results from the union of reality and desire. Although the poem forms part of *Ocnos*, thematically it is as closely related to *Variaciones sobre tema mexicano*.

7. Jaime Gil de Biedma, *El pie de la letra* (Barcelona: Grijalbo, 1980), 329.

8. The phrase appears in "Luna llena en semana santa," Cernuda, *Poesía completa*, 538.

9. Philologists disagree about the etymology of *acorde;* Corominas (*Diccionario etimológico de la lengua castellana*) traces the word back to *cors,* though he acknowledges the "influence" of *chorda.* Spitzer explains: "Due to a particular coincidence not extant in Greek, there was in Latin a *cord-*susceptible to two interpretations: it could be connected not only with *cor, cordis,* 'heart' (which was the original meaning), but also with *chorda,* 'string.' [. . .] Thus psychological harmony and musical harmony (and disharmony: *disc(h)ordia*) were ensconced in one word of poetic ambivalence which allowed for a kind of metaphysical punning" ("Classical and Christian Ideas of World Harmony (Part II)," *Traditio* 3 [1945]: 322). See also Mack Singleton, "Spanish *acordar* and Related Words," *Language* 17 (1941): 119–126.

10. See Gonzalo Sobejano, "Alcances de la descripción estilística (Luis Cernuda: 'Nocturno yanki')," in *The Analysis of Hispanic Texts: Currents Trends in Methodology,* ed. Mary Ann Beck, et al. (New York: Bilingual Press, 1976), 89–112.

11. Cernuda even omitted *Perfil del aire* from the list of first books by poets of his generation in his study of modern Spanish poetry (*Prosa I,* 183). Some of the poems of *Perfil del aire* appear in *La realidad y el deseo* under the heading of "Primeras poesías."

12. In the background of some of Cernuda's references to air lies one of the privileged objects in Romantic iconography, the Aeolian lyre, which joins the musical and elemental senses of the word by making "airs" with "air." Cernuda, who translated Shelley's *A Defense of Poetry* (where Shelley develops the idea that the poet is a harp or lyre), uses similar imagery in several of his poems. In "Instrumento músico," he compares the poet's words to the sounds emitted by the strumming of a lute; in "La gloria del poeta," the poet describes his "pecho sonoro y vibrante, idéntico a un laúd" [vibrant and sonorous chest, identical to a lyre] (233); and in "El arpa," which has been linked to Coleridge's "The Aeolian Harp," the melody of the lyre is described as an "air" made of "rememberings and forgettings" (343). In Shelley, the Aeolian lyre expresses the "harmony" in the poet of objective stimulus and subjective response, as if the lyre were able to "accommodate its chords to the motions of that which strikes them, in a determined proportion of sound." (Shelley, *A Defense of Poetry,* in *English Romantic Writers,* ed. David Perkins [New York: Harcourt, Brace and World, 1967], 1072). Shelley here describes the phenomenon that Cernuda, perhaps echoing *A Defense of Poetry,* would call *el acorde.* In the chapter on Shelley in his *Pensamiento poético en la lírica inglesa* (1958), Cernuda glosses this famous passage (*Prosa I,* 330). More generally, "aire" in Cernuda covers some of the same semantic ground as "wind" or "breeze" in the English Romantic lyric, for which see M. H. Abrams, *The Correspondent Breeze: Essays on English Romanticism* (New York: Norton,

1984). On Coleridge and Cernuda, see Kevin Bruton, "Luis Cernuda's Exile Poetry and Coleridge's Theory of the Imagination," *Comparative Literature Studies* 21 (winter 1984): 382–395.

13. Claudio Guillén, *El sol de los desterrados* (Barcelona: Quaderns Crema, 1995). This is a much expanded version of Guillén's influential essay, "On the Literature of Exile and Counter-Exile," *Books Abroad* 50, no. 2 (spring 1976): 271–280. Guillén's distinction between the Ovidian and Plutarchan, or between exile and counterexile, is itself a Plutarchan maneuver; the father's poems are of a piece with the son's essays. On the significance of *aire* in *Aire nuestro*, see Joaquín González, "Sail Before the Wind *(Aire Nuestro)*," in *Luminous Reality: The Poetry of Jorge Guillén*, ed. Ivar Ivask and Juan Marichal (Norman: University of Oklahoma Press, 1969), 82–89; and Manuel Durán, "Una constante en la poesía de Jorge Guillén: El aire, el aire luminoso y respirable," in *Homenaje a Jorge Guillén*, ed. Justina Ruiz-Conde, et al. (Madrid: Insula, 1978), 223–233. For Jorge Guillén's own views on the role of air in his poetry, see *Guillén on Guillén: The Poetry and the Poet,* trans. Reginald Gibbons and Anthony L. Geist (Princeton: Princeton University Press, 1979), where he remarks that "air is the fundamental element" in his poems (19).

14. In "A mis paisanos," he writes: "En mala hora fuera vuestra lengua / la mía, la que hablo, la que escribo" [It was an evil hour that made your tongue / my own, the one I speak, the one I write] (546).

15. Cernuda, *Prosa I*, 202.

16. Cernuda, *Prosa I*, 204. "El aire" appears in *Aire nuestro* (Milano: All'Insegna del Pesce D'Oro, 1968), 518–523. The last sortie in this air war was to be Guillén's; in *Homenaje,* the last section of *Aire Nuestro,* he includes a eulogy to Cernuda, "Perfil del viento," which begins with a phrase taken from *Donde habite el olvido,* "Hecho aire que pasa" [Turned into air that passes by] (1196).

17. Juan Ramón Jiménez, *Guerra en España (1936–1953),* ed. Ángel Crespo (Barcelona: Seix Barral, 1985), 64.

18. In "Díptico español" he writes: "La poesía habla en nosotros / La misma lengua que hablaron antes, / Y mucho antes de nacer nosotros, / Las gentes en que hallara raíz nuestra existencia; / No es el poeta sólo quien ahí habla, / Sino las bocas mudas de los suyos / A quien él da voz y les libera" [Poetry speaks in us / The same tongue that was spoken before, / and much before we were born, / by the people in whom we are rooted; / It's not only the poet who speaks there, / But the mute mouths of his people / to whom he gives voice and freedom] (503).

19. Cernuda, *Prosa I*, 853.

20. Pedro Salinas and Jorge Guillén, *Correspondencia (1923–1951)* (Barcelona: Tusquets, 1992), 503.

21. For Guillén's warm feelings about Wellesley, see Salinas and Guillén, *Correspondencia (1923–1951),* 480; for Cernuda in limbo, see the poem by the same name (*Poesía,* 460–461).

22. Salinas and Guillén, *Correspondencia (1923–1951),* 512 (letter dated October 8, 1949). This does not mean that Guillén did not feel anguish at

being separated from his mother tongue (for which see a poem such as "Desterrado"), only that it wasn't as much of an issue for him as it was for Cernuda, Salinas, or Juan Ramón Jiménez. Symptomatic of Guillén's lower anxiety level about xenophony are the interlingual rhymes in his exile poetry, often between Spanish and English: Dallas/alas, death/vejez, juice/Jesús, see/así, inglés/yes, etc.

23. Literally, "tragaluces" means "light swallowers." A less literal but more accurate translation of "tragaluces" might be "black holes."

24. Salinas, *Poesías Completas*, ed. Soledad Salinas de Marichal (Barcelona: Barral, 1975), 648.

25. Letters to Katherine Prue (Reding) Whitmore, Pedro Salinas Papers, Houghton Library, Harvard University, bMS Span 107, Folder 165, April 8, 1946. Used by permission of the Houghton Library, Harvard University.

26. On Mexico as maternal space, see Bernard Sicot, "Luis Cernuda, *Variaciones sobre tema mexicano:* El espacio y el tiempo recobrados," in *Poesía y exilio: Los poetas del exilio español en México*, ed. Rose Corral, Arturo Souto Alabarce, and James Valender (Mexico City: El Colegio de México, 1995), 245–252.

27. Philip Silver, *Ruins and Restitution* (Nashville: Vanderbilt University Press, 1997), 117.

28. On the poem's intertexts, see Antonio Monegal, "Pre-texto e intertexto en 'Retrato de poeta' de Luis Cernuda," *Boletín de la Fundación Federico García Lorca* 9 (June 1991): 65–75.

Chapter 4

1. Included are pieces by Jesús Vega, María Zambrano, Italo Calvino, Severo Sarduy, Miguel Barnet, Luis Marré, Luis Agüero, and Humberto Arenal (*Unión* 16 [1993]). In 1970 the inaugural issue of the Cuban-exile journal *Alacrán Azul* included a dossier about Casey, "Calvert Casey, In Memoriam," *Alacrán Azul* 1, no. 1 (1970): 23–33; ten years later, the Spanish journal *Quimera*, in its December 1982 issue, also published several essays about Casey.

2. Calvert Casey, *Notas de un simulador*, ed. Mario Merlino (Madrid: Montesinos, 1997); Casey, *The Collected Stories*, ed. Ilán Stavans (Durham: Duke University Press, 1998).

3. Letter to Guillermo Cabrera Infante, September 11, 1968, Guillermo Cabrera Infante Papers, Manuscripts Division of the Department of Rare Books and Special Collections at the Princeton University Library. All letters to follow from Casey to Cabrera Infante are from this collection and published with permission of the Princeton University Library.

4. Calvert Casey, letter to Guillermo Cabrera Infante, February 21 [1967?].

5. Víctor Fowler, "El siglo XIX de Casey y el proyecto de Ciclón," *Unión* 25 (1966): 14. See also Fowler's perceptive reading of this story in *La*

maldición: Una historia del placer como conquista (La Habana: Editorial Letras Cubanas, 1998), 128–140.

6. Undated letter to Guillermo Cabrera Infante. This is corroborated by Humberto Arenal, who as a young man also worked for the Cuban Telephone Company; see his "Calvert, aquel adolescente tímido, tartamudo y otras cosas más," *Unión* 6, no. 16 (1993): 49–50.

7. "Contributors," *New Mexico Quarterly* 24, no. 4 (winter 1954–1955): 367. In his *Antología del cuento cubano contemporáneo* (Mexico City: Ediciones Era, 1967), Ambrosio Fornet mentions that in his youth Casey published "una apología de Martí que él mismo se encarga de recoger y de la que no queda rastro" [an apology for Martí that he himself picked back up and of which there is no trace] (58). Some years earlier, in a review of the first edition of *El regreso*, Edmundo Desnoes attributed to Casey a novel entitled *Los paseantes*, published under the pseudonym of José de América ("Calvert Casey: *El regreso*," *Casa de las Américas* 2, no. 10 [enero/ febrero 1962]: 126–133). Humberto Arenal also indicates that before leaving Cuba in 1946 Casey wrote a novel entitled *Los paseantes* ("Calvert, aquel adolescente tímido, tartamudo y otras cosas más," 49). Like Fornet, I have not been able to find any trace of the Martí apology, but in the 1940s a "novela breve" entitled *Los paseantes* was indeed published in Havana under the pseudonym of "José de América." Given that the pseudonym could be mistaken for a reference to Martí, the author of "Nuestra América," it is possible that Fornet is thinking of the same book as Desnoes and Arenal. But Casey's authorship of this work is doubtful. Although *Los paseantes* has no date of publication, the text is signed "La Habana, invierno de 1941." In the winter of 1941 Casey was sixteen years old. The copy of the novel that I have seen carries a handwritten dedication by "The Author," whose large elegant lettering does not at all resemble Casey's crabbed script. Moreover, this author's style is unlike anything Casey ever wrote. The novel begins:

Lector: Antes de que empieces a leer estas pocas páginas es mi deseo acercarme a tí para anticiparte que te van a parecer la obra de alguien que, como aquel incorregible soñador de la fábula francesa, se pusiese en medio de un terrible incendio a contarle los pétalos a una rosa . . . Sí, lector, es lo que te van a parecer mis páginas cuando te hable al través de ellas de amores eternos y comuniones espirituales. Sin embargo, en mi condición de humano no puedo menos que dejarle un endeble tributo al Amor, "la más pura síntesis de la Vida" que la llamase Concha Espina, la meta de todas las aspiraciones humanas, el más elevado de los sentimientos. (3)

[Reader: Before you begin reading these few pages my wish is to approach you to warn you that they will seem the work of someone who, like that incorrigible dreamer of the French fable, stands in the middle of a fire counting the petals of a rose . . . Yes, reader, this is how my pages will appear to you when I speak to you about eternal loves and spiritual communions. Nonetheless, as a human being I

cannot but leave a feeble tribute to Love, "the purest synthesis of Life" as Concha Espina has called it, the goal of all human aspirations, the highest of our feelings.]
If Casey wrote this, his talent for *simulación* is even greater than anyone has suspected. But the real simulation may have been claiming the book as his own (if he did) rather than writing it. Still, it is intriguing that the novel's title anticipates that of Casey's story, "El paseo."

8. As quoted in Luis Marré, "Nada menos que todo un amigo," *Unión* 6, no. 16 (1993): 46 47.

9. This is part of the author's note included in the second edition of *El regreso* (1963).

10. Letter to Guillermo Cabrera Infante, February 28, 1967.

11. Rafael Martínez Nadal, "Calvert Casey y notas a una lectura de 'Piazza Margana,'" *Quimera* 26 (December 1982): 85.

12. Letters to Guillermo Cabrera Infante, February 28, 1967 and May 15, 1967.

13. Letter to Guillermo Cabrera Infante, November 12, 1967.

14. Letter to Guillermo Cabrera Infante, undated (February 1968?).

15. Guillermo Cabrera Infante, "¿Quién mató a Calvert Casey?" in *Mea Cuba* (Barcelona: Plaza y Janés, 1992), 150.

16. Cabrera Infante, *Mea Cuba,* 148.

17. Letter to Guillermo Cabrera Infante, undated (summer 1968).

18. Martínez Nadal, "Calvert Casey," 85–86. It was not until twelve years after Casey's death that "Piazza Margana" was finally published in a Canadian literary magazine, *The Malahat Review* (July 1981); its Spanish translation, by Vicente Molina Foix, was published alongside Martínez Nadal's essay in *Quimera.*

19. George Santayana, *The Sense of Beauty* (1896; New York: Dover, 1955), p. 104.

20. Calvert Casey, *Memorias de una isla* (La Habana: Ediciones R, 1964), 90–91.

21. Calvert Casey, *The Collected Stories,* 187. Casey's bilingualism creates a curious editorial situation: On the one hand, *The Collected Stories,* a volume of English translations, includes two stories that were written originally in English, "Piazza Margana" and "The Walk"; on the other hand, the recent collection in Spanish of his fiction, *Notas de un simulador,* includes Vicente Molina Foix's Spanish translation of "Piazza Margana" as well as Casey's own Spanish version of "The Walk." Page references to these two collections will be included in the text; to distinguish between them, I will identify the numbers that refer to *Notas de un simulador.*

22. Martínez Nadal, "Calvert Casey," 85.

23. On the Revolution's persecution of homosexuals, see Ian Lumsden, *Machos, Maricones and Gays: Cuba and Homosexuality* (Philadelphia: Temple University Press, 1996); and Néstor Almendros and Orlando Jiménez Leal, *Conducta Impropia* (Madrid: Playor, 1984).

24. Letter to Guillermo Cabrera Infante, August 17, 1967.
25. Andreu stayed in Cuba and eventually also took her own life. See Reinaldo Arenas, *Antes que anochezca* (Barcelona: Tusquets, 1992), 160–161; also Cabrera Infante, *Mea Cuba*, 144, 194.
26. John and Charles Wesley, *The Poetical Works of John and Charles Wesley* (London: Wesleyan-Methodist Conference Office, 1870), 7: 327.
27. Casey wrote to Cabrera Infante: "Aquí en Roma, todo deja de tener importancia; estoy más cerca de ese quietismo nirvanesco que tú tanto odias y yo tanto ansío. Tres semanas busqué por Madrid las obras del padre Mariana, el gran quietista español excomulgado por esa cocinera incansable que era Santa Teresa y su amiga o hermana San Juan de la Cruz, activistas insufribles" [Here in Rome everything loses its importance; I am closer to that nirvana-like quietism that you hate and that I long for. I spent three weeks in Madrid looking for the works of Father Mariana, the great Spanish quietist excommulgated by that tireless cook Saint Theresa and her friend or sister Saint John of the Cross, insufferable activists both] (May 15, 1967). Casey confuses Miguel de Molinos with the historian Juan de Mariana. For Casey's interest in *molinismo,* see also Vicente Molina Foix, "En la muerte de Calvert Casey," *Insula* 272–273 (julio-agosto 1969): 40; and María Zambrano, "Calvert Casey, el indefenso," *Quimera* 26 (diciembre 1982): 60.
28. Of the dozen "subjects" he finds, only one is female. "Notas de un simulador" is based on an earlier story, "La plazoleta," included in the Spanish edition of *El regreso,* where all of the narrator's subjects are male.
29. George Steiner, *Extraterritorial* (New York: Penguin, 1971), 16.
30. It would be interesting to know whether there is any connection between Casey's stutter and his bilingualism. In "El regreso," the protagonist traces his stuttering back to "some obscure and unknown tragedy of his earliest years" (83). In a letter to Cabrera Infante, Casey mentions that when he lived in Canada, in the late forties, he didn't stutter.
31. Cabrera Infante, *Mea Cuba*, 137.
32. Karl Vossler, *The Spirit of Language in Civilization*, trans. Oscar Oeser (New York: Harcourt, Brace, 1932), 123.

Chapter 5

1. Jason Wilson, "Guillermo Cabrera Infante: An Interview in a Summer Manner," in *Modern Latin American Fiction: A Survey,* ed. John King (London: Faber and Faber, 1987), 309.
2. Wilson, "Guillermo Cabrera Infante: An Interview in a Summer Manner," 309.

3. Steven Kellman, *The Translingual Imagination* (Lincoln, NE: University of Nebraska Press, 2000), 12. Kellman does not include Cabrera Infante in his extensive "roster" of translingual writers (117–118).

4. Among them: *Delito por bailar el chachachá* (1995), *Mi música extremada* (1996), *Cine o sardina* (1997), and *El libro de las ciudades* (1999). He has also published English translations of several of his books—*A Twentieth Century Job* (1991), *Writes of passage* (1993), *Mea Cuba* (1994)—and a Spanish translation of *Holy Smoke, Puro humo* (2000).

5. Rita Guibert, *Seven Voices*, trans. Frances Partridge (Alfred A. Knopf, 1973), 397–398.

6. Suzanne Jill Levine, "Wit and Wile with Guillermo Cabrera Infante," *Americas* 47, no. 4 (July-August 1995): 29.

7. When Levine was translating *Vista*, he asked her: "Do you think that the vignettes (or whatever they're called) are coming out too Hemingwayan in English? I'm worried about that with some of them, particularly the older ones (like those you are translating now, the one with the two generals), that were written around 1963 or even before. It worries me because of the possible American reader (and especially critic)." As quoted in Suzanne Jill Levine, *The Subversive Scribe: Translating Latin American Fiction* (St. Paul, MN: Graywolf Press, 1991), 106. On Cabrera Infante and Hemingway, see Terry J. Peavler, "Guillermo Cabrera Infante's Debt to Ernest Hemingway," *Hispania* 62 (1979): 289–296.

8. Guillermo Cabrera Infante, *Vista del amanecer en el trópico* (New York: Penguin, 1997), 194. Other page references to the Spanish edition will be included in the text.

9. Guillermo Cabrera Infante, *Tres tristes tigres* (Barcelona: Seix Barral, 1967), 9.

10. Cabrera Infante's phrase from his interview with Rita Guibert in Guibert, *Seven voices*, 414.

11. Levine, *The Subversive Scribe*, 103.

12. Raymond Souza, *Guillermo Cabrera Infante: Two Islands, Many Worlds* (Austin: University of Texas Press, 1996), 118.

13. Wilson, "Guillermo Cabrera Infante: An Interview in a Summer Manner," 321

14. Levine, *The Subversive Scribe*, 104.

15. Guillermo Cabrera Infante, "Cronología a la manera de Laurence Sterne . . . o no," in *Infantería*, ed. Nivia Montenegro and Enrico Mario Santí (Mexico City: Fondo de Cultura Económica, 1999), 42.

16. Cabrera Infante, "Cronología," 45.

17. Souza, *Guillermo Cabrera Infante: Two Islands, Many Worlds*, 81. See also Isabel Álvarez Borland, "Challenging History from Exile: Guillermo Cabrera Infante's *View of Dawn in the Tropics*," in *Cuban-American Literature of Exile: From Person to Persona* (Charlottesville: University of

Virginia Press, 1998), 28–38; and Nivia Montenegro, "¿*Qué dise/mi/ nación?*: Island Vision in Guillermo Cabrera Infante's *Vista del amanecer en el trópico,*" *Cuban Studies* 28 (1999): 125–53.

18. Cabrera Infante, "Cronología," 42.

19. Guillermo Cabrera Infante, *View of Dawn in the Tropics* (London: Faber and Faber, 1988), 47. Other page references to this edition will be included in the text.

20. "When I write I always try to make the sentence, the phrase, and the word sound right to me. I of course pay more attention to sound than sense. If the sound, the written sound, is right I don't particularly care about the sense. In fact, if there is no sense, more power to the prose. All it can become is nonsense" (Levine, "Wit and Wile with Guillermo Cabrera Infante," 28–29).

21. Guillermo Cabrera Infante, *View of Dawn in the Tropics* (New York: Harper & Row, 1978), 86. Other page references to this edition will be included in the text.

22. See Peavler, "Guillermo Cabrera Infante's Debt to Ernest Hemingway"; also Terry J. Peavler, "Cabrera Infante's Undertow," in *Structures of Power: Essays on Twentieth-Century Spanish-American Fiction,* ed. Terry J. Peavler and Peter Standish (Albany: State University of New York Press, 1996), 125–143.

23. There is also an orthodox, not to say faithful, translation of this story by Suzanne Jill Levine: "A Nest of Sparrows on the Awning," in *The Eye of the Heart,* ed. Barbara Howes (Indianapolis: Bobbs-Merrill, 1973), 357–363.

24. This story has appeared in several anthologies, though to my knowledge it has never been included in any of Cabrera Infante's books; it was published originally in *London Tales,* ed. Julian Evans (London: Hamish Hamilton, 1983), 108–43.

25. Guillermo Cabrera Infante, *Writes of Passage* (London: Faber and Faber, 1993), x.

26. Cabrera Infante, *Tres tristes tigres,* 9.

27. Cabrera Infante, *Tres tristes tigres,* 61.

28. Guillermo Cabrera Infante, *Three Trapped Tigers* (New York: Harper & Row, 1871), 55. The title page states that the novel was "translated from the Cuban by Donald Gardner and Suzanne Jill Levine in collaboration with the author."

29. Wilson, "Guillermo Cabrera Infante: An Interview in a Summer Manner," 307.

30. John Updike, "Infante Terrible," *The New Yorker,* June 29, 1972, 93.

31. Regina Janes, "Up in Smoke," in *Guillermo Cabrera Infante, Assays, Essays, and Other Arts,* ed. Ardis L. Nelson (New York: Twayne, 1999), 186.

32. Guillermo Cabrera Infante, "The Phantom of the Essoldo," in *London Tales,* ed. Julian Evans (London: Hamish Hamilton, 1983), 108.

33. Letter to Guillermo Cabrera Infante, undated (summer 1968). Guillermo Cabrera Infante Papers, Princeton University Libraries.
34. The epigraph of Cabrera Infate's *El libro de las ciudades* (Madrid: Alfaguara, 1999), refers to the *Collins English Dictionary*, as does the title of one of the essays in the book (123).
35. Nabokov, *Strong Opinions* (New York: McGraw-Hill, 1973), 98.
36. Levine, "Wit and Wile with Guillermo Cabrera Infante," 27.

CHAPTER 6

1. Respectively in: Ágata Gligo, *María Luisa (Sobre la vida de María Luisa Bombal)* (Santiago de Chile: Editorial Andrés Bello, 1985), 124; Lucía Guerra-Cunningham, "Escritura y trama biográfica," in *Literatura como intertextualidad, IX Simposio internacional de literatura,* ed. Juana Alcira Arancibia (Buenos Aires: Instituto Literario Cultural Hispánico, 1993), 134; Gloria Gálvez Lira, *María Luisa Bombal: Realidad y fantasía* (Potomac, MD: Scripta Humanistica, 1986), 9; Kimberly A. Nance, "Contained in Criticism, Lost in Translation: Representation of Sexuality and the Fantastic in Bombal's *La Última niebla* and *House of Mist,*" *Hispanófila* 130 (September 2000): 42.
2. Page numbers refer to María Luisa Bombal, *Obras completas* [*OC*], ed. Lucía Guerra (Buenos Aires: Editorial Andrés Bello, 1996).
3. The movie starred Libertad Lamarque. Indulging the genre's appetite for spectacle, the plot even included a duel. "¡A mí me encantan los duelos!" [I love duels!], Bombal said (*OC*, 333).
4. Roberto Ignacio Díaz, *Unhomely Rooms: Foreign Tongues and Spanish American Literature* (Lewisburg: Bucknell University Press, 2002). Díaz is the only critic to date to take seriously Bombal's anglophone fiction. My comments on *House of Mist* are indebted to his incisive reading of the novel.
5. Marjorie Agosín, *Las desterradas del paraíso, protagonistas en la narrativa de María Luisa Bombal* (New York: Senda Nueva de Ediciones, 1983), 123.
6. Lucía Guerra Cunningham, *La narrativa de María Luisa Bombal: Visión de la existencia femenina* (Madrid: Playor, 1980), 8.
7. María Luisa Bombal, House of Mist *and* The Shrouded Woman (Austin: University of Texas Press, 1995), viii.
8. María Luisa Bombal, *House of Mist* [*HM*] (New York: Farrar, Straus, 1947), 245. Other page numbers will refer to this edition.
9. Díaz, *Unhomely Rooms,* 152, 183.
10. Elizabeth Klosty Beaujour, *Alien Tongues: Bilingual Russian Writers of the "First" Emigration* (Ithaca: Cornell University Press, 1989), 37.

11. Cedomil Goic, "La última niebla: Consideraciones en torno a la estructura de la novela contemporánea," *Anales de la Universidad de Chile* 121 (1964): 59–83.
12. Goic, "*La última niebla*: Consideraciones en torno a la estructura de la novela contemporánea," 62–63.
13. Daphne du Maurier's *Rebecca*, which also turns on the arrival of a second wife to her new husband's home, had been published in 1938 and made into an award-winning movie in 1940. On the similarities between *House of Mist* and *Rebecca*, see Díaz, *Unhomely Rooms*, 147, 149, 152.
14. As quoted by Ester Matte Alessandri, "María Luisa Bombal o la búsqueda del amor," in *Maria Luisa Bombal: Apreciaciones críticas*, ed. Marjorie Agosín, Elena Gascón-Vera, Joy Renjilian-Burly (Tempe, AZ: Bilingual Press, 1987), 15.
15. As quoted in Gligo, *María Luisa*, 139.
16. Calvert Casey, *The Collected Stories* (Durham: Duke University Press, 1998), 192.
17. Regina's name paraphrases Bombal's father's nickname for his daughter, "reina." According to Bombal, she identified both with the protagonist of *La última niebla* and with Regina: "Me identifico con las dos mujeres que aparecen, con la soñadora y con Regina, la apasionada" [I identify with the two women who appear, with the dreamer and with Regina, the passionate one] (*OC*, 450).
18. Díaz, *Unhomely Rooms*, 146.
19. It is conceivable that some may have understood the allusion, however, since Bombal's attempted murder of Sánchez was reported in *The New York Times* under the heading, "Foe of Chilean Reds Shot Down by Writer" (28 January 1941, p. 3). The leader of a right-wing militia, Sánchez was a well-known figure in Chilean politics.
20. As quoted in Gligo, *María Luisa*, 100.
21. Gálvez Lira, *María Luisa Bombal*, 9.
22. "Fracasaron con el libreto. El primero fue un disparate muy intelectual. El segundo lo encargaron a otra inglesa. Fue un disparate menos intelectual. Nunca me dejaron ayudar, porque allá todo está canalizado. Al novelista le corresponde escribir novelas, no adaptarlas. Un día se les ocurrió que sería un buen tema para Audrey Hepburn, pero a la actriz nunca le agradó. Cada cierto tiempo me invitaban a cenar para comunicarme que alguien iba a filmar *La última niebla,* pero todo quedó en proyectos" [They failed with the script. The first one was a very intellectual piece of nonsense. The second one was done by another English woman. It was a less intellectual piece of nonsense. They never let me help, because there everything is compartmentalized. The novelist writes the novels, she doesn't adapt them for the screen. One day it occurred to them that it would be a good vehicle for Audrey Hepburn, but she wasn't interested. Every once in a while they would invite me to dinner to tell me that

someone was going to film *House of Mist,* but it never got beyond the planning stages] (*OC,* 398). According to the account of the sale of the film rights in *The New York Times* (27 July 1946, p. 7), Hal Wallis originally bought the script with the idea of having Jennifer Jones star in the movie.

Chapter 7

1. Esmeralda Santiago, *When I Was Puerto Rican* (New York: Vintage, 1994), 43.
2. Julia Alvarez interview with Mike Chasar and Constance Pierce, *Glimmer Train Stories* 25 (winter 1998): 140–141.
3. Julia Alvarez, *The Other Side* (New York: Dutton, 1995), 3.
4. I am paraphrasing Roland Barthes's definition of connotation in *Elements of Semiology,* trans. Annette Lavers and Colin Smith (New York: Hill and Wang, 1968), 89–90.
5. Ernst Rudin, *Tender Accents of Sound: Spanish in the Chicano Novel in English* (Tempe, AZ: Bilingual Press, 1996), 152–181.
6. Walter Benjamin, "The Task of the Translator," in *The Translation Studies Reader,* ed. Lawrence Venuti (London: Routledge, 2000), 15.
7. Sandra Cisneros, *Woman Hollering Creek* (New York: Random House, 1991), 153.
8. Sandra Cisneros, "Dulzura," in *Loose Woman* (New York, Vintage, 1995), 27. From LOOSE WOMAN. Copyright 1994 by Sandra Cisneros. Published by Vintage Books, a division of Random House, Inc., and originally in hardcover by Alfred A. Knopf, Inc. Reprinted by permission of Susan Bergholz Literary Services, New York. All rights reserved.
9. Cisneros, *Loose Woman,* 4–6.
10. Paul De Man, "Autobiography as Defacement," *MLN* 94 (1979): 920.
11. Richard Rodriguez, *Hunger of Memory* (New York: Bantam, 1983), 179. Further page references will be incorporated in the text.
12. For discussions of the reference to Caliban, see Ramón Saldívar, "Ideologies of the Self: Chicano Autobiography," *Diacritics* 15, no. 3 (1985): 26–27; and Lauro Flores, "Chicano Autobiography: Culture, Ideology and the Self," *The Americas Review* 18, no. 2 (1980): 86.
13. Saldívar, "Ideologies of the Self," 27.
14. Paul John Eakin, *Touching the World: Reference in Autobiography* (Princeton: Princeton University Press, 1992), 117–37.
15. In act I, scene 2 of *The Tempest,* Prospero says to Caliban:
    When thou didst not—savage!—
    Know thine own meaning, but wouldst gabble like
    A thing most brutish, I endowed thy purposes

With words that made them known . . .
To which Caliban makes his famous reply:
You taught me language, and my profit on't
Is, I know how to curse. The red plague rid you,
For learning me your language.

16. Richard Rodriguez, "An American Writer," in *The Invention of Ethnicity*, ed. Werner Sollors (New York: Oxford University Press, 1989), 4.

17. Calvert Casey, *Notas de un simulador* (Madrid: Montesinos, 1997), 227.

18. Rodriguez, "An American Writer," 8.

19. Tomás Rivera, "Richard Rodriguez's *Hunger of Memory* as Humanistic Antithesis," *Melus* 11, no. 4 (1984): 10. On Paz and Rodriguez, see José Limón, "Editor's Note on Richard Rodriguez," *Texas Studies in Literature and Language* 40, no. 4 (winter 1998): 391.

20. For an energetic queer reading of Rodriguez, see Randy Rodriguez, "Richard Rodriguez Reconsidered: Queering the Sissy (Ethnic) Subject," *Texas Studies in Literature and Language* 40, no. 4 (winter 1998): 396–423. Issues of sexuality (his own) are somewhat more visible in Rodriguez's second book, *Days of Obligation: An Argument with My Mexican Father* (New York: Penguin, 1992), particularly in the chapter "Late Victorians," a discussion of the AIDS epidemic in San Francisco that is also Rodriguez's characteristically reticent coming-out piece; but it is only in *Brown* (New York: Viking, 2002) that he describes himself as "a queer Catholic Indian Spaniard" (35). In a recent interview, Rodriguez explained that he kept his homosexuality out of *Hunger of Memory* because its inclusion would have induced too "sociological" a reading of the book (Timothy S. Sedore, "Violating the Boundaries: An Interview with Richard Rodriguez," *Michigan Quarterly Review* 38 [1999]: 424–446). But one might say just the opposite: that the exclusion of his homosexuality from the memoir tips the balance toward race and class rather than gender.

21. For a perceptive Derridean reading of the distinction between writing and reading in *Hunger of Memory*, see Henry Staten, "Ethnic Authenticity, Class, and Autobiography: The Case of *Hunger of Memory*, PMLA 113 (1998): 103–116; see also Rolando J. Romero, "Spanish and English: The Question of Literacy in *Hunger of Memory*, *Confluencia* 6, no. 2 (1991): 89–90.

22. The spelling gaffe (in Spanish the word is *propio*, not *proprio*) occurs in a wrenchingly appropriate context. Visiting from Mexico, young Richard's uncle is outraged by his nephew's inability to speak Spanish: "After listening to me, he looked away and said what a disgrace it was that I couldn't speak Spanish, '*su proprio idioma*.'" Recounting the incident, the adult Rodriguez confirms his uncle's judgement.

23. Rodriguez, *Days of Obligation: An Argument with my Mexican Father*, xv. This wrenching episode occurs while Rodriguez is in Mexico, where he has

gone to film a documentary for the BBC. Red and green are two of the colors of the Mexican flag.

24. Richard Rodriguez, "Going Home Again," in *The Norton Book of Personal Essays,* ed. Joseph Epstein (New York: W. W. Norton, 1997), 410–411. This essay was originally published in *The American Scholar* in 1974.

25. Richard Rodriguez, "The New, New World: Richard Rodriguez on Culture and Assimilation," interview with Virginia I. Postel and Nick Gillespie, *Reason* 26, no. 4 (August-September 1994): 41.

26. Judith Ortiz Cofer, "Lesson One: I Would Sing," in *Reaching for the Mainland and Selected New Poems* (Tempe, AZ: Bilingual Press, 1995), 60. Copyright Bilingual Press/Editorial Bilingüe, Arizona State University, Tempe, AZ, used with permission.

27. Judith Ortiz Cofer, *Woman in Front of the Sun* (Athens: University of Georgia Press, 2000), 120.

Index

192 ❖ INDEX